YOUNG AND UNDOCUMENTED

Young and Undocumented

Political Belonging in Uncertain Times

Julia Albarracín

NEW YORK UNIVERSITY PRESS

New York

NEW YORK UNIVERSITY PRESS
New York
www.nyupress.org

© 2025 by New York University
All rights reserved

Please contact the Library of Congress for Cataloging-in-Publication data.
ISBN: 9781479819072 (hardback)
ISBN: 9781479819089 (paperback)
ISBN: 9781479819102 (library ebook)
ISBN: 9781479819096 (consumer ebook)

This book is printed on acid-free paper, and its binding materials are chosen for strength and durability. We strive to use environmentally responsible suppliers and materials to the greatest extent possible in publishing our books.

The manufacturer's authorized representative in the EU for product safety is
Mare Nostrum Group B.V., Mauritskade 21D, 1091 GC Amsterdam, The Netherlands.
Email: gpsr@mare-nostrum.co.uk.

Manufactured in the United States of America

10 9 8 7 6 5 4 3 2 1

Also available as an ebook

To Cohen

CONTENTS

Introduction

Framing the Issue

I'm like, "here we go again." It's just like a never-ending roller
coaster, that's how it feels like, you know? . . . The worst part
is to feel like someone is playing with your life.
—Zoe, 25, Interview

On November 14, 2023, I participated in a day of action in Washington, DC, to advocate for work permits for long-term undocumented residents and DREAMers. In a moment when the prospects for congressional immigration reform were nonexistent, a coalition of nonprofits and businesses asked President Biden to use his parole power, which allows the Executive "to parole any noncitizen applying for admission into the United States temporarily for urgent humanitarian reasons or significant public benefit."[1] I, along with a group of thirty-seven students from Western Illinois University, and nine employees and volunteers of the nonprofit I direct, traveled to Washington, DC, on two chartered buses. The day of action consisted of visits with congresspersons and a rally in front of the White House.

The events in Washington were energizing. Some 2,200 people, including long-term undocumented residents, DREAMers, and allies from around the country waved flags from Latin American countries and carried signs indicating the number of years they have resided in the country. The colorful crowd chanted, "What do we want? Work permits! When do we want them? Now!" DREAMers who came to the country as children were there to advocate for their undocumented parents but also for a solution to their situation. To this day, 20 percent of the almost eleven million undocumented are under twenty-four years of age.[2] Even the hundreds of thousands who benefited from Deferred Action for Childhood Arrivals (DACA), a work permit, and deferment of deportation passed by President Obama in 2012[3] are probably exhausted from their roller-coaster lives so far: discovering they were undocumented, obtaining DACA, and remaining in limbo after multiple court and other decisions following the Trump administration's attempt to terminate the program in 2017.[4]

Attempts at comprehensive immigration reform providing a path to citizenship for noncitizens failed during the presidencies of Trump, Obama, and George W. Bush.[5] The prospects for comprehensive immigration reform in December 2024 remain bleak. "Wheeling and dealing on the various issues related to immigration and border policy had been a familiar part of the congressional landscape, particularly in the Trump era, when Republicans got deeply obsessed with the alleged civilizational threat of 'open borders.'"[6] Republicans now demand increased border security in exchange for a Biden-requested supplemental spending bill that includes time-sensitive aid to Israel and Ukraine.[7] For years, a deal that would increase border security in exchange for a path to citizenship for DREAMers seemed likely.[8] Now, immigration bargaining has excluded these and other long-term undocumented residents and replaced them with aid for Israel and Ukraine.

This book uses the incorporation framework to analyze the ups and downs of thirty-six young DACA recipients who, while forming their identity in the only country they know, had to come to terms with their immigration status, its implications, and changes. Although the literature on DREAMers and undocumented youth is profuse,[9] with the notable exception of work by Roberto Gonzales,[10] past studies have failed to provide a clear theory to understand how DACA recipients' cultural, legal, and political identities are shaped by unique legal changes and shifting contexts during the course of their lives.

Incorporation refers to the acculturative process through which immigrants come to feel part of the host society.[11] This book argues that incorporation can be *typical*, *disrupted*, or *roller-coaster*. In the typical incorporation, immigrants arrive in the country, learn the language, and develop a sense of connection with their ethno-racial group; later (likely) develop some sense of commonality with members of the dominant group; progress socially and economically, and acquire permanent residency; and finally, if they so choose, become citizens of the host country, and integrate some aspects of the new culture into their cultural identity.

In contrast to *typical incorporation*, the process for undocumented immigrants is severely *disrupted* by limited social and economic opportunities, hostile public opinion, constant threat of deportation, and legislation that curtails their chances for advancement in society.[12] Despite these limitations, adult undocumented immigrants made the decision to migrate, are aware of the drawbacks of illegality, and enjoy a certain stability in their desolation. *Roller-coaster* incorporation, I argue, is typical of DACA recipients, who may be unaware of their lack of papers and/or its implications; are sometimes asked to lie about their place of birth from an early age; realize the obstacles they face when coming of age; obtain protection from deportation and a work permit; and later risk losing this protection. The question addressed in this book is: What are the consequences of the United States' delaying deportation but also not delivering full integration into American society to a group of undocumented immigrants who arrived in the country as children and are protected by DACA?

This book proposes a framework that links incorporation to real and perceived changes in the position of DACA recipients in relation to the border and law. The growing body of literature on DREAMers draws primarily on the stories of Latino/a youth of Spanish-speaking origin in California.[13] This study draws on a sample of DREAMers in Illinois and includes three Polish DACA recipients, thus allowing for a comparison of the experiences of White versus non-White DACA recipients. It first analyzes the premigration stage, including the hardships the family faced in the country of origin, the trauma of separating from family and friends when migrating, and the distress caused by the act of migration when crossing the border. It then assesses the different pathways for cultural incorporation DACA recipients follow in the postmigration stage, including their integration into American schools, the process of English language acquisition, social integration, and support received from teachers and counselors. This book also addresses the consequences of the different perceived and actual immigration status changes on lives, identities, dreams, and hopes of DACA recipients, including the realization of their lack of documents, the acquisition of DACA, and the hardships caused by the announcement of DACA's termination in 2017. Finally, it addresses the political incorporation of DACA beneficiaries and the different ways in which they assert their voices. This exploration is done through an examination of DACA re-cipients' experiences shared during in-depth interviews.

Immigration and DACA

The United States is defined as a country of immigrants, "but not just any immigrants."[14] Since its consolidation as a modern nation, the United States has selected potential immigrants. Important restrictions to immigration were passed in the late nineteenth century to exclude the Chinese, those likely to become a public charge, those without pre-arranged work contracts, the criminal, the diseased, and the politically undesirable.[15] In 1921 and 1924, the so-called Quota Laws were passed with the intent of insuring that Northern and Western Europeans would be more numerous than other groups, such as Jews, Italians, Slavs, and Greeks.[16] The quota system ended with the passage of the Nationality Act of 1965, which is essentially in place today.[17] Prior to 1965, there were no quantitative restrictions on migration from Mexico.[18] While the 1965 law was celebrated as liberal, it imposed a numerical restric-tion on immigration from the Western Hemisphere for the first time. Mexican immigrants, the most numerous group of immigrants in the United States, were originally exempt from the quota system.[19] Major legal changes since 1965 have created severe restrictions on the "legal" migration of Mexicans.[20] Due to congressional inability to pass compre-hensive immigration reform, an estimated 10.5 million undocumented immigrants lived in the United States in 2021.[21]

On June 15, 2012, the Obama administration announced a program called Deferred Action for Childhood Arrivals (DACA). This program allowed people who came to the United States as children before the age of sixteen, and who were in the country since 2007, to apply for de-ferred action, which protected them from deportation, and to obtain a two-year work permit.[22] DACA-eligible individuals are those currently in school, those who have graduated or obtained the equivalency of a high school diploma, and certain honorably discharged veterans of the US military.[23] This group of young individuals was previously baptized as DREAMers, in reference to the Development, Relief, and Education for Alien Minors (DREAM) Act of 2001, which gained approval from the US House of Representatives on December 8, 2010, but not from the

Senate.[24] Unlike the DREAM Act, which would have provided a path to citizenship, DACA allowed individuals to apply for renewals if they are in good standing and can produce the necessary documents required by the United States Citizenship and Immigration Services (USCIS), but not to secure permanent residency or citizenship.

Authors have referred to the rights awarded by DACA as liminal legality or status.[25] Liminal legality partially protects beneficiaries from social exclusion associated with illegality, but it does not necessarily lead to social inclusion.[26] Moreover, rather than guaranteeing access to resources that would encourage social inclusion, liminal legality is a form of "legal violence" that generates fear, uncertainty, and social exclusion.[27] Although the efforts to characterize the situation of undocumented individuals after acquiring DACA are commendable, this book avoids giving Deferred Action for Childhood Arrivals names that obscure its legal nature. For this reason, this book uses the term deferred action.

Deferred action is a form of prosecutorial discretion. Prosecutorial discretion, also used in criminal law, is the authority of an agency to refrain from asserting the full scope of its enforcement authority in a particular case.[28] Although it was applied in the past to both individuals and groups who met qualifying criteria, deferred action was born out of the five-year legal battle by the late former Beatle John Lennon, when he and his wife Yoko Ono attempted to stay in the United States despite Lennon's earlier drug conviction.[29] This legal battle shined light on an internal practice of allowing INS officials to assign low-priority status to a proceeding, essentially avoiding further action to remove the noncitizen.[30] Deferred action is only available at the discretion of the agency, which decides to use this discretionary power on a case-by-case basis.[31] Although the outcome of an application for deferred action is clear (an application can be granted, denied, or unresolved), deferred action, like most forms of prosecutorial discretion, has traditionally operated without a formal application form or fee, or a process for appealing a denial.[32]

By 2011, when the inability of the Obama administration to get the DREAM Act approved became clear, Democratic members of the House and Senate began to push for the use of deferred action, prosecutorial discretion, and other administrative means to protect the DREAM Act students from deportation, especially considering that hundreds of them were outspoken about their status during the DREAM Act deliberations.[33] On June 15, 2012, DHS (the US Department of Homeland Security) issued a memorandum creating DACA, which used traditional humanitarian factors to outline its parameters, such as tender age and longtime residence in the United States. This program was intended to address the humanitarian crisis after Congress faced a stalemate to approve the DREAM Act.[34] Although the number of DACA-eligible individuals was estimated at 1.9 million, approximately 800,000 immigrants benefited from DACA.[35] Ninety percent of DACA recipients are from Latin America.[36] The top four countries of origin are Mexico (79.4%), El Salvador (3.7%), Guatemala (2.6%), and Honduras (2.3%).[37] Nearly half (45%) of current DACA recipients live in just two states: California (29%) and Texas (16%). Illinois has a little over 42,000 DACA recipients and is the third state in its proportion of DACA recipients (5%), together with New York (5%).[38]

After the Trump administration's attempt to terminate the program, DACA went through several legal challenges, and the Biden administration's August 30, 2022, memo to strengthen DACA has been declared unlawful by a Texas court.[39] At the time of writing, DACA recipients can apply for renewal, but new DACA applications are not being processed.[40] In March 2021, the US House of Representatives voted to give young people who came to the country as children a path to citizenship.[41] In a vote of 228 to 197, the House voted to set up a permanent legal pathway for more than 2.5 million undocumented immigrants, including those brought to the United States as children (DREAMers) and others granted Temporary Protected Status for humanitarian reasons.[42] The congressional vote nearly followed party lines and only nine Republicans voted yes. Some unsuccessful version of the DREAM Act has been proposed virtually every year since its introduction in 2001.

DACA, Its Attempted Termination and Legal Challenges

DACA has gone through a large number of legal changes and court challenges. At the time of writing, the fate of a memo by the Biden administration issued by the Department of Homeland Security on August 30, 2022, to strengthen DACA was still pending due to legal challenges brought by Texas and other Republican states.[43] Donald Trump promised the end of DACA during his 2016 presidential campaign.[44] Despite this, he was ambiguous and contradictory about his intentions toward DACA because he had a soft spot for its beneficiaries.[45] The Trump administration was characterized by radical, restrictionist actions undertaken to reduce legal immigration, to enact harsher enforcement policies against unauthorized immigration, and to undertake nativist policies impacting certain groups.[46] These policies were laid out by his transition team before his inauguration.[47] These actions included restricting travelers from predominantly Muslim countries, ramping up workplace raids, reducing the number of refugees allowed to enter the country annually, rescinding the Temporary Protected Status that had been in place for several Caribbean and Latin American countries, and enacting a zero-tolerance policy that separated migrant parents from their children.[48] In 2017, Attorney General Jefferson B. Sessions advised DHS to rescind DACA.[49] In a letter, Sessions warned then Acting Secretary of Homeland Security Elaine Duke that leaving DACA in place would risk litigation. On September 5, 2017, Acting Secretary Duke issued the "Duke Memorandum" instructing DHS to stop accepting new DACA applications.[50]

The memorandum justified this decision in one sentence: "Taking into consideration the Supreme Court's and the Fifth Circuit's rulings in the ongoing litigation, and the September 4, 2017 letter from the Attorney General, it is clear that the June 15, 2012 DACA program should be terminated."[51] During the first six months of his administration, President Trump sent mixed messages about the fate of DACA, praising DACA-recipient students on one day and deporting one of them the next day.[52] During the rescission announcement, Attorney General Sessions referred to DACA recipients as "illegal aliens" and declared this rescission to be in the national interest.[53] The rescission triggered a legal battle that continues to this day, following years of efforts by opponents to dismantle the program and by supporters to preserve it.[54]

Under the terms of the rescission announcement, DACA recipients retained their deferred action and work permit until it expired, unless it was terminated or revoked for a specific reason.[55] Renewals were limited to those whose DACA permit expired on or before March 5, 2018, but had to be filed by October 5, 2017.[56] Given the limited time to renew permits, an estimated 20,000 DACA beneficiaries were unable to renew. In June 2018, Congress failed twice to enact legislation that would have allowed the DREAMers to have a path to citizenship.[57] Soon after the rescission announcement, different states and immigration advocates filed lawsuits against the proposed DACA rescission.[58] The primary challenges took three different paths, originating in litigation filed in California, New York, and the District of Columbia.[59] Plaintiff groups claimed that DACA's rescission was arbitrary and capricious under the Administrative Procedure Act (APA) and violated the equal protection guaranteed by the US Constitution's Fifth Amendment's Due Process Clause.[60]

In January 2018, a federal district court in California issued a preliminary injunction and ordered DHS to continue the DACA program.[61] This court determined that Attorney General Sessions' decision was reviewable by an Article III court and noted that the government made no effort in its briefs to challenge any of the foregoing reasons why DACA was and remained within the authority of DHS.[62] Even though this court decision allowed for two-year renewals, it did not allow for new DACA applications or for DACA recipients to apply for advance parole, a permission that allows DACA recipients to leave the country and, in some cases, adjust their status.[63]

In February 2018, a federal court in New York delivered a similar decision, concluding that the Trump administration's decision to end DACA was a mistake of law.[64] This decision, like the one in California, applied only to the youth who were granted DACA in the past and not to those who had never applied. In April 2018, in a case brought by Princeton and several other elite universities, as well as the NAACP, the American Federation of Teachers, and the American Federation of Labor (AFL-CIO), a third federal court in the District of Columbia issued a ruling but gave the Trump administration ninety days to provide a fuller explanation of why DACA was unlawful.[65] This decision termed the rescission of DACA "arbitrary and capricious" because it failed to adequately explain why the program was allegedly unlawful.[66] Complying with the decision, DHS Secretary Kirstjen Nielsen submitted a three-page memo that reiterated earlier arguments that DACA was illegal. She also reasserted the administration's position that DACA was not nuanced or individualized and therefore amounted to a large-scale amnesty.[67]

In September 2018, attorneys general from seventeen states took issue with the Nielsen memo, stating that it had not been made part of the appellate record and that the word(s) missing was insufficient to address the defects of the original September 5, 2017, letter.[68] They also argued that President Trump's anti-immigrant and anti-Mexican tweets and public comments, together with his participation in the decision to end DACA, raised a plausible inference of invidious discrimination.[69] In the meantime, Congress was unable to act, and even though thirteen DACA and DREAM Act bills were introduced in the period 2017–2018, only two came to an unsuccessful vote in the House and none in the Senate.[70]

The US Supreme Court granted the government's cert petitions from these rulings on June 18, 2020.[71] By a five to four vote and in an opinion written by Chief Justice Roberts and the four liberal justices, it held that DACA's rescission was arbitrary and capricious. The Court's decision involved four holdings: two about the federal courts' authority to consider challenges to the Trump administration's DACA rescission and two about APA's arbitrary and capricious review.[72] The Court first rejected the argument that the DACA rescission was unreviewable as "agency action committed to agency discretion by law" under APA Section 701(a)(2).[73] The Court also rejected the argument that the courts lacked jurisdiction to review the DACA rescission, emphasizing the importance of judicial review and the narrowness of its exceptions.[74] The Court then turned to the arbitrary and capricious review and stated that the agency could not rely on post hoc explanations given by Secretary Nielsen.

Finally, the Court turned to the merits of the arbitrary and capricious issue by relying on its famous airbag case, *State Farm*, which states that the agency action that fails to consider "an important aspect of a problem before it" is arbitrary and capricious.[75] The Court stated that DHS violated the *State Farm* principle in two ways. Although DHS had considered the illegality of benefits, such as work permits, as sufficient to end DACA, it offered no arguments to terminate the deportation protection.[76] Justice Roberts further noted that the consequences of terminating DACA would "'radiate outward' to DACA recipients' families, including their 200,000 US citizen children, to the schools where DACA recipients study and teach, and to the employers who have invested time and money in training them."[77] The Court did not address DACA's legality nor did it order DHS to maintain DACA if it terminated the program in a lawful way.[78]

DHS did not provide immediate guidance on how they would implement the June 18, 2020, Court decision. But on July 28, 2020, DHS released a memo titled, "Reconsideration of the June 15, 2012 Memorandums Entitled 'Exercising Prosecutorial Discretion with Respect to Individuals Who Came to the United States as Children,'" known as the Wolf Memo.[79] This memo stated that DHS was "considering anew the DACA policy" to assess "whether the DACA policy should be maintained, rescinded, or modified."[80] The Wolf Memo also instructed USCIS to: (1) reject all initial requests from applicants who qualified for DACA but never received it before; (2) reject all advance parole applications from DACA recipients except where there are exceptional circumstances; (3) shorten the DACA renewal and work authorization from two years to one.[81]

On December 4, 2020, the Eastern District of New York issued an order vacating the Wolf Memo, because Chad Wolf was not lawfully serving as the Secretary of Homeland Security and thus had no lawful authority to issue the memo.[82] This court restored DACA to its pre-September 5, 2017, status, the date the Trump administration originally attempted to terminate DACA. The December 4 order required DHS to accept first-time DACA applications and renewals, to grant two-year DACA and work authorizations, and to accept advance parole applications under the pre-September 2017 standards.[83]

On July 16, 2021, the US District Court for the Southern District of Texas stated that the DACA program was unlawful.[84] The court prohibited the federal government from granting DACA to new applicants (although it could still accept submissions). Today, USCIS continues to accept and grant DACA renewal requests from individuals who have previously had DACA and continue to be eligible for these benefits.[85] At the end of August 2022, the Department of Homeland Security issued a memo to strengthen DACA which would provide lawful presence to DACA recipients in the United States but would leave the program unchanged and fail to clear the way for the acceptance of new DACA applications.[86] In its latest blow, a court in Texas decided that the Biden administration's Final Rule, which attempted to give DACA recipients a firmer legal standing, was unlawful.[87]

Undocumented Youth and the States

Although immigration law is a federal matter, states can decide how much to cooperate with the federal government on immigration enforcement.[88] Illinois is a state "welcoming" of undocumented immigrants. The 2017 Illinois Trust Act prohibits local law enforcement from participating in immigration enforcement.[89] Before 2017, Illinois local authorities had the ability to enter into 287(g) agreements with Immigration and Customs Enforcement (ICE) and collaborate in raids and other enforcement measures. However, Cook County, the largest county in Illinois, limited their own ability to cooperate with ICE in 2011 through the Cook County Detainer Ordinance; this ordinance became the model and inspiration for the adoption of the Trust Act.[90] Further, Chicago has been a sanctuary city since 1985, prohibiting any city employee from "asking about or assisting an investigation of the 'citizenship or residency status of any person' unless ordered to by a court or federal law."[91]

The federal government protected undocumented K-12 students. The 1981 *Plyler v. Doe* US Supreme Court decision ruled that all children, regardless of immigration status, shall have the same right to access free public K-12 education.[92] However, this decision did not guarantee access to higher education for undocumented students.[93] Thus, undocumented and DACA students have no educational protections after high school. These students lack access to federal financial aid and loans. Some states offer additional protections for undocumented and DACA students, but these protections vary greatly across states.[94]

Twenty-four states and Washington, DC, have state and other provisions allowing undocumented students to pay in-state tuition at state colleges and universities.[95] Four states, Delaware, Iowa, Michigan, and Pennsylvania, provide limited access to in-state tuition in some public schools. Only DACA recipients qualify for in-state tuition in colleges and universities in Arkansas, Idaho, Maine, Mississippi, and Ohio.[96] Alaska, Louisiana, Montana, North Dakota, Puerto Rico, South Dakota, Vermont, West Virginia, and Wyoming have no policy concerning DACA and undocumented students.[97] Indiana, Missouri, New Hampshire, North Carolina, Tennessee, and Wisconsin bar in-state tuition for undocumented and DACA students.[98] Finally, another three states—Alabama, Georgia, and South Carolina—prohibit undocumented students from enrolling at all or at certain public postsecondary institutions.[99]

In 2003, the Illinois Acevedo Act (Public Act 93–0007) allowed undocumented students who reside in the state of Illinois to receive in-state tuition if they live with a parent or guardian in the state of Illinois, have attended an Illinois high school for at least three years, and/or graduated with a high school diploma or equivalent in the state.[100] Other states have also established different rules to increase access to higher education by undocumented and DACA students. The Illinois Dream Act (SB2185) of 2011 made scholarships, college savings, and prepaid tuition programs available to undocumented students who graduate from Illinois high schools.[101] It also mandated that counselors be trained to assist undocumented students in gaining access to higher education. However, this mandate is not enforced, and this research shows that school counselors lack the resources (and sometimes the will) to guide undocumented students through the application process. Finally, the Rise Act (HB 2691) of 2019 allowed undocumented (and transgender) students who do not qualify for federal financial aid because of their lack of legal status to receive state financial aid.[102]

Methods

For this study, I interviewed a sample of thirty-eight DACA recipients between July 2018 and September 2020. Two participants later withdrew from the study for fear of being identified. Participants were recruited through announcements at different universities, DREAMers' clubs, events where DREAMers congregated, and key contacts who knew DREAMers. Participants had the option of answering the questions in English or Spanish. Key contacts were especially helpful in identifying non–college track DACA recipients. Given their age, interviewees were undocumented when they were part of the K-12 school system but later acquired DACA. Interviews were conducted in person, via Skype, or over the phone. Interviews lasted around forty minutes. All participants selected a pseudonym by which they are identified in this study.

Interviews were open-ended, and after stating their dreams and aspirations, level of education, and income and occupation of their parents, participants were asked the following questions: How did your parents decide to come to the United States and why? Do you have a memory of your arrival to the United States? What do you remember about it? How were your interactions with neighbors, family members, and others? How did you feel when you started school? How did your interactions with other schoolchildren change your perception of who you were? How were your interactions with teachers, school administrators, and counselors? When did you find out you were undocumented and under what circumstances? How did this affect your perception of who you were? How about your dreams? What was the impact of your acquisition of DACA status on your sense of self-worth? How did this new status affect the way you thought about yourself and others? What was the impact on your life of the announcement of the termination of the DACA program in September 2017? How did this change the way you thought about yourself and others? Can you describe interactions that you may have had with police and law enforcement? What other changes and turning points in your life have affected your identity? All the materials for this study were approved by Western Illinois University's institutional review board (IRB).

The interviews were transcribed by a bilingual, bicultural DACA recipient in the original language of the interview. The data were analyzed question-by-question, and the answers were classified by themes, categories, and patterns. Feedback on drafts of the chapters was provided by the bilingual, bicultural transcriber. Numbers and percentages are offered when available and should be interpreted with caution given the small sample of this study.

Description of the Sample

Illinois is the third state in its proportion of DACA enrollees (5%). DACA recipients tend to live in metropolitan areas such as Los Angeles-Long Beach-Anaheim (89,900), New York-Newark-Jersey City (47,200), Dallas-Fort Worth-Arlington (36,700), Houston-The Woodlands-Sugar Land (35,800), and Chicago-Naperville-Elgin (34,100).[103] Most of the interviewees in this study attended K-12 public schools located in urban

TABLE I.1. DACA Recipients by Country of Origin

	Percentages of DACA Recipients	
Country	DACA Enrollees	Study's Sample
Mexico	79	81
El Salvador	4	3
Peru		3
Guatemala	3	3
Asia (China)	3	3
Europe (Poland)	1	7
Other	10	—

Note: Percentages rounded up.
Source: Orozco, Gustavo López, and Jens Manuel Krogstad, "Key Facts about Unauthorized Immigrants Enrolled in DACA," *Los Dreamers ante un Escenario de Cambio Legislativo: Inserción Social y Económica en México* (2020): 123.

settings, including Chicago and its suburbs. Some interviewees attended K-12 public schools in Beardstown and Monmouth, two small towns in rural Illinois.

Most DACA recipients interviewed for this study were from Mexico, followed by El Salvador, Guatemala, and Peru (see table A.1 in the appendix for complete details). Thus, this study's sample roughly reflects the national origins of DACA recipients, as it comprises four of the top five of DACA recipients' countries of origin.[104] With 183,000 undocumented immigrants, Chicago is home to 36 percent of Illinois's undocumented population.[105] Most of these immigrants come from Mexico and Latin America, 9 percent of them from Asia, and 5 percent from Europe. To honor this diversity, this study included one participant from China and three from Poland.

The mean age in my sample was 24.2 and the average age of arrival in the United States was 5.6. My sample was 55 percent female and 45 percent male (see table A.1 in appendix for complete details).

Not all DACA recipients obtain college degrees. In my sample, 70 percent have attended college and 30 percent have not. At the national level, 44 percent of DACA recipients do not pursue higher education.[106] Non-college track students were invited to participate by other participants who knew them. For this reason, non–college track students were slightly underrepresented in my sample compared with college track students.

Interviewees in this study were given the option of doing the interview in English or Spanish, and most respondents chose the first option (85%), which is proof of the high level of acculturation of the DREAMers in the sample. Finally, we also asked participants if they had children, and the answers were no (88%) and yes (12%). The interview also included other questions that are addressed thematically in the appropriate chapters.

Plan of the Book

Chapter 1 addresses the premigration stage, including the economic and other hardships facing the family in its country of origin, the reasons why the family came to the United States, the family preparation for migration, including parents' separation from the children, and the possible impact of these experiences on the children. Within the act of migration, it analyzes the separation from the extended family in their country of origin—sometimes to join the parents, the different strategies for crossing the border, the dangers and hardships faced during the crossing, and the impact of these factors on the lives of these youth. Both stages are addressed in relation to my sample.

Chapter 2 discusses the cultural incorporation of the immigrant youth during the postmigration stage. This chapter addresses the process of language acquisition and the integration into schools, as exemplified by interactions with other schoolchildren. In doing so, it pays attention to the school's diversity and the availability of different resources for language learning, such as English as a Second Language classes, and the level of inclusion experienced by my participants.

Chapter 3 addresses the support by teachers and other school personnel, including guidance counselors. It explores the level of support and assistance provided by these staff as perceived by my interviewees.

Chapter 4 analyzes the ways undocumented youth in this study found out they were undocumented and the impact of this discovery on their lives, expectations, and identity. It shows that, after a partial inclusion during the early school years, the undocumented youth hit a low point upon discovering they were undocumented or upon understanding the implications of such a realization.

After analyzing DACA's history, chapter 5 reviews the impact of the acquisition of DACA on my participants. It pays particular attention to the practical, psychological, and cultural implications of this new status. It further argues that despite DACA's limitations, its impact was positive and represented a high point in the *roller-coaster* incorporation of my participants.

Chapter 6 depicts the termination of DACA and the subsequent court decisions and administrative responses, including the August 2022 memo by the Biden administration to strengthen DACA.[107] It then describes the impact of the announcement of the termination of DACA on the lives of DREAMers among my sample. It shows that DACA's termination announcement threatened to throw DACA recipients back into a space of exclusion and caused an array of negative implications, emotions, and feelings of exclusion.

Chapter 7, after discussing the importance of political incorporation, assesses the level of political incorporation among participants in the sample. Whereas some DACA recipients have continued to be fearful of revealing their status and have remained private about it, others have been open about their immigration status and engaged in different groups supporting the DREAMers' cause, all the way from just showing up for a rally to assuming leadership positions in groups of DREAMers. This chapter analyzes these differing political cultures and their impact on the participants' sense of identity and lives.

The conclusion offers an overview of what was discussed in the book, develops its theoretical implications, and offers some final remarks.

1

The Crossing

Reasons for Migrating

Cynthia's dream is to run her own day care facility someday. She came to the United States from Mexico with her mom, dad, and one of her four siblings when she was twelve years old. Cynthia and her family moved for personal and family reasons more than economic ones, because her parents had gotten back together after a breakup. Cynthia and her family crossed the border without inspection, an experience that was very difficult and caused great fear. When she arrived in the United States, she did not know anyone and spoke no English. But her history of family violence in Mexico was left behind and Cynthia embraced this second chance in life.

The school that Cynthia attended upon arrival placed her in seventh grade, although she had been in eighth grade in Mexico. "And this is how my life started in the United States," she said sarcastically, as she described the moving experience in Spanish. The school system in the United States seemed very different from Mexico: more technologically advanced but lagging behind in math and science. Cynthia was part of an English as a Second Language (ESL) program throughout her schooling. Despite the support her teachers provided, she felt excluded because ESL students could not take elective classes. Nonetheless, Cynthia worked really hard on her English skills, which allowed her to place out of ESL classes in her senior year. This would allow her to have "the real high school experience."

Cynthia always knew she was undocumented because she remembered crossing. Even though undocumented students in Illinois have had the right to get in-state tuition since 2003,[1] she was told that as an undocumented student her only option was a community college. Cynthia wanted to achieve the American Dream and become a teacher and, with no financial aid, attended a community college near her home. Her college dream came to an end during her last year because of economic difficulties and the arrival of her son. Obtaining DACA gave Cynthia a sense of stability in her life. This sense of stability was replaced by fear and uncertainty with the announcement of the termination of DACA. "What would happen to my son?" Cynthia wondered.

Cynthia's life was transformed when her son was born. Even though she had to stop studying, and even though being a single mom was not part of her plan, it gave her a new sense of purpose. Getting ahead in life became a must. The fear of being sent to Mexico by President Trump and being separated from her son, an American citizen, consumed her. But she is hopeful her son will have the opportunities she lacked in Mexico. Cynthia tries to work hard, remain positive, and avoid being afraid.

As Cynthia's story shows, immigrants go through different stages in the process of incorporation into the host society. These stages are premigration, act of migration, and postmigration.[2] This chapter reviews the premigration stage, which begins with the decision to migrate, and the act of migration.[3] Potential immigrants consider both the socioeconomic situation of the family and their opportunities in their country of origin and the potential risks and rewards of migrating.[4] During this stage, the family engages in the first concrete moves toward migration, including studying the conditions in the host country, filing applications for visas, or hiring coyotes or smugglers. This chapter first reviews the literature on the complex economic, individual, and political reasons that lead people to migrate and assesses the extent to which this literature sheds light on why the families of the youth in my sample migrated to the United States.

The physical act of migrating occurs in the migration stage of incorporation into the new society. As this chapter will show, the migration experiences vary by age and immigration pathway.[5] Cynthia was twelve when she crossed the border without inspection, and she retained a memory of this crossing for the rest of her life. Her experience was very different from that of families who arrive with a visa through airports. For the immigrants like Cynthia, the migration stage can involve considerable risk and exposure to trauma.[6] Further, like many families,[7] Cynthia's parents apparently left three of their children in Mexico. The second part of this chapter describes the relationship between immigration and the border, efforts at border enforcement and the process of militarization of the US-Mexico border. It reviews the act of migration for respondents in my sample, including different strategies for crossing the border, dangers and hardships faced during the crossing, separation of families, and its impact on the lives of these youth and the family members left behind.

The Premigration Stage: Why Do People Migrate?

In 2020, 281 million people were living outside of their country of origin, and 50 million of those were living in the United States.[8] In the same year, Mexicans living in the United States accounted for 24 percent of all immigrants, a decline from 30 percent in 2000.[9] In turn, immigrants from India and China accounted for 6 percent of the foreign-born population, those from El Salvador, Vietnam, Cuba, and the Dominican Republic for 3 percent, and those from Guatemala and Korea for 2 percent. Combined, immigrants from these eight countries accounted for 57 percent of all immigrants in the United States in 2019.[10] Different global, systemic, and political reasons explain why people decide to move to a different country. Stephen Castles[11] classifies these as factors that: (1) are linked to globalization, transnationalism, and North-South relations; (2) arise from the migratory process; and (3) exist within the political system.

Globalization, Transnationalism, and North-South Relations

Common knowledge tells us that migration is determined by differences in income, employment, and other opportunities, usually between North and South countries.[12] Push-pull theories identify economic, environmental, and demographic factors that are assumed to push people out of their places of origin and pull them into destination places. If rational calculations on income gains were the only consideration when a person decides to emigrate, then the poorest in a society would move at higher rates. Data on migration to the United States, however, provide mixed evidence on the idea that poverty pushes immigrants (negative selection) out of their country.[13] The high levels of income inequality in Mexico would seem to suggest that negative selection should prevail, and that the poorest, least educated in society would migrate to the United States.[14] However, both early[15] and recent research[16] found that migrants from Mexico were in the middle of education distribution. Overall, the evidence on the selection of immigrants from Mexico is inconclusive.

Global theories provide more complex explanations for international migration. The current dynamics of South-North migration flows can be explained by the ongoing process of capitalist restructuring,[17] which has deepened social inequalities, poverty, and marginalization within undeveloped nations. For instance, the North American Free Trade Agreement (NAFTA) was a major driver of the migration from Mexico to the United States, turning Mexico into the world's primary emigration country.[18] NAFTA was also sold to the American public as a means to deter emigration by speeding economic and job growth in Mexico, but it has done neither.[19] Even though immigration from Mexico slowed down after 2010, this change can be attributed to other factors, such as the 2008 recession.[20]

Factors Arising from the Internal Dynamics of the Migratory Process

Other theories point to factors related to the social dynamics of the migration process. One such theory is that bureaucratic rules to regulate the admission of foreign citizens effectively shape migration. These theories, however, fail to pass the historical test. For instance, the securitization of the border had the unintended effect of making immigration from Mexico more permanent by raising the cost, both human and economic, of crossing the border for seasonal work.[21] Another case in point are the immigration reforms in the United States initiated in the 1960s, thought to open the door to mass immigration from Asia and Latin America by eliminating past discriminatory policies established by quota laws from 1921 and 1924.[22] While this may be true for Asians, it is not the case for Latin Americans, who were earlier exempted from the application of the quota laws and faced more restrictions to legal migration after 1965, because of the cap established for immigration from the Western Hemisphere. The boom in Latin American migration occurred *in spite* of rather than *because* of changes in US immigration law.[23]

Migration network theory addresses how immigrants create and maintain social ties with other migrants and with family and friends back home, and how this can lead to the emergence of social networks that encourage immigration.[24] Chain migration describes the way in which the initial migration of certain individuals is usually followed by the migration of family and community members.[25] Today, scholars emphasize the role of migrant networks in aiding the process of migration by providing help with work, housing, and other needs soon after immigrants' arrival into a new county.[26] These networks are also referred to as social capital.[27] Migration network theory speaks to the cumulative causation of migration as a result of reduced social, economic, and emotional costs of migration due to the existence of networks pursuant to the formation of migration networks.[28] Because of its sociological aspects, it superseded the economistic "push and pull" conceptions that prevailed earlier.

Factors within the Political System

Political factors also seem to be important in explaining immigration. To be sure, overpopulation, poverty, and economic stagnation have a role in pushing immigrants out of their country,[29] but these explanations are often overly simplistic. Saskia Sassen provides the example of the Dominican Republic to prove this point.[30] At first sight, the high levels of overpopulation, poverty, and economic stagnation would seem to explain emigration from this country. A closer look, however, reveals that these factors were present before the mass exodus from the Dominican Republic to the United States. "What, then, accounted for the sudden surge?" Sassen asks.[31] In the case of the Dominican Republic, the surge seems to be linked to relationships between the two countries that were formed during and after the occupation by US Marines in 1965, in response to the election of left-wing presidential candidate John Bosch, which resulted in the growth of political and economic ties as well as the subsequent networks created by the political refugees that emigrated to the United States.

In turn, Mexican migration to the United Sates is related to countless linkages between the two countries. Until the 1848 Treaty of Hidalgo, which ended the Mexican American War, much of the Southwest of the United States belonged to Mexico.[32] From 1900 to 1914, labor flowed more or less freely from Mexico to the United States, and Mexican workers provided much needed labor for agriculture and the building of infrastructure in the Southwest.[33] Later, the Bracero Program, a set of agreements launched in 1942 by a small group of government administrators, provided a framework for the importation of agricultural workers.[34] By the time the Bracero Program ended it had supplied an "endless army" of cheap labor to Southwest growers.[35] In addition, it had created a steady flow of immigrant laborers and a system of networks, which continued to sustain the immigration from Mexico to the United States.

Parents' Decision to Migrate

Participants in my sample were asked, *How did your parents decide to come to the United States and why?* All but four respondents (13%) were able to answer this question (table 1.1). The main reasons for the parental decision to migrate to the United States were economic and also wanting to provide a better future to the children (more than just economic), followed by family reunification, political problems, and violence. Four interviewees stated that the move to the United States was not planned. I classified answers as *economic* if the main reason for migrating had to do with insufficient income, lack of jobs or well-paid jobs, desire to save, and problems with family business. I classified the answers as *beyond economic* if the main reason for migrating included considerations such as better opportunities, starting something new or a new start, to have a better life, and a comment that said that life in Mexico was difficult without specifying the reason.

I classified the answers as *family* if the main reason given for migrating was reuniting with family, such as a spouse, father, uncle, or cousin. I classified the answers as *violence* if the specific reason given for migrating was related to the violence and insecurity experienced in the country of origin. I classified the answers as *political* if the main reason for migrating was related to a specific government and the

TABLE 1.1. Reasons for Migration, My Sample

Reasons	Count	%
Economic	9	27
Beyond Economic Calculations	9	27
Family	6	18
Political Problems	1	3
Violence	1	3
Was Not Planned	4	13
Unclear /No Answer	4	13

family's relationship with it. Finally, I classified as *unplanned* the answers that stated that the parents did not envision living in the United States, that migration wasn't planned, or that the family decided to stay while on a visit or vacation. When the reasons given were mixed, for instance, economic problems and reuniting with family, I chose the one that seemed the most immediate reason to migrate.

Economic Reasons

Economic theories of migration tell us that people move to a different country because of rational calculations about economic gains. One-quarter of my respondents cited economic reasons as the main driver of the family's decision to move to the United States (table 1.1).

Even though to a degree my respondents' families migrated to the United States in search of a better income, this explanation alone is too simplistic. For starters, if income is a main driver of migration, the poorest is society should move at higher rates. However, my data corroborated historical data on German migration showing that the persons who migrated were not the poorest in society.[36] More specifically, many of the families had businesses in Mexico and were therefore members of the middle class. Also, as I show below, moving for *better opportunities* means more than just economic opportunities, and most parents had the future of their children in mind in addition to their own. Finally, at times the economic considerations were intertwined with family and personal ones.

Ismael's comments are significant because they exemplify three of the four characteristics described previously:

> My parents decided to come to the United States because of the economic situation in Mexico at the time in the 1980s or the 1990s. Despite my mom having gone to a technical school and having a job, it wasn't enough to provide for me and the family. My dad was working as a dental assistant making dental molds for dental offices. But it wasn't enough, so my parents decided to leave for the U.S. in search of better opportunities and for me.

Ismael was well-informed about the economic situation in Mexico during the 1980s and 1990s. In 1979, the US Federal Reserve Board raised the federal funds rate and as a consequence of this increase, borrowing costs for Mexico rose substantially.[37] In 1982, Mexico suspended debt payments.[38] In 1983, Mexico signed an agreement with the International Monetary Fund (IMF) to implement neoliberal economic policies.[39] These policies continued to be followed by different presidents through the 1990s and beyond, causing a 30–40 percent decrease in wages and salaries and a 12 percent rise in unemployment and precarious jobs.[40] The Zapatista rebellion in 1994 was primarily an opposition to these policies and the implementation of NAFTA.[41] As these facts show, the crisis in Mexico was influenced by actions initiated by the US government and multilateral institutions like the IMF.

Classic economic approaches suggest that the poorest in society are the most likely to migrate. However, many of the parents of the youth I interviewed seemed to belong to the Mexican middle class. Many definitions of middle class are based on income, but some definitions are still based on occupation.[42] Unfortunately, my study lacked information about the income of the undocumented youths' parents in Mexico, but did include information about occupations. Classic sociological theory tells us that professional and technical occupations constitute the upper middle class, other white-collar occupations of the middle class proper, and manual occupations the working class.[43] According to these definitions, Ismael's parents belonged to the Mexican middle class: His mom had a technical degree and his dad was a dental assistant. Other parents referenced in my sample also seem to have belonged to the middle class in their country of origin. For instance, Ernesto's mom ran a store, Luna's dad managed a rancho, and Ana's and Nathaniel's families had businesses.

Despite both parents having jobs, in Ismael's words, their income "wasn't enough." This is the part of Ismael's explanation of his parents' reason to migrate that fits into the classical theories that argue that income gains calculation in the host country makes people more likely to migrate.[44] Other interviewees also referred to the slim income their parents made in their countries of origin despite their efforts. Ernesto, for example, explained, "I remember my mom had a store that she used to manage and make ends meet. And basically, bartending at night to supply for myself and the family." In turn, Luna said, "because we are like from a small rural town and he [her dad] always tells me that they don't really have work or that they don't really have well-paid jobs . . . I guess my dad just wanted more." Similarly, Marcos explained that his dad, who was a construction worker, could not find work in Mexico. Obviously, economic reasons at least partly explained why families moved.

More Than Just Economics: The Search for Better Opportunities and a Brighter Future for the Children

"Since early times man has been on the move, always looking for new places, better opportunities, easier living conditions."[45] One-quarter of my interviewees gave reasons for migrating that went beyond economic considerations to include a search for better opportunities and a better future for the children (table 1.1). As Ismael mentioned at the end of his comments, his parents came to the United States "in search of better opportunities and for me." Do better opportunities strictly mean economic prospects? When the reason for migrating is the children, can we consider parents as maximizers of their own utility function?

Certainly, better opportunities may mean more than just jobs and income differentials between countries of origin and destination. A study among immigrants in New Zealand found that immigrants moved for better opportunities in several areas, including (1) better future for the

TABLE 1.2. Main Reasons for Migrating

Reasons	%
Relaxed Pace of Life	44
Climate or Clean Environment	40
Better Future for the Children	39
Friendly People	28
Employment Opportunities	28
Safety from Crime	27
Join Family Members	23
Educational Opportunities	18

Source: John Bryant and Paul Merwood, "Reasons for Migrating and Settlement Outcomes: Evidence from the Longitudinal Immigration Survey New Zealand," *Labour, Employment and Work in New Zealand*, 2008; New Zealand Statistics, "Longitudinal Immigration Survey: New Zealand (LisNZ) Wave 1," Wellington: Statistics New Zealand, 2008.

children, (2) educational opportunities, and (3) economic conditions.[46] Further, the same study found that employment opportunities ranked fourth among the reasons why people migrated, preceded by a relaxed pace of life, the climate or clean environment, a better future for the children, and the availability of friendly people (table 1.2).[47]

Among respondents in my sample, the meaning of better opportunities differed. Certainly, a better future or better opportunities was sometimes described in economic terms. In this sense, Hugo explained, "So my dad wanted, I guess, a brighter future for me because of the way he grew up in an already big family. And there wasn't really anything to go around, even my grandpa was working the hardest. So he just wanted something different for me and my mom." As this comment shows, even though Hugo cited a brighter future for him as a reason to migrate, he later referred to hardship suffered by a big family that didn't have "anything to go around."

Other interviewees, however, expressed that the reasons for migrating to the United States went beyond strictly economic ones. Mary, for example, recounted,

Like I said, I come from a *pueblecito* in Mexico. There is nothing there, just like three houses. Coming to the United States kind of opened my possibilities and gave me that chance in life. Before when I got here it was kind of odd because of the language and everything in general is very different, but once you get a little accustomed to it, you get used to it as well. You get used to having, I don't know, internet and pretty much every comfort you have here.

In this comment, Mary referred to several differences between her *pueblecito* (small village) and the place she made her home in the United States. Her home village was tiny: "There were like three houses," in her words. In contrast, the United States is "very different" and offers internet and "every comfort." Even though some of these issues, like having access to the internet, may be related to economic opportunities, Mary seemed to be referring to a generally better quality of life that she believes the United States offers.

Others also referred to the opportunities the United States grants for a different or new life. Andrés explained, "I don't remember how my parents got here, but I do remember my mom telling me that she wanted for me to start a better life." Even though Andrés was not very specific about what he meant by "a better life," it is unlikely that he was just referring to economic opportunities. In a similar vein, Cynthia stated, "my mom wanted a new start." In this case, Cynthia seems to be discussing more of a personal need for a new start than simply a new economic start. These findings corroborate previous research that found that immigrants move for better opportunities in several areas, including reasons that go beyond economic conditions.[48]

The youth interviewed in this study lacked a role in the decision to migrate. Despite this, in many cases they were a major consideration in their parents' decision. This fact also runs counter to the argument that people migrate in response to rational calculations about their own well-being. The second part of Ismael's statement cited above exemplifies this. Ismael stated his parents moved "in search of better opportunities" and "for me." A few other interviewees made similar comments. Julio explained his mom wanted to have a better future for him and for his sister. Daniel reported that his mom wanted the children to have a better life. In turn, Jessica said, "My dad was planning since I was born, and was like, 'what am I gonna give to my daughter?' So he was like, I need to go over there." As these comments show, the children in the family were an important factor in the decision to migrate.

Family Networks and Reunification

Networks of friends and family increase the likelihood of international migration because they lower the costs of migrating and increase its expected gains.[49] One-fifth of my interviewees cited the presence of a family member in the United States as the reason for migrating (table 1.1). Several interviewees reported coming to the United States to reunite with their father. Ignacio, for instance, stated, "I first came here when I was a kid. I was pretty young. I remember that. It was the three of us and then we went [back] to Mexico. Then my dad came back to the United States and then he brought me with him ... I came with my uncle when I was thirteen years old." As this comment shows, Ignacio's family's process of migration took time, and the main reason for migrating was to reunite with his dad. Hugo, in turn, explained, "In terms of deciding to come, my dad was already here, and he wanted to be with his family, so he asked my mom if she wanted to come here, obviously to be together as a family." Being "together as a family" was a major consideration for many in the decision to come to the United States.

Similarly, Justice explained, "We came here to somehow reunite with my father because he worked here, back and forth." Justice's dad was a seasonal worker for a while until he decided to bring the rest of the family to the United States. Mary's mom had migrated with her brother and the reason she gave for the family's migration to the United States was to reunite with her mom and brother. Ernesto's mom had a boyfriend who came to the United States first. In this sense, he explained,

> When I was born, my mom had a boyfriend named Leo, as I called him. And they were about twenty-three years, twenty-four years old. And he worked at the mercado in the city. When I was four, he left his job in Mexico to come to Illinois and send us money. So he left, I want to say, in January or February of 2001 ... I just remember one day, my mom got our passports, we got on a greyhound, and we came to Illinois.

In the case of Ernesto, even though they had economic reasons to migrate, the immediate reason for migrating was that his mom's boyfriend was already living in the United States.

In some cases, more distant family members were in the United States. Carmen, for example, explained that her uncle told her dad about a job. Lucio said his father had a cousin who lived in the United States legally and that this was the reason why they migrated. In turn, Andrés explained how confused he was when upon arrival he met his family members who were already in the United States. "I didn't really know who they were until my mom started saying, 'this is your uncle, this is your aunt.'" Luna was similarly confused when meeting family members who were already living in the United States. She explained,

> But the only thing I do remember about my arrival and I think it is really funny . . . Is that I was in a vehicle and we had already arrived in the home where I was going to live at with my parents. And this man, he was my uncle, he opened the door and he was just making silly faces and he was just smiling at me. And I was just so confused because I didn't know where I was and, obviously, I didn't recognize anybody. But that's when I realized they were just excited to see me for the first time.

As these examples show, several interviewees had family members who were already in the United States who likely influenced or eased the process of migration.

Politics and Violence

Many times, reasons inside of the political system generate migration. This was the case for two interviewees in my sample: one from El Salvador and one from Peru. Andreíta, for instance, referred to the situation mentioned above, which places El Salvador as one of the countries with the highest rate of violence in the world.[50] In this sense, discussing the reasons why her parents moved to the United States, Andreíta explained,

> Immediately, prior to moving here, I know they took other factors into their decision as well, like the violence. I was only six years old at the

time, so I didn't see much of it, I didn't experience much of it, but I know that my brother who is nine years older than me had already been experiencing like muggings in specific areas where my aunts used to work. He felt like it was controlled by gangs.

As this comment shows, gang violence in El Salvador was a major factor in favor of emigrating for Andreíta's family.

Another interviewee, Melody, whose parents migrated from Peru, described the reasons why she believed her parents migrated to the United States. Melody's mother worked for a bank in Peru and her father was in the army for a while and then became a police officer working alongside President Fujimori. According to Melody, there was a lot of backlash against Fujimori even though she didn't know exactly why her parents had to leave Peru. In 2000, with increased authoritarian control over the legislative and judicial branches along with constitutional reforms to allow for his reelection, President Alberto Fujimori campaigned for a third term in office.[51] Amid protests, Fujimori tried to resign but was finally impeached at the end of 2000. Melody's father likely had to leave Peru because he had worked for President Fujimori. Even though Melody offered no additional details, it is clear that political reasons were the driver of the family's migration.

Polish Interviewees

My sample included three interviewees from Poland, analyzed separately in this book to allow for a clearer comparison between White and non-White DACA recipients (Latino/a and Asian). Overall, the reasons for migrating among Polish families were similar to those of the non-White, predominantly Latino/a families. For Mateusz's family it came down to an economic/financial decision. He explained,

Like for most people, I think, it was a financial decision. So, for a while my parents were doing very well, had a nice house and everything was going well. My dad had his own business. But then the business went under. And they got in a lot of debt and sort of, you know, started looking for places to emigrate.

Mateusz's family was in a good economic situation at some point but as the family business failed, the family considered migrating. Mateusz's case also illustrates my previous point that the families who migrated were not the poorest in their societies.

The other two interviewees from Poland, Peter and Ali, provided reasons for migrating that went beyond economic considerations. Peter's family sent him to the United States to live with his grandmother. He explained, "Just to get a better life than you did in Poland, you know. There [in Poland], I wouldn't have as nice of a future as I could here. So they made a choice to have me just come here and hopefully, you know, become someone one day." Not unlike some of the Latino/a families, Peter was sent to the United States alone to have a better future and to "become somebody" one day. Ali's family, in turn, came to the United States in search of better opportunities. She recalled,

Yeah, so I was nine years old when we arrived here. My parents decided to drop their life in Poland and come to the US, that typical search of a better life. It was mostly my father's decision to come here, because he knew we'd have better opportunities for them as far as work. And for me and my little brother as far as education and just our life here.

Ali's statements show that the better life her family was looking for included not only a better job for her parents, but also educational and other life opportunities for the children.

It is worth noting that all of the interviewees from Poland knew people in the United States who helped them lower the cost of migration. Notably, Peter came to live with his grandmother, and several of his uncles were also in the United States. Mateusz and Ali also had connections who helped them settle in the United States. Mateusz explained how a friend of a friend helped them settle here:

So we didn't have family here. I think my mom had an old friend in Poland that lived in America for about twenty years before he went back to Poland. So he had some friends who were American citizens. And he contacted some friends that lived in Chicago, an older couple, who rented out their basement to us when we first moved here . . . So we rented there from them for the first six months that we lived in the United States for

$400 a month. And then eventually my parents were able to get an apartment in Chicago after six months.

As this comment shows, Mateusz's family relied on a "friend of a friend" to settle in Chicago, helping them to get housing in their first months in the country.

Immigration and the Border: The Crossing

International migration is inherently a *political* process that arises from the organization of the world into categories of mutually exclusive sovereign states, commonly called the "Westphalian System."[52] Some authors believe that restrictive immigration policies prevail worldwide because they constitute a sine qua non condition for the maintenance of the international state system.[53] Borders have long signified a sharp division between here and there, inside and outside, us and them.[54] Perhaps the most iconic borders are the boundaries between the United States and Mexico or the high seas or rugged landscapes of the European Union or Australia.[55] Nicolas de Genova assigned the label of Border Spectacle to the "enduring and durable hegemony of the body of immigration law (and its history of legislative debate and law-making) that has produced, for each 'national' state, the very premises and predicates of a whole regime of migrant 'legality' and 'illegality.'"[56] Thus, immigration policies reinforce territorial identities and re-legitimize the boundaries of the imagined community.[57] Apprehension, threats of detection, interception, detention, and deportation contribute to produce the border.[58]

Immigrants, especially those who cross the border without inspection, experience violence, abuse, trauma, and even death during the crossing.[59] In recent years, border enforcement strategy has centered on the development of a militarized logic and an enforcement plan that emphasizes pain, suffering, and trauma as deterrents to undocumented migration.[60] Increased enforcement measures have not deterred unauthorized crossings. Between 2005 and 2012, an estimated average of 570,000 Mexican-born migrants attempted to enter the United States each year.[61] Further, the unprecedented militarization of the border had the paradoxical effect of turning migration from a circular, seasonal flow of male workers to a settled population of families.[62] If border enforcement is not effective at

deterring border crossings, why spend billions on it? Immigration policies and the borders that define them have strong symbolic meanings and
serve as a tool of demarcation and control.[63]

After an increase in unauthorized migration during the 1980s, the US
government intensified border enforcement efforts due to this perceived
"Latino Threat."[64] The most well-known politician contributing to the
Latino Threat Narrative was President Ronald Reagan, who in 1985 declared that undocumented migration was a threat to national security,
warning that "terrorists and subversives [are] just two days away from
the [border crossing at] Harlingen, Texas" and that "communist agents
were ready to feed on the anger of recent Central and South American immigrants who will not realize their own version of the American
dream."[65] The Latino Threat Narrative reached its peak with Donald
Trump, who exploited (and continues to exploit) the anxiety of a non-
college-educated White electorate, falsely declaring that immigrants
from Mexico are criminals and rapists.[66] This rhetoric was accompanied
by an astounding number of immigration restrictions.[67]

In theory, border enforcement works by raising the economic and
human cost of crossing the border and offsetting expected gains from
crossing.[68] However, from 1986 to 2008, the undocumented population
in the United States grew from three million to twelve million persons,
despite astronomical increases in the number of Border Patrol officers,
hours spent patrolling the border, and nominal funding.[69] The Immigration Reform and Control Act (IRCA) from 1986 and the Illegal Immigration Reform and Immigrant Responsibility Act (IIRIRA) from 1996
enhanced immigration enforcement by penalizing employers who hire
undocumented immigrants, and by granting the Immigration and Naturalization Service (INS) wide-ranging authority to arrest, detain, and remove immigrants.[70] The implementation of preventive measures to deter
border crossings, later heightened by the September 11 efforts that treated
immigration as an international security issue, was not effective and, in
fact, raised the economic and human cost of crossing the border.[71]

The Crossing

Immigrants and travelers normally enter countries through different
border security checks by land, sea, or airports. Migrants can also cross

the border without inspection through unauthorized border crossings. The US-Mexico border is close to 2,000 miles long from southern California to the southern tip of Texas at the Gulf of Mexico.[72] The United States has 167 land ports of entry, 47 of which are on the Southern border.[73] The US Customs and Border Protection (CBP), a branch of the Department of Homeland Security, is the primary agency responsible for overseeing trade and travel in and out of the country, along with the Transportation Security Administration (TSA) and Drug Enforcement Administration (DEA).[74] Seaports were commonly used during the nineteenth and early twentieth centuries.[75] Most travelers now come through airports. Before the pandemic, in 2018, 233.6 million people traveled in and out of the United States through airports.[76]

Overland Crossing without Inspection

Immigrants attempting to enter the United States via overland travel at the Southern border have the most dangerous and potentially traumatic experiences.[77] The efforts to deter unauthorized border crossings in urban areas, such as Operation Hold-the-Line in El Paso in 1993, and Operation Gatekeeper in San Diego in 1994, diverted immigrant crossing to more dangerous areas such as the Sasabe-Arizona Desert, the All-American Canal, or the Rio Grande, eventually raising risks to the immigrants, including death.[78] Threats to physical health include heat stroke, rattlesnake bites, long-distance walks without food, water, and shelter, lack of sanitary facilities, and lack of medical care.[79] Undocumented immigrants are also vulnerable to physical, sexual, and verbal abuse by members of the local population, authorities, and organized crime, and are commonly exposed to expressions of racism, xenophobia, abuse, and violence.[80] A study of Latino adults in the United States found that 16 percent experience anxiety-related disorders and 4 percent experience post-traumatic stress disorder (PTSD) during their lifetimes.[81]

Authors and advocates refer to immigration law's "shadow" to describe the extent to which undocumented immigrants have to live, work, study, or function in society in hidden ways.[82] As this research shows, undocumented youth's first stories and memories about coming to the United States also frequently include hiding. Because of their young age, some of my interviewees did not remember crossing the border. This was the case for Ana, who came to the United States at the age of four through the desert with a coyote, her mom, and her uncle. Ana's parents had been living in the United States for several years but decided their children should be born in Mexico. When their father had saved enough money to bring the rest of the family, he sent for them. Ana explained,

> Oh, I don't remember anything. I just have stories that my mother would tell me about hiding in these little sheds and having to be really quiet; they didn't want anyone to hear us. And my brother was in a kangaroo so he was attached to my mom's chest and my uncle was the one who would hold my hand.

Even though Ana did not remember crossing, her family's stories about coming to the United States were passed on to her.

Similarly, Zoe had only partial memories of the crossing. She did not recall crossing the river, but she did remember other details.

> Hmm, so my dad was carrying my older sister that at the time was nine, I was three about to be four. And the guy who transports people, the coyote, he was carrying me and then my mom who was pregnant . . . so, I remember that image and I also have another image, I, still an image, hmm, I remember being like hiding in these bushes and I don't know if it was ICE that drove by us, but I do remember it was a van . . . I do remember being really, really thirsty and kept telling my dad, "Can we go now? Or can I drink something?" I remember just being super thirsty and didn't understand why I couldn't get some water. Hmm, so that's probably the only images that always stayed with me.

Despite being only three at the time of crossing, Zoe remembered being carried by the *coyote*, a border smuggler that immigrants use to help them enter the country.[83] It is estimated that out of those who decided to cross the border without inspection, 66 percent used a coyote.[84] Cynthia also remembered hiding in the bushes from what was likely the US Border Patrol, and not Immigration and Customs Enforcement (ICE), the agency dedicated to the internal enforcement of immigration laws.[85] She may have been dehydrated after crossing the border but nonetheless was denied water. One can only wonder about the impact of this experience on the life of a three-year-old.

Although Hector was only four years old when he came to the United States, he also remembered the traumatic crossing that involved sleeping in a dumpster, a separation from his mom, and a car accident. He remembered,

> And at first it was a little weird for me because I remember the entire trip from leaving Mexico, to sleeping in a dumpster at one point, to being separated from my mom. And then being in an accident, me and my cousin, and my cousin being detained by the police. And me sitting outside and talking to the cops the best I could even though I could only speak Spanish at the time. And then ultimately being released from the police station. And then meeting up again with my mom and driving over here to Illinois. So that entire trip, I could distinguish everything that happened.

Hector had vivid memories of his crossing despite his age. It is unclear why he had to sleep in a dumpster, but it is apparent the accident and subsequent detention by the police was traumatic, especially because his mom was not with him. Hector's crossing also included his first encounter with language barriers.[86]

Mary also crossed the border without inspection when she was thirteen. She explained to me,

> I came in and crossed the border just like many other people. What I remember is that I left my house in Mexico in the beginning of December, and I didn't make it to Chicago until the beginning of January. I got here January 19th. It took me almost a month to get to the United States. The reason why it took us almost a month is because the people who were taking us here . . . you know immigration officers kept getting us and sending us back. They kept sending us back and those people kept bringing us back here. It just took a while to cross the border.

Mary and her group used coyotes to cross the border, "the people who were taking us here," as she puts it. It took them a month to get to the United States because they were apprehended by Border Patrol and sent back to Mexico multiple times. After they were sent back, they would cross again until they succeeded. It is not uncommon for immigrants to make several attempts to cross the border.[87]

Crossing through Ports of Entry

Despite the myth that most undocumented immigrants come to the United States without inspection, crossing through ports of entry remains the most common method.[88] In 2017, the number of immigrants who overstayed their visas was double the number of people caught trying to cross the US-Mexico border.[89] The ports of entry must serve as a filter that differentiates among entrants.[90] The ideal port should have an efficient, rapid detection process to sort out law-violating from non-law-violating entries, register entries, and assign regulations and tariffs as appropriate.[91] The bulk of illegal drugs seems to enter through commercial shipments at land, air, and seaports.[92]

La Línea

The documentation needed to enter the United States is very rigorous, but land border checkpoints may have been less strict at the time my interviewees crossed the border. For example, US citizens were able to cross into the country at land borders with a declaration of citizenship until January 31, 2008.[93] Two of my interviewees crossed what immigrants refer to as "*la Línea*." Although the phrase *la Línea* (the line) is often used to refer to the border itself, crossing la Línea means crossing the border by legitimate security checkpoints, usually by car, using counterfeit IDs, somebody else's ID, or by simply hiding.[94] In the case of children, many times they pose as somebody else's children, including relatives or smugglers. Laura, for example, came with relatives, as she described,

> I remember, my dad did actually cross the border, but my sibling and I crossed what is called la Línea, like by car with some of my relatives' papers, but immigration didn't ask us much when we were crossing just because we were asleep and we were young. So, my aunts were actually the ones who helped us cross, and they just pretended we were their kids.

We were just coming back from a vacation from Mexico, that's what I've been told.

Apparently, Laura's father crossed the border without inspection but sent his kids to cross through la Línea, presumably because it is safer. Because the children were young and sleeping, border agents did not ask for much. Being with a relative likely made the experience much less frightening than crossing with a coyote.

Marcos was five years old when he crossed the border through la Línea, probably with a coyote. As Laura's did, his parents crossed separately, without inspection.

> My mom didn't cross the border with us. She actually left us at the border because we passed through what is called The Line meaning that we don't actually pass through the desert or something. Ah, we passed in a car hidden from border agents or giving a form of ID that says we are from here. A fake ID or something. I was five at the time so we were put to sleep so that we wouldn't wake up while we were crossing the border. So next thing I know I am in a house with my sisters and random people, and we were asking for my mom. This lasted around, I want to say about five days, it's my recollection and we would be waking up at late hours at night and said, "we need to go, we need to go." Meaning we needed to move to a different house. What I'm guessing, what I gathered, is because immigration was on our tails or something. So, we would move, my sisters and I would move to different houses until we got to California.

As this description by Marcos depicts, his crossing was similar to Laura's but the arrival to the United States seemed upsetting given that he and his siblings continued to be separated from their mom for five days. Being woken up "by random people" in the middle of the night to change hiding places was probably also traumatic.

Crossing through Airports

One of the major challenges facing the Department of Homeland Security is scrutinizing the number of authorized travelers that enter and leave the country every day.[95] The United States requires a tourist visa issued by the traveler's country's American Embassy or Consulate for most countries in Latin America. It is estimated that 30–40 percent of undocumented immigrants come to the United States through airports with a visa and later overstay their visas.[96] Visa requirements vary by country of origin. To obtain a visitor visa, people must provide a passport, a photo, an application, and money for a fee.[97] Often, travelers need to present evidence of purpose of the trip, intent to depart the United States after the trip, and ability to pay the cost of the trip.[98]

Several of our interviewees came with a visa through airports. For geographic reasons, most of the youth who came by plane were from countries other than Mexico, including Peru, Guatemala, El Salvador, and China. Nonetheless, their experiences seemed to be traumatic. Benita, for instance, came from Mexico by plane with a coyote when she was four.

> I come at the age of four. I would have come earlier but circumstances couldn't . . . I do remember crossing and everything. I remember like, my mom took me . . . con el coyote, so I went with a stranger. She was American and my mom paid her. At the moment [I] passed for one of her nieces because I kind of looked like her. I looked kind of white, like I had light skin and like brown hair. She passed me. So, my mom took me with her. Before I used to cry . . . My mom, you know, kind of me dio terapias, like, "oh she's your aunt, you know." Like, I kind of had to tell that to the police officer that she's my aunt. You know, I had to study that. So yeah, my mom left me with her . . . I think it was three weeks in total I didn't see my mom, until I got contact with her . . . So we crossed there, and I saw my mom again.

Benita was very young when she came to the United States with a coyote, who she called "a stranger." Because she was light-skinned, Benita was able to pose as the coyote's niece. Benita had to be coached to lie to law enforcement agents, what she calls "me dio terapias," and tell them she was the coyote's niece. Benita began disguising her identity at an early age, and even today, she never discloses her immigration status.

Melody's trip to the United States from Peru was probably easier than that of most interviewees. She and her family took a plane from Lima, Peru, and she was told they were coming to the United States to visit

Disney World. In reality, though, they were moving to the United States and did not visit Disney World after all. Melody explained,

> Yeah. I was actually eight years old when we came to United States. We came via airplane. We came on a tourist visa. My parents told us that we were going to Disney World . . . So when people would ask us, we would tell them, "Oh, we're going to Disney World for vacation." And it was normal, we didn't really think much of it. I genuinely didn't think we were moving. I thought it was just a vacation trip because we used to travel all the time. But it was myself, my sister, my older brother, and my dad who came to United States via plane. And then when we landed in Miami, the day after, we flew here to Illinois, to meet up with my mom. We came in August of 2001, so just a month before 9/11 happened. So, we've been here for quite some time and lived in Illinois the whole time and haven't moved. But my parents did sacrifice a lot; they would tell us how . . . we would ask them, "Oh, when are we going back home?" Because, you know, I thought it was just a vacation, but it was a permanent, a permanent move.

Melody's family had a more comfortable premigration socioeconomic situation than most of my other interviewees, reflected in the fact that they "used to travel all the time." She and her siblings must have been confused, and even disappointed, when the supposed trip to Disney World turned into a move.

Two of my interviewees got lost when arriving in the United States. Andreíta was left in her native Guatemala for two years until she came to join her parents at the age of five. She described the trip:

> And when I came here, I came with my grandma and my uncle. They were the ones who dropped me off and I pretty much remember the whole experience of just leaving Guatemala. Traveling . . . I don't know where we went to . . . I don't know what is called, think we went to Texas or something. When we first went to Texas, and we waited for a little bit, and then we switched planes. I remember getting to the airport and like, it was huge. This is massive . . . I had no idea where I am and let alone my grandma or my uncle, they had no idea where they are. But we went to the airport and my uncle rented a car. He was so confident thinking

he knows where he was going but then we got so lost (chuckles). And I just remember falling asleep in the back of the car and thinking, "we are never going to make it."

Andreíta has a vivid memory of her arrival in the United States. It was probably comforting to travel with her grandma, the person with whom she had lived for the last two years. Her experience of getting lost, however, even though she chuckled when talking about it, must have been a little upsetting. After the family changed plans because her uncle couldn't find the meeting place, Andreíta was finally reunited with her parents.

José also had a confusing experience at an airport. He came with his family from El Salvador at the age of six, after experiencing losses due to the 2001 earthquake and the insecurity and violence in his country. He clearly remembered the trip to the United States.

> We had several stops that I don't really remember but the first thing was really getting lost at O'Hare airport. I remember we were at the airport trying to find my uncle who was picking us up. I think we were there for about four hours just trying to get out. It was confusing. Obviously, the airport is much larger than what we had back home. And I remember we got there late at night. Our uncle picked us up and brought us to our first apartment in Carol Stream, Illinois. Not too far from me.

José's crossing experience was likely not too stressful, considering he was with his parents and came by plane. The four-hour period during which they could not find his uncle, however, was probably worrisome.

Migration and Family Reunification

The process of migration is an "economic, social and political process that affects the person who moves, those who stay behind, and the places where they go."[99] The process of migration of an entire family can be painful and stressful, take years, and entail the separation of family members, sometimes on a permanent basis.[100] Because this study deals with first-generation immigrant children, the family reunification most likely took place when the children arrived in the United States.

TABLE 1.3. Persons Who Migrated First, My Sample

Person Who Migrated First	%
Father	57
Mother	3
Mother and Father	14
Father and Sister	3
Brother and Mother	3
Brother	3
All Together	18

Typically, males migrate first and are later joined by working-age sons and then by wives and younger children.[101] In these cases, wives and children join the father once he has found a job, a home, or has acquired some stability, or a clearer sense of what the family migration would entail.[102] But the migration process can take multiple forms, including wives migrating first, or the couple migrating first and leaving children behind.[103]

Even though interviewees in my study were not asked which member of the family migrated first, this issue came up in all but four interviews. The classification of interviewees' statements can be found in table 1.3. More than half of the interviewees in my sample stated that their father migrated to the country first, and close to one-fifth reported that both parents came first. Only one interviewee said that her mother migrated and she, her dad, and siblings stayed in Peru. Several others reported that the whole family migrated together, and in these cases, the family usually had some sort of visa that later expired (table 1.3). Other forms the process of migration took included the father and a sister coming first, the mother and a brother coming first, and a brother migrating first (table 1.3).

Likely, the most painful form of migration was one that involved the separation of the children from the parents. Several interviewees described the impact of this type of migration. Andrea, for example, remembered,

> My parents came first in 1997. They came alone and left us with our grandparents in Mexico for five years. They came due to the lack of resources, to have a better life because life in Mexico is difficult, and at the time, we

couldn't come together. They left us in Mexico for five years, and, well, it is hard to live with a strange (*ajena*) family, they don't give you the same life. They treat you differently, it is sad to be without your parents for five years . . . When they finally brought us . . . well, it was very hard because I didn't want to come. I was crying. At the same time, I did want to see my parents, but I didn't want to come to a country I didn't know because they spoke a different language. It was very hard for me to leave my friends, my school. A whole life there.

As these comments show, Andrea had a difficult time living without her parents. Even though life in Mexico was difficult, it was likely painful to be separated from her grandparents after living with them for five years. Not surprisingly, Andrea also had a hard time adjusting in school.

Liz was also left in Mexico with her grandparents, and she explained,

[B]ut my parents always tell me stories about like when I left Mexico. My grandparents were really upset because I was their first and only grandchild from both my mom and dad's side. And so, I was their bundle of joy and I left. What's it called? When I left, I kept calling for my grandma, my grandma Mary. Like I kept asking for her because she was basically like my second mom.

Like Andrea, Liz had a strong bond with her grandparents after living with them for a year and it was hard for her to leave Mexico. Migration affects both those who move and those who stay behind.[104] Liz's departure from Mexico was probably even more difficult for her grandparents, for whom she was the only grandchild and "bundle of joy."

Polish Interviewees

Unlike most of my Latino/a and Asian interviewees, two out of the three Polish interviewees, Mateusz and Peter, came to the United States through airports and with a valid tourist visa. It's unclear to me how Ali's family entered the country. Ali told me,

It wasn't an easy journey, he [Ali's father] was not able to receive visas to the US, so he decided to move us to Canada first. We actually tried that out for about a year. My parents didn't quite like it. And my dad was still trying to work towards that dream to come to America. So, we ended up immigrating over into the US through New York. So that was my dad's decisions. Like, listen, "This is just what we have to do this way, and we'll figure everything out once we get there." So, we immigrated without a legal status, obviously. Right? So, we immigrated over into New York and settled here in Chicago.

After unsuccessfully requesting a tourist visa to come to the United States, the family decided to emigrate to Canada, where they stayed for a year before coming to the United States. After a year they entered the country in New York, likely by land. Ali stated the family immigrated without a legal status. I wonder if they had a tourist visa or just crossed the US-Canadian border without inspection. The traumatic experiences of crossing the border without inspection that were so common among the Latino/a interviewees were, however, absent among my Polish interviewees. Mateusz, for instance, shared the following memories from his "crossing": "So, I remember arriving at O'Hare. You know, December 17, it was very snowy. And this big old, you know, United States. My dad was trying to buy us McDonald's at the airport. And we went to this little suburban house." Mateusz's experience seems like a pretty typical airport experience.

In one respect Peter's experience of family separation resembled that of so many of the Latino/a interviewees, and even Daniel's, from Asia, whose mother was deported when he was still a minor. Peter was sent to the United States alone to live with his grandmother and uncles. He said,

Yeah, so my parents stayed in Poland. So, I came to my grandma. Okay. Yeah. So, I actually came by myself. I'm from Poland, my parents live in Poland. So, I came to my grandma . . . No, I just had like a lady on the plane that just, you know, took care of me, but I came alone . . . So when I arrived, you know, I just came. I got to see my uncle that I haven't seen since he left, since I was like one or two. I got to see my other uncles and aunts and my grandma that lived here. And then they were not sure if I was gonna stay in the US or not, just because of the status. They knew that I was going to be illegal if I stayed. So, I was kind of on and off debating if I should go back to Poland or stay here. And they ended up making a choice for me to stay here. So then they signed me up to school, and I began my life here.

Peter's migration experience involved separation from his parents. This experience was likely as traumatic as it was for the non-White interviewees in my sample.

Conclusion

Over the course of this chapter, I have reviewed the vast body of literature addressing the global, systemic, and political reasons explaining why people migrate. Past research provides only partial support for the idea that differences in income and employment opportunities between developed and developing countries drive immigration.[105] For instance, only one-fourth of the non-White interviewees in my sample cited economic reasons as the main cause for the family's migration to the United States, and only one Polish interviewee reported coming to the United States for economic reasons alone. Additionally, a good share of my interviewees' families seemed to belong to the middle class back in their countries of origin. Overall, my evidence provided support for the contention that the opportunities immigrants migrate for involve much more than just jobs and income differentials, to include a better future for the children and an improved quality of life.[106]

The evidence presented here provided support for the roles of networks of family members and friends in encouraging immigration.[107] These networks work to facilitate both the process of immigration and settlement.[108] This was true for non-White and White interviewees alike. One-fourth of the interviewees in my sample stated that their families immigrated to reunite with a relative who was already residing in the United States. Most often, that relative was the father who had been working in the United States on a permanent or seasonal basis. In some other cases, however, the relatives in question were more distant. Several interviewees, for instance, recounted meeting their aunts and uncles after moving to the United States.

Political reasons such as turmoil and natural disasters in their home countries were also influential in the families' decision to migrate.[109] This was true for the participants from El Salvador and Peru. The political turmoil followed by insecurity in El Salvador explained the migration of Ana's family to the United States. In turn, the political involvement of Melody's father with a president who was removed from power in Peru explained the migration of her family to the United States. Although these two cases were different in that insecurity was important in the first case but not the second, political reasons were nonetheless at work in explaining the families' decision to leave their country of origin.

Immigration policies and borders are state tools for population demarcation and control.[110] Immigration rules determine who can be admitted and as such produce legality and illegality and reinforce territorial identities. Even though the militarization of the US-Mexico border in recent years has not stopped immigrants from crossing the border without inspection, it has raised the economic and human cost of crossing the border[111] and has made undocumented immigration more permanent.[112]

The border crossing experiences of this study's participants varied by national origin, age, and the time and type of crossing. The Polish interviewees, for the most part, had non-traumatic crossings. The youth who came without visas and crossed without inspection through overland travel had the most traumatic experiences, including spending time with coyotes, hiding from border patrol, accidents, dehydration, and separation from their parents. The memories of these youth from before they were five were likely accurate.[113] The ones who came through la Linea by car probably had the second most traumatic experiences, which included lying to authorities, hiding, or both. Finally, the participants who came to the United States with visas and through airports mostly had the best experiences, despite some minor problems.

The process of migration can take years and entail separation from family members, sometimes on a permanent basis.[114] Many participants, non-White and Polish alike, experienced pain when separated from their parents, either being sent alone to the United States, or because their parents moved to the United States first and the children were left behind, usually with grandparents, for five years in one case. This separation also led to a catch-22 situation in which reunion with parents also led to pain for leaving the grandparents behind. Overall, the migration experience of my interviewees was plagued by trauma, pain, and loss.

2

Finding One's Place

Pathways to Cultural Integration

Ali's dream is to raise a family and develop a career in business, especially one that gives back to the community. Born in Poland, she came to the United States when she was ten, after spending a year in Canada with her family. She and her family were unable get a visa to the United States when they lived in Poland, so the family emigrated to Canada for a year instead, after which they emigrated to the United States, "but not legally," as Ali put it. Ali and her family settled in Chicago and lived in a basement apartment for a while until they could get a place of their own.

Ali was scared when she started school in fourth grade because she knew no English. She was lucky to attend a school with a high proportion of Polish kids like her and a great ESL program. According to Ali, the teachers encouraged the other students to befriend her. With this support, after just three months, Ali was fluent in English and had no trouble making friends on her own. Teachers also helped Ali become acculturated in the United States and learn about "how everything works."

Ali's immigration status became real to her when her friends started getting driver's licenses and jobs at the age of sixteen. At this point, Ali felt frustrated because even though the United States is all she knows, even though she feels like an American, she could neither get a driver's license nor work. She was very happy when DACA came out during her senior year because it would help her and her brother get an education, get a job, and be part of the community. With the help of a school counselor, Ali was able to start college and later obtained her bachelor's degree in business.

Ali was devastated when the termination of DACA was announced. She remembered it was the day of her birthday and her mom called her with the news. However, Ali married her US-born boyfriend a year later and was able to apply for a green card. She could not have her dream honeymoon in Europe though, because of her travel restrictions, so they honeymooned in Florida instead. Ali worries about her younger brother, who has DACA and "should not rush into marriage because of this." She found out she was pregnant at the time of our interview.

Ali's incorporation in school went smoothly: She attended a school with other Polish children, had helpful teachers and a great ESL program, and was integrated after three months. This book argues that the process of incorporation of DACA recipients follows a roller-coaster pattern. As this chapter shows, the arrival and initial interactions in schools were excellent for some and not very smooth for others. In particular, the experiences of my non-White participants differed sharply from Ali's. Overall, however, compared with later periods, thanks to *Plyler v. Doe*, DACA recipients found spaces of belonging in schools.

This chapter discusses the cultural incorporation of immigrant youth during the postmigration stage. The first part explores the process of language acquisition and the ease/difficulty with which my participants learned English, points to some factors facilitating language acquisition, and discusses the perspective of some participants who were critical of English language classes and styles. The second part explores the sense of belonging immigrants experienced upon arrival, as exemplified by interactions with schoolchildren, and classifies different paths to incorporation into *assimilation*, *separation*, *integration*, and *marginalization*. In the next chapter we delve into the relationships between immigrant children and their teachers and counselors.

Incorporation: Dimensions and Stages

Gary Gerstle defines three different dimensions of incorporation: cultural, legal, and political.[1] Cultural incorporation refers to the process through which immigrants come to feel part of the host society.[2] This feeling develops through language acquisition, exposure to the host country's culture and people, and socialization in different institutions in society. Legal incorporation refers to the place immigrants are located on the immigration status continuum.[3] Political incorporation can be defined as the extent to which group interests are effectively represented in policy making.[4]

To a large degree, cultural incorporation involves a process of sustained interaction between newcomers and the societies in which they live. Although part of this process may be voluntary, cultural incorporation is also determined by the opportunities and barriers present in society. For instance, the values and prejudices of the host society are likely to influence the process of adaptation in the new society.[5] Immigrants face different challenges when growing up in a new country, including negotiating cultures of origin and of the host society, settling into the new society, and establishing new social relationships.[6] Through these processes, immigrants come to feel American and part of the host society.[7] Schools are particularly important to this study because of the age of its participants and because public schooling provides them with an experience of inclusion atypical for undocumented immigrants.[8]

Immigrants can follow different acculturation paths in the host society. Socialization into the new society is an essential part of incorporation.[9] Following John W. Berry, I classify the pathways to incorporation as: (a) *assimilation* (b) *separation*, (c) *integration*, and (d) *marginalization*.[10] In the *assimilation* pathway individuals do not seek to maintain their culture of origin, and engage in daily interactions with the dominant group. In the *separation* pathways individuals place a value on holding on to their original culture and wish to avoid interaction with others. In the *integration* pathway there is an interest in both maintaining one's original culture and engaging in daily interactions with other groups. Finally, in the *marginalization* pathway, there is little possibility of or interest in cultural maintenance, and little interest in having relations with others, sometimes due to discrimination. This classification assumes that people are free to choose their acculturation strategies, but this is not always the case. A mutual accommodation is required for integration to occur.[11]

The Role of Schools

This study places particular emphasis on the incorporation of DACA recipients in schools through learning English, making friends, and relating to teachers and counselors. Schools are central institutions of community life and have an essential role in the social integration of newcomer immigrant and refugee youth.[12] "It is in school where, day in and day out, immigrant youth come to know teachers and peers from majority culture as well as newcomers from other parts of the world. It is in schools that immigrant youth develop academic knowledge and, just as important, form perceptions of where they fit in the social reality and cultural imagination of their new nation."[13]

While schools have the potential to engender a sense of belonging and membership for undocumented immigrant students, they often fall short of this promise.[14] Historically, the public school has been one of the most important institutions in the lives of immigrant children, having the power to either replicate societal inequalities or equalize the field.[15] As such, schools function as sites of both inclusion and exclusion.[16] When newcomer youth settle in a community, they have the double status of youth and new immigrants.[17] Schools are the main institutions where newcomer youth develop cultural knowledge, build relationships, acquire social capital, and begin to participate in their communities.

Latino/a and Black youth are concentrated in schools with low academic performance outcomes as measured by standardized test scores and graduation outcomes.[18] The academic success of immigrant-origin children and youth is in large part determined by several factors associated with the family's premigration conditions and postmigration experiences. A family's premigration economic, educational, social, and psychological resources provide differing starting points for immigrant children. In turn, the postmigration labor market, legal, neighborhood, and school contexts offer different challenges and opportunities for success.[19] Factors such as low levels of parental education and employment, poverty, newcomer status, language barriers, racialization as a visible minority group, and undocumented status of self or parent endanger educational and economic outcomes.[20] Other impediments to immigrant children's and youths' school integration include low expectations from teachers, low levels of parental involvement, and isolation.[21]

Research shows that students who attend racially and socioeconomically diverse schools are more likely to obtain higher test scores and grades, graduate from high school, and attend and graduate from college.[22] Schools that are integrated and have little segregation can promote all students' feelings of safety, interethnic group cohesion, and trust in teachers.[23] Classrooms in these schools are likely to provide culturally relevant pedagogy that both engages students and offers visions of immigrant students as part of the social fabric.[24] Upon arrival in a country, immigrants need to learn the local language to communicate effectively.[25] Newcomer children and youth also need to make sense of the sociolinguistic environment of their new school. Therefore, the process of language acquisition and identity formation during the formative years are intertwined.[26] Schools in linguistically diverse districts usually offer programs for newcomer schoolchildren, termed in this book English as a Second Language (ESL). One in ten students enrolled in high school in the United States is an ESL student.[27] Most ESL students in the United States were born in the United States and are citizens.[28]

Relationships and Identity

During adolescence and early childhood, undocumented immigrant youth must navigate their process of identity formation. The process of acculturation challenges immigrants' ethnic identity. In her seminal work, Jean S. Phinney defined ethnic identity as a dynamic and multidimensional construct that includes identification of oneself as a member of a particular ethnic group, positive evaluation of and involvement in the group, preference for the group, sense of belonging, and involvement in group activities.[29] Immigrants are forced to reconcile exclusionary and discriminatory messages and their sense of belonging to their ethnic group. A positive sense of ethnic identity plays a protective role against these messages.[30] The process of acculturation of undocumented immigrant children into a new society produces stress.[31] Immediately after migration, however, the stress is not significant because this initial honeymoon period involves reconnecting with family members, enrolling in schools, learning a new language, and experiencing a new culture.[32]

The process of acculturation or cultural incorporation also entails a negotiation between the culture of origin and the culture of settlement.[33] Social integration is the degree to which an individual is connected to other individuals in a social setting.[34] This sense of connectedness, in turn, shapes the identity of the immigrant youth.[35] Successful adaptations among immigrant students appear to be linked to the quality of relationships they forge in school settings.[36] Positive relationships provide several protective functions, including a sense of belonging, emotional support, assistance and information, cognitive guidance, and positive feedback.[37] This chapter focuses on the interactions of immigrant youth with their peers.[38]

Relationships with peers are essential for social integration.[39] The most common friendships in multicultural societies are among members of the same ethnic or cultural group.[40] Early studies of school desegregation showed that relatively few interethnic friendships emerged in desegregated schools.[41] Further, children showed a bias toward selecting children of the same ethnic background as friends.[42] Researchers attribute this preference for same-ethnic friends to homophily.[43] People who belong to the same ethnic or cultural group share similar experiences, values, and attitudes when compared with members of the outgroup. This similarity in turn improves mutual understanding and results in stronger emotional support and social affirmation.[44] According to John Berry, individual factors such as immigration status, cultural pride, and racist victimization are also predictors of friendship choices.[45] We therefore expected that the youth investigated in this study would prefer befriending others of the same cultural or ethnic group.

School Diversity, Language Acquisition, and Belonging

Research shows that students who attend racially and socioeconomically diverse schools perform better academically, socially, and psychologically than students who attend homogenous, predominantly White schools.[46] Even though my interview did not include a question on the diversity level of the school the students attended, all but two interviewees provided information about it. Responses show that more than three-quarters of the youth in my sample attended diverse schools. The two interviewees who failed to provide this information were excluded from the total. Additionally, two of my Polish participants attended schools with other Polish students, and the third, Peter, attended a school that was predominantly Latino/a. The evidence shows, however, that attending a diverse school provided for a better social and psychological experience than attending a nondiverse one.[47]

The experiences of students who grew up in the Chicago area exemplify the social and psychological benefits of attending a diverse school. For instance, Angel, who later moved to the Chicago suburbs, explained,

Well, I think I was kind of fortunate to have classmates who were also La-tino/Mexican-American/Chicano because I kind of identified with some of them . . . I'm not sure how familiar you are with Chicago but there were a lot of Polish folks in the area so I would say the majority of my classes were 60–70% Latinos and the other 40% were Polish. So, a lot of immigrant families.

In a similar vein, Andrés stated,

My school had a lot of minorities. African Americans, Puerto Ricans, Mexicans, and other Latin countries . . . So it wasn't too hard; we kind of grew up in the same culture. Yeah, a lot of the faculty were either His-panic, Latin or African American. They just knew who we were basically, so I didn't feel like a minority at all.

Ismael, who also attended school in Chicago all his life, concurred.

So, some kids spoke Spanish, others spoke English. Kids that were White, kids that were Black. Literally, the other kids that spoke Spanish were from Mexico, so I didn't feel like I was out of place. My first and second grade teacher was Mexican and spoke Spanish. I never felt out of place during my education.

As these experiences show, students who attended diverse schools devel-oped a sense of commonality or shared identity with other students of similar backgrounds, and did not feel like a minority or out of place.

The experiences of the undocumented who attended predominantly White schools were less positive. For example, Angel moved from Chi-cago to the suburbs and was able to reflect on this change:

And then in fifth grade is when we moved out from Chicago to the sub-urbs outside of Chicago and there things were a little bit different because the suburbs were more predominantly White. Moving out from Chicago and all the way to public high school from eigth grade was not as positive. I think that's when I felt more out of place. There were fewer Latinos and then I didn't really feel like I fit in with those schools.

Angel's move to a predominantly White area in the Chicago suburbs was not a positive experience for him. Rather, it made him feel out of place, like he did not belong.

Zoe also had a negative experience after moving, in her case, from Georgia to Illinois. She explained,

> I think the hardest thing for me, and I don't know if it is an identity piece, but in Georgia you would see mostly teachers who were African American. And here [in Illinois] you mainly saw White teachers and I think that was uncomfortable for me. It was just weird because I wasn't used to it. In Georgia I mainly grew up with African American and Hispanic kids. There was literally only one White kid.

Zoe grew accustomed to a school in Georgia with diverse faculty and students, and moving to a predominantly White school in Illinois made her "uncomfortable." One can only wonder at the impact this move had on the development of her identity.[48]

José was also enrolled in a predominantly White school and was able to reflect on an experience he had when asked to provide a writing sample.

> It was rough at times because they also weren't used to having someone who only spoke Spanish. I remember, my parents love this story, and it is so embarrassing. But in first grade, only a month or two after I got here, we were doing a writing sample and I decided to copy the girl next to me. So, I think that I ended up writing that my hobbies were painting my nails and hanging out with my mom or whatever. So obviously, they realized that I didn't understand the assignment. I think it was the principal who came by and asked me if I liked to play basketball but since I couldn't understand him, he actually brought a basketball, started bouncing it, and asked me if I liked this. So, they tried to communicate the best way they could, but I don't think they had the resources to have a fully Spanish-speaking administrator to sort of bridge that gap. But they tried.

José must have been stressed out trying to come up with something to turn in to his teacher when he could not understand the assignment, so he just copied from a classmate. Although it is commendable that the school administrator did not admonish José for copying his assignment, it is nonetheless clear that the school lacked the necessary resources to accommodate a child who spoke only Spanish.

As this section shows, diverse schools had a positive impact on the youth interviewed in our sample. Angel, Andrés, and Ismael developed a sense of commonality or shared identity with other students of similar backgrounds they met in their schools, experiences that gave them a sense of belonging. This racial/ethnic identity comes with understanding one's position in the larger social structure and protects the individuals' self-esteem by helping them distinguish discriminatory practices directed toward them as an individual versus those focusing on them as a member of a certain group.[49] In contrast, attending school in a predominantly White school environment made Angel and Zoe feel uncomfortable, and like they did not fit in, which probably conflicted with the process of identity formation. Part of the literature, however, argues that attending a so-called integrated (White) school in a higher socioeconomic status neighborhood helps the academic performance of undocumented youth.[50]

Schools and English Language Programs and Acquisition

Linguistically diverse schools usually offer ESL programs to accommodate students from different linguistic backgrounds.[51] In these programs, teachers do not need to be fluent in the students' languages.[52] ESL models can be of three kinds: ESL pullout, ESL class period, or ESL resource center.[53] In the pullout model, students, usually from elementary schools, spend most of the day in mainstream classes but are pulled out for part of the day to receive English as a Second Language instruction. In the ESL class period model, students, usually from middle schools, receive English instruction during a regular period. In the ESL resource center model, students are brought together from several classrooms and schools to receive English instruction.[54] In contrast, bilingual programs use both children's native language and English for instruction.

This study did not specifically ask participants if their school provided English language programs, but all except two interviewees discussed such programs in their answers regarding their school experience. Also, most participants had a basic understanding of the language programs offered in their schools but did not provide specific details about them. For this reason, those programs are generically identified here as "ESL." More than three-quarters of the participants attended schools that offered some sort of ESL program. Because more diverse districts are likely to offer English language programs, it is not surprising that this number is identical to the number of participants who reported attending a diverse school. All three Polish DACA recipients attended schools that offered some sort of English language classes.

This study also investigated the process of language acquisition and classified respondents either as those who *struggled* to learn English or those who *did not struggle*. I classified as *struggled* those who said they had difficulty, felt overwhelmed, out of place, or otherwise made a major effort to learn English. I classified as *did not struggle* those who said they learned English easily or took some time to learn but did not seem stressed out about the language learning process. Close to 60 percent of respondents struggled to learn English and just over 40 percent did not struggle. Although my sample was small, it is worth mentioning that two of the three Polish interviewees did not struggle with the language and one did.

Students Who Struggled

Zaide had a difficult time trying to learn English. She explained,

> I do have flashbacks of going to school. I remember I had a hard time with the language, which is English. I think that was the most difficult part. I was trying to make friends and I didn't understand, so I kind of got frustrated. So, when I tried to tell my mom, "I don't want to be here anymore," I didn't want to be here because I couldn't understand the language. Like, being away from the family that I was used to seeing; being around new people and in a new setting; but I would say language was the most difficult for me.

Zaide got frustrated that she could not communicate and make friends to the point that she no longer wanted to be in school. She grew up in a small town, which was unprepared to receive large numbers of English language learners at the time and offered few English classes. Students from the same town who attended school in later years received more support and resources, including a dual immersion program where the students attend classes in both English and Spanish throughout the day.[55]

Melody also struggled when trying to learn English. She recounted,

> I remember being in third grade, which is the first school year I did here. I remember vividly just sitting down during class and not really knowing what was going on and feeling really out of place and dumb. I think it was during reading time, when all the kids were reading out of their reading books. I had absolutely no idea what they were saying but I felt so out of place because I was reading ABC books that are made for babies, and they were reading a lot more in-depth content. So, what I did was I stood up in the middle of class and I was about to grab an extra book and I just stared at it pretending like I knew what I was reading, and my teacher came up and said, "oh, no, no" like, "this isn't for you." I think she spoke a little Spanish. "This is for English readers. You need to read this one." So, my teacher was very nice, very understanding.

Melody was understandably upset when asked to read ABC books in third grade, which probably contributed to making her feel "out of place" and "dumb." To be sure, integrated language and content instruction has been proven effective in developing second language proficiency,[56] but both language and content objectives need to be appropriate, including age-appropriate, for instruction to be effective.[57] The teacher probably humiliated Melody even more when she replaced the book Melody pretended to read in front of the whole class. Despite this, Melody thought her teacher was very nice and understanding.

Melody's teacher's behavior contrasts with José's, who made him feel accepted, despite his language limitations. José explained,

> The first time was a little odd since there was that language barrier and I had to re-start the first grade, which didn't set me back too far but . . . So I was in first grade. The only things that I remember is that I befriended the one person who was bilingual at the time because they did teach you English back at El Salvador, but it was very basic. Like I knew some colors, I knew some small phrases but didn't really know the language at all. So, I befriended the only child in my class who was bilingual, but I remember my teachers were kind of interested. I remember one day they allowed me

to read a book in front of class that was entirely in Spanish. I'm not sure what the other kids got out of it, but they were accepting, and they tried to make it work with the language barrier.

The decision to put José back in first grade was not the best. According to established literature, subtractive schooling that assesses students only on their English skills and fails to consider other resources acquired during their schooling in their countries of origin is a bad practice.[58] Asking José to read out loud in Spanish to the rest of the class was, however, a good decision, which likely encouraged positive attitudes about belonging to his ethnic group.[59] Further, a robust finding in the literature shows that ethnic affirmation promotes positive physical and mental health, and educational outcomes.[60]

Peter, a DACA recipient from Poland, also seemed to have some difficulty learning the language. He told me,

> It was hard, you know, making friends at first, especially not knowing the language. When I went to school, you know, I had to take ESL classes and start from scratch so I couldn't really have any friends still until I learn English . . . So you know, good two years until I was actually able to learn the language and start meeting some friends.

Compared to other students in my sample, and especially his fellow Polish citizen Ali, who as we see below learned the language in "two to three months," Peter took a while to learn the language. It was likely stressful for him to not be able to make friends for two years.

Students Who Learned the Language Right Away

Forty percent of this study's participants reported having no difficulty learning English. Several participants described these experiences. Ernesto, who came to the United States when he was five years old, learned English at school but with no special support. He recalled,

> So in school, I started when I was in first grade. I went to a school called Oakland Park. Again, this was a rural town of about ten or twelve thousand people. But I think I learned English pretty fast. Honestly, we never

had anyone who taught English as a Second Language or anything. English was my first language at school and Spanish at home. I honestly didn't even notice.

Ernesto learned English fast and without ESL classes. He easily understood that English was the language for school and Spanish the language for home. Maybe Ernesto was lucky, because not having language resources for English language learners can threaten their educational success.[61] Further, research shows that students enrolled in dual language programs outperform those in English-only ones.[62]

Other participants, including Andrés and Luna, also learned the language easily. Andrés, who came to the United States when he was two years old, explained, "I'm pretty sure I spoke Spanish, that's what my parents have told me. But as a kid, I was a quick learner and picked up English really quick. But it is not my first language, of course."

It is not clear from the interview if Andrés had special school support to learn English. It is clear, however, that he had an easy time learning English. Luna, who came to the United States when she was one year old, also learned English easily, but in her case, she learned from her cousins who were born in the United States.

> Thanks to cousins . . . they were born here, and I would say that the family that was already here was already Americanized. So, most of them were already speaking English. When I got to kindergarten, it was so easy for me to understand and learn English compared to the rest of my classmates who only spoke Spanish.

It is not uncommon for immigrants to learn the language outside of a classroom setting, such as by making friends and interacting with family members.[63] It is worth noting that most of the participants who did not struggle learning English arrived in the United States when they were five years old or younger.

Ali, featured in the beginning of this chapter, attended a predominantly Polish school. She told me,

> But going to school here in Chicago was very helpful, because there are a lot of Polish people around. They had a great ESL program with teachers

that would help kids that didn't speak English . . . So within I say, in two to three months, I was already feeling much more comfortable.

Despite being terrified starting fourth grade in the United States without knowing much English, Ali had a good experience in the school she attended in Chicago. Apparently, having immigrant-background classmates and an ESL program facilitated her quick language acquisition process.

Support for Language Learning

Some interviewees acknowledged the support they received from their school's programs, teachers, and/or classmates who helped translate for them. Mary, who moved to the United States when she was thirteen years old, described the support she received:

> So, when I came in before I knew how to speak English, school was different. I started in middle school and obviously everybody speaks a different language. I had awesome teachers that really cared. I was in the EL, the bilingual program. And I think that helped as well because there were a lot of kids that spoke my language. I think that kind of helped me adapt better. I couldn't communicate with people because I couldn't speak their language. I couldn't communicate. I couldn't even ask for something as easy as food. Again, the language barrier was a huge thing for me.

Mary came to the United States at an older age than most of the other participants. Despite this, her supportive teachers and classmates who spoke Spanish helped her overcome the language barrier, and that was "huge" for her. Further, the relationship with her classmates helped her adapt better.

Andreíta, who came to the United States when she was five years old, found support in a school in a small town that was not accustomed to receiving English learner students. She explained,

> And the other thing I remember is going through some lessons with my . . . ESL teacher. They [the school] didn't have a program where they taught English to kids from the Latino/Hispanic population. The town

was very, very small so they didn't see any need for it. But there was a teacher, this ESL teacher that wanted to give it a shot. She tested everything she could possibly think of and did research on me, and it worked. Like, in three years, I learned English and praise God because she is the only reason why I'm here. So, I remember some lessons, the one that is most clear is . . . Since we were like seven years old everything in the classroom was tiny while she was big, so she was sitting on the table and I was sitting down on this little table. She had this sheet that was laminated with the alphabet. What we did a lot was go through each letter and the different sounds that they make. And that's all I remember from those lessons.

Despite being in a small town, Andreíta had a dedicated teacher who through research and probably some trial and error taught her English in three years. Andreíta is grateful to her teacher for where she is today, graduated with a master's degree in design from a major public university in Illinois.

Several interviewees received support from classmates who interpreted for them. These interpreters are termed in the literature as language brokers, described as somebody who acts as "an agent for one party in a conversation."[64] Unlike a professional interpreter who is independent, impersonal, and detached, a language broker is there to support someone. Sometimes language brokers translate for their own parents and sometimes for their classmates. Benita, who came to the United States when she was four years old, described the help she received from a classmate and a teacher.

I didn't really talk to people because when I left Mexico, I was just starting kindergarten, the second semester of kindergarten, so it was really hard because I didn't know English. They were talking to me and I didn't know what to say. And I remember I had one friend that helped me through it; she helped me translate. Yeah, like I said, it took me a while to learn English. Because first of all, I was scared. I didn't want to talk so I had an ESL teacher for like years, for like seven years because I had trouble with my English. I had trouble speaking. You know, comfortable like you and me are speaking, I wasn't able to do that seven years ago. I wouldn't say a word.

Benita was scared not knowing English and did not "say a word." Luckily, she had a friend who helped her translate. Despite this help, it took seven years of English instruction for her to be comfortable speaking English.

Alejandro and Mary became good friends with their language brokers. Alejandro, who came to the United States when he was eleven years old, explained, "The truth is I didn't have friends. I didn't have friends because I would stay away from other children. But there was this student who translated for me. She was the one I talked to the most."

Mary, who came to the United States when she was thirteen years old, said,

> I think at the beginning, because I didn't speak any English at all . . . it was really hard to make friends. I remember a good friend, my neighbor. I remember we used to take the same bus to go to school and she used to translate for me. But even my Spanish wasn't good; it was hard. I felt like I didn't fit in. I hated it. I wanted to go back home but I knew that my mom was doing the best for us. She was just looking for something better.

Both Alejandro and Mary benefited from the help of classmates who interpreted for them and also became their friends. Despite this support, Mary hated being in the United States.

Students Who Were Critical of Their ESL Classes

Some interviewees thought classes for English learners set them back. Ana, who came to the country when she was four years old, had a difficult time adjusting to her "all English" classes when her parents were deported and she was transferred to regular English classes by her aunt and uncle. Ana stated,

> Yeah, so other stories that I've heard, and I don't remember this myself, but when I was in kindergarten, I was very upset. I think I was having a very hard time adjusting, so I cried a lot and always asked for my parents, but they said that after some time, I started adjusting. I was first enrolled into the ESL program and so it wasn't until fifth grade when my parents were deported, and I moved in with my uncle and aunt. My aunt pushed

us to change into all English classes. So, I was terrified. "You know, I'm not ready for this. My English is not good enough." But it turns out it was probably the best decision that was made for me.

Ana struggled in her transition to all English classes. The pain she felt upon her parents being deported likely also made the stress in this transition even greater. But Ana is grateful her aunt and uncle made this decision for her, because it forced her to learn English.

Five of my interviewees did their interviews in Spanish. Two of them resented their ESL and/or Spanish classes. Andrea, who came to the United States at fifteen years old, explained, "The teachers spoke only Spanish. I arrived here in middle school and all my classes were in Spanish. And in high school too. Only the last two years were mostly in English, but I didn't learn enough [English]. I learned English when I started working." Andrea arrived in the United States when she was in middle school and she had predominantly Spanish classes until her junior year of high school. She felt this hurt her chances for speaking better English.

Cynthia, who came to the United States when she was twelve years old, resented her Spanish classes for several reasons. She told me,

I arrived in a group that was bilingual where we spoke Spanish and learned English as a Second Language. The adaptation was easier because they talked to us in Spanish. But the process of learning English was difficult because we were not out of our comfort zone and forced to learn English. In these circumstances, my classmates and I were the targets of mockery by our [English-speaking] classmates because we didn't speak English and we couldn't understand. And in high school the bilingual group was excluded because we couldn't take electives because we had to take English . . . To be sure, my teachers were very supportive . . . but it was difficult for me. When I started college, the major obstacle was the language one.

Nothing justifies the English-speaking students' mocking the ESL students. But sometimes, pulling students out of the regular classroom to provide them English language instruction may have a negative impact on the integration of students in school.[65] On certain occasions, students resist school-sanctioned ESL identities.[66] As soon as she could, Cynthia studied hard and signed up for all English classes so that she could have the real high school experience.

Relationships with Peers

Socialization into the new society is an essential part of incorporation.[67] As discussed earlier, I follow Berry, classifying the pathways to incorporation as: (a) assimilation, (b) separation, (c) integration, and (d) marginalization.[68]

Berry describes the situations in which people are not free to choose their group of belonging:

> When the dominant group enforces certain forms of acculturation, or constrains the choices of non-dominant groups or individuals, then other terms need to be used. Most clearly, people may sometimes choose the Separation option; but when it is required of them by the dominant society, the situation is one of Segregation. Similarly, when people choose to Assimilate, the notion of the Melting Pot may be appropriate; but when forced to do so, it becomes more like a Pressure Cooker. In the case of Marginalisation, people rarely choose such an option; rather they usually become marginalised as a result of attempts at forced assimilation (Pressure Cooker) combined with forced exclusion (Segregation); thus no other term seems to be required beyond the single notion of Marginalisation.[69]

These insights were helpful in developing predictions. I expected that in some cases, *assimilation* would be a choice and in others it would be forced (pressure cooker). I expected that in some cases *separation* would be a choice but in other cases it would be the result of *segregation* by the dominant group. I also expected that cases of *marginalization* would occur because of failed attempts at forced assimilation, sometimes combined with forced exclusion (segregation). My findings show that among my participants, the most common path to incorporation was separation, followed by integration, marginalization, and assimilation.

The Polish interviewees, not included in this breakdown, followed three different paths in their incorporation: Ali, assimilation; Mateusz, separation; and Peter, integration.

Assimilation: Becoming Part of the Dominant Group

In the *assimilation* pathway, individuals do not seek to maintain their culture of origin and engage in daily interactions with the dominant group. Fewer than 10 percent of my participants reported being mostly integrated with members of the dominant group. Lucio, despite the differences between the school systems in Mexico and the United States, learned English and made friends in a school in the deep South. He explained,

> I was smart. I was smart since I was a little kid. I was good in school. And when I moved to the US everything was very different from what I was learning. The learning system was very different to the one we had in Mexico. When I moved here, I couldn't understand because I only spoke Spanish. But I kept on watching TV. It was odd for me at first seeing White kids for the first time; we moved to Alabama first when we got to the United States. They had a good system. I think it was called ESL, where teachers . . . spoke English and Spanish . . . Yeah, like I said, the kids were just kids. They played; they went to class. We had activities and whatnot. So, for me, there was the language barrier but pretty much I talked to the kids, played, and went to school just like I did in Mexico.

Lucio's school was likely predominantly White. Perhaps Lucio's assimilation was a case of "pressure cooker" more than "melting pot" given the school lacked other Latino/a children,[70] but Lucio seemed to assimilate to the school environment without major problems.

Ali, from Poland, also integrated into the dominant group, but in her case, this was her own racial group. She explained, "They [the teachers] basically made other kids be friendly to me and help me out and say, you know, 'please sit with her, please help her as much as you can.' And I would say that was, I still remember my fourth-grade teacher to this day, because she helped me so much."

Ali made friends quickly and had an easy transition in her predominantly White school with a significant proportion of Polish children. The teacher's request to her classmates to be friendly and helpful toward her likely helped her assimilate into the dominant group.

Estela was somewhat forced to assimilate when she lived in Phoenix, but she chose to have Latino/a friends when she moved to Illinois.

> Ah yeah, it was a little difficult. I didn't speak English so in the school that I attended in Phoenix . . . I did feel a little weird. I did feel a little discriminated. Even my sisters do remember, they are older than me and they were, I want to say in middle school, and it was hard . . . the teachers didn't want you to speak Spanish and it was a little hard to blend in the beginning because I didn't know the language, so I started picking up a lot of it from my cousins. I have a lot of cousins that were around our ages. But yeah, we made friends . . . Like, friend-wise, it was easy to make friends. I don't know, for me it was. I know that for my sisters it wasn't. I don't really know anything to be honest, but I really felt a little like an outcast with the teachers. But it was a little different when I moved here [Illinois] because we were living in a community of Hispanic people so a lot of them spoke Spanish and I just feel like I did fit in.

The dominant group's cultural norms were imposed on the students, who were forced to speak English.[71] It is not clear what Estela meant by feeling like an "outcast" with the teachers, but it seems as though the teachers failed to help students of diverse backgrounds feel welcome. Despite this, unlike her older sisters, Estela made friends easily. This finding is consistent with research showing that younger children are less likely to perceive discrimination than older ones.[72] It may be that Estela's siblings perceived discrimination more acutely than she did.

Ernesto also assimilated into the dominant group. In his case, even if the rural, small town he lived in had few to no Latinos/as, he did not feel like an outcast or different from other children. Ernesto told me,

> In school I started when I was in first grade . . . Again, this was a rural town. I never really felt different from anyone. I found friends

immediately, I hang out with the same group of friends from first to eighth grade. And then obviously branched out to high school, but I always had the same friends.

Unlike the two previous interviewees, Ernesto's assimilation into the dominant group seemed less the result of a pressure cooker. He learned English fast and made friends. Maybe, despite being a rural, small town, the context of reception was more favorable to allow for the integration of Latino/a immigrants.[73]

Separation from the Majority Group

In the *separation* pathway, individuals place a value on holding on to their original culture and wish to avoid interaction with others.[74] Forty-two percent of my participants followed a separation strategy in their incorporation. Participants who followed this strategy were of three types: those who chose separation by choice; those who separated because of a reason beyond their control, such as a language barrier; and those who separated because of segregation by the dominant group. The first and second options were considered in Berry's original work.[75] Some participants naturally chose to befriend the children with whom they had more in common. José, for instance, who was quoted earlier, was allowed to read a book in Spanish and felt accepted despite the language barrier.

Even if José primarily befriended the only bilingual child in his class, his teachers and classmates were accepting and tried to work with his language barrier. Further, the teacher permitted José to read a book in Spanish to the whole class, which provides evidence that the dominant group in José's school accepted that members of the nondominant group wished to maintain their heritage culture and allowed them to become an integral part of the society by engaging in relationships with them.[76]

ESL classrooms and practices help develop immigrant children's English language skills, but they serve other important social purposes as well. Becoming part of a community is critical for young people and even more so for immigrant youth who can experience psychological distress due to leaving relationships behind.[77] Culturally diverse spaces provide opportunities for interethnic friendships but can also increase the preference for same-ethnicity friendships or ethnic homophily.[78] This research shows that ESL classes gave participants a sense of belonging and an opportunity to befriend members of their ethnic group. Ana, for instance, explained,

> Elementary was a little bit easier because I was put in ESL courses and other students were also Hispanic and so they spoke the language. So, it was easy for me to hang out with them and to kind of pick up on the stuff that they were talking about and probably learn.

Ana felt she could hang out with other children who were Latino/a and spoke Spanish, understand them, and learn with them.

Luna was more explicit about the connection between ESL classes, identity, and belonging.[79] She stated,

> I just remember interacting with a lot of Hispanic kids like me, so I didn't feel any different. But when I got to second grade, that was when I had more exposure to more kids who spoke English because they actually transferred me to a different class because my English was good, so they decided to put me in a class with English speakers.

Luna emphasized the identity match with children taking ESL classes when she said, "I didn't feel any different." The use of the word "but" in the second sentence implies that Luna did feel different when she was transferred to the classes with English speakers.

Research shows that a higher quantity of cross-ethnic friendships, defined as those between individuals from different ethnic minority groups, moderated the negative effects of perceived ethnic discrimination among schoolchildren.[80] Results suggest that cross-ethnic friendships are beneficial for minority children by functioning as a protective factor from the negative effects of discrimination within a multiethnic context.[81] Brianna, who attended a diverse school, had the opportunity to make friends from a different nondominant ethnic group. In this sense, she said,

> Well, I guess I was more of a shy kid. I barely spoke to people unless they spoke to me. But they were very welcoming to me. They would try to

include me in their activities. One of my first friends was actually Indian; she grew up here, so she knew English and everything. She was one of my first friends who was not a Hispanic, not a white or anything like that.

Even though Brianna was shy, she was able to make a friend of color who grew up in the United States and spoke English. These friendships likely helped her become acculturated and acted as a buffer against the prejudicial effects of ethnic discrimination.

Some participants, including Zaide, made friends within their own ethnic group because of the language barriers experienced when trying to communicate with the dominant group. I argue this option was not contemplated in Berry's original work because it is not a completely free choice,[82] but it is not required by the dominant society either, as in the case of segregation. I call this option separation by force. Zaide explained,

Yeah, usually most of my friends were the other Hispanic girls that were there as well. I think that again, because of the language barrier, it was harder for me to, like, make friends with the English-speaking girls. So, probably it was after the third or fourth grade when I started engaging more with the all-American students.

Zaide originally befriended other children who spoke Spanish and progressed toward a stage of integration with the dominant group as she acquired the necessary English language skills.

In other cases, participants remained separated from the dominant group because of explicit action by the dominant group, such as segregation.[83] Zoe, for instance, attended a diverse school, but gravitated toward other Latino/a children. As she explained, the White majority made discriminatory comments directed to Latino/a children, like "go back to your country" and "Go back to Mexico." Zoe explained, "Hmm . . . I think when you are starting high school is like a whole big change, everything is more difficult. But I think I made friends right away and there were also a lot, a lot of Hispanic kids there so I think it was easy for me to just kind of make friends."

Zoe was fortunate that she made Latino/a friends right away. The commonalities between Zoe and the other Latino/a children likely improved mutual understanding and resulted in stronger emotional support and social affirmation.[84]

Choosing Integration with the Majority Group While Maintaining Original Culture

In the *integration* pathway there is an interest in maintaining one's original culture, while also engaging in daily interactions with other groups.[85] Twenty-one percent of my participants followed this incorporation strategy. Ana, for instance, was forced to integrate with the Anglo-American students when her parents were deported, and she and her siblings lived with their aunt and uncle. Although it was challenging at first, she found her way toward integration through sports. Ana explained,

> My aunt pushed us to be very involved, so I was a part of the track team; most of those in track were American students. I was pushed to do softball and almost all the softball players were American. We didn't have soccer at the time, so it was not an option. So, I found that I got along with them well but there was always there that kind of cultural difference . . . I think I was just so close and tight to my Mexican side that sometimes it was hard for me to want to interact with Americans until I became a teammate. When you become a teammate, then you need to help one another to succeed in a softball game or whatever it was.

Participation in sports is an important socializing agent for youth.[86] Participation in sports may reinforce understanding and respect of cultural diversity and foster the integration of migrants.[87] Even though Ana was aware of cultural differences with the Anglo-American students, she was able to bridge these differences by becoming a teammate, where cooperation and reciprocity become the norm.

Proficiency in the national language predicts the social inclusion of immigrant children.[88] Abraham had told his parents he wanted to live in the United States to learn English. He attended ESL classes and learning English allowed him to make Anglo friends. Abraham explained,

But I didn't really feel out of place even though I didn't speak English; I felt that I was welcome. I never felt out of place because I didn't speak English or that I didn't belong. I wanted to learn English so for me, it was just like, "oh I'm going to school to learn English," you know? So, once I got the hang of it . . . I decided to talk to different people. That's how I made American friends. You know, kids that are from here that didn't know Spanish.

Abraham never felt out of place in his school but was nonetheless driven to learn English. After he did, he was able to count American children among his friends.

Marcos explained how who he was or where he came from was not an obstacle to making American friends. He said,

Oh absolutely, I actually, like I said, some of my best friends are, and I still talk to them until this day, from when I was in grade school in first grade. You know, we're really good friends. Most of them were actually born here but at that time we didn't normally see that: we were just friends. And yeah, I've been making friends ever since. It's not like it stopped me because of who I am or where I come from.

Marcos was able to befriend children born in the United States. At least, "At that time we didn't normally see that," he stated. Apparently, Marcos always had an easy time making friends but was aware that at a later age it would not be as easy. Whereas primary school friendships are based on play and other activities, secondary school friendships are more likely to be based on mutual sharing and intimacy.[89] Perhaps this is why ethnic and cultural differences become more salient as children grow older.

Finally, Peter, from Poland, made friends outside his Polish coethnics. He recalled, "So once I learned a little bit of English. I got to, you know, meet Latino children then through sports. We had common interests. So we started playing soccer together. So that's how I kind of started hanging out with them." Peter was open to making friends from other ethnic groups. Through common interests, he got to know the Latino/a children who played soccer. As the literature shows, friendships at this age are based on play and common activities.[90]

Marginalization

In the *marginalization* pathway, there is little possibility or interest in cultural maintenance, and little interest in having relations with others, sometimes due to discrimination.[91] Fifteen percent of my participants followed this incorporation pathway.

Benita had trouble making friends, and although she eventually made one friend, I classified her as a case of *marginalization* because she said she didn't have any friends until middle school. She was discriminated against by her classmates.

> I didn't have many friends; they couldn't understand me. They couldn't understand my accent and my English. My English was very poor. I only knew the basics. And it was hard because I thought I was dumb because I couldn't read or write . . . It was definitely different than Mexico. It was harder because of the language. I had trouble reading, I had trouble writing, I had trouble speaking. Like, I didn't want to talk to the students, and they would just make fun of me because I didn't speak English. Like I did make a friend. She became my best friend for like . . . she became my best friend throughout middle school.

Children become aware of the discrimination they suffer by around the age of ten.[92] Discrimination can have negative ramifications for the development of young children's sense of self and social identity and is particularly harmful in the early years, when children are in the process of developing a sense of self.[93] As a college student, Benita remains isolated.

Alejandro also felt discriminated against in Miami, but in his case, by his Latino/a classmates.

> The truth is I didn't have friends and I always separated from the rest. In the school, they had bad ideas about Mexicans; I had fights several times because of this. And they would tell me things like "Mexicano this, Mexicano that." So I would get in fights to defend myself. But finally, my father

pulled me [from the school]. And then we moved to Reno, where I had friends because there was no racism there.

Four and a half million immigrants lived in Florida in 2020.[94] However, Mexican immigrants ranked fourth in the state after Cuban, Haitian, and Colombian immigrants.[95] Florida's ethnic composition and the role of Mexican immigrants as a smaller immigrant group partly explains the discrimination against Mexican immigrants in this state.

Other factors likely influenced the treatment that Alejandro received in South Florida, as well. For instance, the Cuban immigrants who arrived in South Florida in the 1960s self-identified as White.[96] Mexican immigrants, on the other hand, have been racialized throughout the history of the United States.[97] Vilma Ortiz and Edward Telles offer the following analysis about Mexicans and Mexican Americans:

> Their long and continuous history as labor migrants destined to jobs at the bottom of the economic hierarchy and their historic placement at the bottom of the racial hierarchy, preceded by the conquest of the original Mexican inhabitants in what is now the US Southwest, have created a distinct racial category of "Mexican" in the popular imagination. While not as heavily excluded from economic and social integration as African Americans, Mexican origin persons have encountered severe racial barriers, which have structured opportunities for them.[98]

Mexicans and Mexican Americans have historically been discriminated against by Whites and other groups. To be sure, Latinos/as in general have been perceived as unintelligent, uneducated, and unproductive by White individuals,[99] but research shows that being ascribed as Mexican increases the likelihood of experiencing discrimination relative to being ascribed as White or Latino/a.[100] Thus, Mexicans and Mexican Americans are one of the Latino groups that is most discriminated against.

Andreíta also felt isolated after her arrival in the United States. She explained,

> With the kids, it [the relationship] was almost non-existing. I honestly don't remember anything right away, but my parents constantly mention

how I would cry every time that it was time for me to go to school because I couldn't . . . I kept saying that I just couldn't talk to them, interact with them because I couldn't understand and they couldn't understand me. So it was this whole bundle of confusion. And I honestly don't remember any of that but they [my parents] do. Maybe I suppressed memories, who knows. What I do remember is just two years [later], this was probably third grade. I remember just playing in the playground and actually having someone to hang out with during playtime. It was just so exciting because I didn't have anyone for I don't know how long. Maybe the first year and half or so.

Language barriers may have been the main factor hindering Andreíta's school adaptation, but in a different part of the interview, she mentioned moving apartments a lot and going to her babysitter's house in the middle of the night because of her parents' busy work schedules. Instability takes a toll on children's lives.[101] Children's residential instability, for instance, has a prejudicial impact on their academic and social outcomes.[102] Likely, this instability also played a role in Andreíta's initial difficulty finding friends.

Hector was also marginalized during school. He attributes this isolation to the fact that his parents asked him to lie about where he was from:

My mom would always advise me, "Hey, never mention where you came from. If they ask, you were born here." I feel like back then, and even now, there is the stigma that I grew up with that you do not want to be honest with people because you don't know where that conversation may lead you to. Being undocumented, I didn't know what that was until I was in seventh or eighth grade . . . I remember even in school projects where they would be like, "oh, where are you from?" Like, I would always just point to Illinois because that's what I was taught . . . That really prevented me from having like a close relationship with most of my classmates when I was growing up, even, even my classmates when I was in a bilingual class.

Around third grade, I actually graduated from a bilingual class because my teachers noticed that I was retaining everything, I was reading and speaking English perfectly fine to them. They thought that I would benefit from being in an all-English class. And that's where I started to build, you know, I guess more barriers around me because at a young age I realized that most of the students weren't different ethnicities, you know, they happened to be, you know, all White. And that for me was very interesting and that's when I honestly didn't make that many friends ... But with moving on I realized I needed to be more private about my life, and I couldn't share. I thought I couldn't share my heritage. That always really bothered me because I didn't want to, you know, keep that hidden because honestly even now that I'm an adult like I am happy where I came from and I wouldn't have it any other way.

Hector felt that having to lie about where he was from isolated him from other schoolchildren. It is not uncommon for undocumented and mixed-status families to conceal their immigration status to avoid its potential consequences, including deportation.[103] Lying affects how children interact at school with friends, as well as in romantic relationships.[104] "For those individuals who feel they cannot be sincere and open to others, another layer of discord is created that affects their sense of being in the world."[105] The impact of lying not only isolated Hector, but also made him question his identity, which he values as an adult.

Conclusion

In this chapter, I have reviewed the immigrant youths' language acquisition process and the development of relationships with peers. It showed that schools are essential in the cultural incorporation of immigrant youth.[106] The majority of the schools that students in my sample attended were diverse. Usually, diverse schools helped students develop a sense of belonging and shared identity with other schoolchildren.[107] Most of the schools my interviewees attended offered some sort of English as a Second Language program. Despite this, the process of language acquisition was challenging for the majority of my participants. In many cases, the process of language acquisition was intertwined with the process of social incorporation, and students who struggled to learn the language also struggled to make friends.

Teachers and classmates alike supported the process of language acquisition. The next chapter addresses the role of teachers and other support staff in the incorporation of youth in schools. Suffice it to say, even in the absence of resources, teachers managed to make a difference in the immigrant children's lives by supporting their English language development. It is also important to note that several students acted as language brokers for participants in this research, helping them with translation and interpretation.[108] Moreover, in several cases these supportive classmates became important friends in the lives of the immigrant youth.

Some students learned English fast. In many cases, the resources provided by the schools proved appropriate to facilitate the language acquisition process.[109] But students also managed to learn the language outside of the classroom, by watching TV.[110] In many cases, the process of language acquisition and social integration were intertwined. I mentioned previously that students who struggled with the language also struggled to make friends. In contrast, students with good command of the language made friends more easily. At the same time, immigrant children sometimes learned the language from their peers who spent time with them. This research therefore showed that the processes of language acquisition and social integration reinforced each other.

Some students were critical of the language classes because they felt the classes set them back. This finding is consistent with previous research showing that adolescents feel ESL settings do not challenge them enough, and instead they aspire to be placed into mainstream classes.[111] Some students in my sample had as a main goal transitioning out of the ESL classroom to a mainstream one.[112] Others were ridiculed by other students for being in ESL. Still others felt they would learn English faster if they were immersed in all-English classes. Maybe experts ought to consider students' desires and expectations more often when making decisions about when to transfer students into mainstream classes.

Friendships proved vital to the incorporation of immigrant youth in the United States.[113] This study followed Berry's classification of the paths to acculturation as assimilation, integration, separation, and marginalization.[114] Most participants chose the pathway of separation, followed by integration, marginalization, and assimilation. Some participants assimilated into the dominant group, but in most cases, the schools either lacked a diverse body of students or the cultural norms were imposed on the participant. Participants who followed integration usually first went through a stage where they had friends of their own ethnicity while learning the language. Participants who chose the pathway of separation were of three types: those who separated by choice, those who were forced to separate by a factor outside of their control, and those who separated due to segregation. Finally, participants rarely chose marginalization as a path, but rather were forced into it due to discrimination and segregation. Importantly, none of the Polish interviewees followed this path.

3

Searching for Support

The Role of School Teachers and Counselors

Laura's dream is to become a pediatrician. She came from Mexico when she was three years old with her two siblings because things in Mexico were "difficult for the family." She and her siblings crossed the border with their aunt, who claimed Laura and her siblings as her children. Laura's family first arrived in a small town in Iowa. She started pre-K at the age of four and, even though Spanish was her first language, English "came easily to her" and she did not struggle with the language.

Later, Laura attended a diverse school in a small town in Illinois. Her experience in school was, however, less than optimal. In fifth grade, a school librarian told her and her friends not to speak Spanish. In middle school, her classmates called her names, which made her think they did not see her as an equal. These experiences hurt Laura even more deeply when at the age of thirteen she discovered she was undocumented and could not legally work in the United States, and when in high school her guidance counselors, who were supposed to help her achieve her college dream, gave up on her for not having documents. Fortunately, however, Laura did have two outstanding teachers who inspired her to continue her education.

Laura was happy when DACA came about because this meant she and her siblings would be able to work and drive without hiding from the police or using back roads. She was also thrilled that she could achieve her college dream. When DACA's termination was announced in 2017, however, Laura was devastated because somebody had decided that after all their hard work and paying taxes, she and the other DACA recipients were not "worthy of being in this country." She was also fearful that now the government knew "everything" about her and her family: where she lived, where she worked, where she attended school, and that her parents were not in this country legally.

Despite her struggles, Laura was able to earn her BS in a private school thanks to a Pritzker Scholarship that provided her with support throughout college. When studying, Laura always remembered what her parents told her: "No one can take your education away from you." Laura is now attending graduate school in Chicago in preparation to apply for medical school. Someday she expects to help her father quit his rough second job, where he works in ninety-degree weather and carries sixty-pound bags of food.

As Laura's story shows, her incorporation into school did not go smoothly. Despite attending a diverse school with a dual immersion program where students switched between classes in Spanish and English throughout the day, she had negative experiences with her peers, support staff, and counselors. This book argues that the incorporation of undocumented immigrant youth follows a roller-coaster pattern. In comparison to the discovery of their lack of documents and exclusion from certain milestones undocumented youth experience during their adolescence, such as the inability to attain a driver's license and/or a first job, schools provide a space that should foster a certain level of inclusion.[1] As we saw previously, though, not every undocumented child enjoyed the same level of inclusion in their early schooling. This chapter first explores the role of teachers in facilitating or hindering this sense of inclusion, then moves on to the role of counselors. For example, school counselors should maximize students' success and foster the well-being of all students, as well as guide them toward a career path.[2] Importantly, the college dream for undocumented students has been a possibility in the state of Illinois since 2003.[3] For this reason, the second part of this chapter explores the role of guidance counselors in facilitating/hindering success both in school and in the path to college.

The Role of Teachers and Counselors

Schools have an essential role in the social incorporation of newcomer immigrant and refugee youth.[4] The achievement gap between Latino students and their counterparts is of concern in the United States.[5] Individual learning is associated with social relationships and interactions that affect educational outcomes. "In education, this is demonstrated in the experiences, interactions, and relationships of students with their teachers, mentors, community, and family, and how this sociocultural matrix impacts who they are, what they believe of themselves, how they think, and how they learn."[6] The nature and strength of relationships with teachers can affect an immigrant child's developmental and acculturative outcomes.[7] Research also shows that relationships with school personnel are important because the lack of school-based networks can prevent undocumented students from pursuing higher education, due to lack of development of supportive student-teacher relationships, higher education mentoring, and lack of information on financial aid options.[8]

A US study found that teachers held lower expectations for and offered less positive encouragement to ethnic minority students, excluding Asian Americans.[9] The consequences of teacher bias can be devastating and are related to the negative outcomes associated with discrimination experiences, including decreased sense of academic competence and belonging in school.[10] This sense of belonging allows students to view schooling as essential to their long-term well-being and is reflected in their participation in academic and non-academic pursuits.[11] Students with a greater sense of belonging at school often have higher intrinsic motivation and higher academic performance.[12] Students with a greater sense of belonging in school also have fewer mental health and social problems, including lower rates of delinquency, reduced social rejection, decreased depression, fewer incidences of dropping out of school, and less drug use.[13]

The attitudes and behaviors of school principals, support staff, and counselors can also influence immigrant children's sense of belonging in school.[14] In particular, school counselors are educators who work to maximize student success by implementing comprehensive counseling programs that foster academic, socioemotional, and career development.[15] Yet the findings in the literature about the role of counselors in serving DACA and undocumented students are mixed. A study that surveyed ten school counselors in California who serve undocumented students found that counselors acknowledged their role in delivering college information and resources, connecting with parents, communities, and colleges, and counseling students. However, these counselors reported facing challenges, including inadequate training and resources, time constraints, difficulty in identifying undocumented students, and lack of support from district and administrative leaders.[16]

Negative experiences with school professionals were also reported in the literature. One study found that many undocumented students experienced discrimination and prejudice from high school and college faculty and staff, either due to ignorance or personal bias.[17] Another study found that high school counselors sometimes misinformed students and discouraged undocumented students from attending college.[18] Further, when counselors and teachers treated "all students the same," they were unable to serve undocumented students because counselors ignored their specific needs.[19] The same study found, however, that when educators were genuinely involved, they could make a difference in helping DACA and undocumented students access college.[20]

The Role of Teachers

The relationships between students, schoolteachers, and staff are essential for achievement because they influence the development of students' identities, sense of self-worth, thinking and learning processes.[21] This study included an open question that asked participants to describe their interactions with teachers, administrations, and counselors. Participants indicated that over 70 percent believed their teachers were supportive and helped them throughout their schooling. The other 30 percent felt teachers were not supportive. The Polish respondents had more positive experiences. Two of them had positive experiences with their teachers and the third one did not explicitly discuss this information.

Teachers Who Inspired Students to Achieve Their College Dream

Education is the path to prosperity par excellence in America.[22] Teachers who believe in undocumented students' abilities and worthiness can positively impact the college process.[23] Students' teachers in our sample inspired students to work hard and pursue their college dreams. Despite Laura's negative interactions with school staff and counselors, she had two "awesome" history teachers who pushed her to keep going. This is what Laura said about her history teachers:

> When they heard bad things in the news, they would ask me, "how are you holding up?" When they saw I was getting discouraged, especially my

senior year when I didn't have funds to go to college, they pushed me and were very encouraging. "You can't give up. You have a great future ahead of you, keep going, don't stop, keep fighting." They would always check on me and follow the DACA news, they talked to me and pushed me to keep fighting and not give up even if it seemed like doors were closing for me. So I appreciate them a lot for talking to me.

Laura's story shows how her teachers kept up with the immigration news, checked on her, and encouraged her to keep fighting when she was discouraged. Laura decided to be open with them about her immigration status. This openness allows teachers and other support staff to penetrate the world of fear and uncertainty undocumented students navigate and to support them.[24]

Similarly, José described the support he received from his science teacher:

I think honestly, the one thing that really helped me get to where I am today was my science teacher, chemistry teacher. My sophomore year, prior to being in his class, my parents had always had this sort of this subconscious message, "You don't really want to stand out in the situation that we are in." So that led me to be as average as possible, to blend into the background as much as I could. But when I got to this teacher's class, he's the one who said, "Hey, what's your plan after high school?" At the time, I didn't really have one. I was going to be a carpenter though I wasn't even a handy person, but that was my plan. He was like, "No, that's not what you should do." He wanted me to go into some sort of engineering field or some kind of science field . . . He basically told me that college was what I needed to do. He was really the reason why I started trying harder in school. Without that, I wouldn't have gotten the scholarships and wouldn't have been able to turn it around. Through his guidance, I could achieve more. So that's really the turning point in my life from trying to be as invisible as possible to deciding that I could really do something good here.

The college decision process for undocumented students is plagued with difficulties.[25] Undocumented students rely on high school staff to provide the necessary information and encouragement they need to apply for college.[26] Sometimes this role is filled by teachers. José was lucky he had a teacher who instilled the college dream in him. When I last spoke with him, he was completing an MBA at a public university in Illinois.

Overcoming Language Barriers: Communication

Some students valued those teachers who communicated with them effectively. Three of their comments referred to ESL teachers, but Zaide's did not. Zaide had good experiences with teachers, despite language barriers. She told me,

> I never had, like, any problems with the teachers. I think they were all very nice to me. They were very helpful as well. Some teachers that I remember like in kindergarten or first grade, didn't know Spanish, so they tried their best to communicate with me, but they are the ones who did help me try to learn the language.

Even the teachers who did not know Spanish were able to help Zaide learn English. This finding may support evidence that shows that English immersion programs are effective at teaching English language skills, even at the expense of losing the potential for bilingualism in school children.[27]

Alondra also had good experiences with her teachers in learning English, but unlike Zaide's, her teachers were bilingual.

> As I said, my school was very diverse, and I was enrolled in the bilingual program. I was studying English and Spanish at the same time. It was a beautiful experience. I could talk to my teachers in Spanish and English. When I didn't know something, they would help me . . . Yes, they helped me practice Spanish and English. I communicate with them to this day. I have them on Facebook and they watch me grow up and develop my career.

Alondra developed a powerful bond with her teachers who instructed her in English and Spanish. Besides literacy and language skills, bilingual education programs provide the opportunity to learn a heritage language, develop at least some proficiency in another language, and attain the cognitive benefits of bilingualism.[28] Further, her teachers' flexibility to switch between English and Spanish has additional advantages, offering equitable, empowering educational and language learning opportunities to minorities to develop bilingual identities.[29]

Ignacio made similar remarks in reference to his Spanish-speaking teacher. In this sense, he explained,

> It was tough. I mean I didn't know English so I would get bullied a lot for not knowing how to speak English. The good thing is that my middle school had a program for people who didn't know English, ESL. So I was with people who didn't know English either, that was kind of cool. But it was weird, you know? . . . A teacher who knew Spanish would help us a lot with homework and stuff. Other than her I didn't speak to anyone else.

Ignacio seemed to be isolated but communicated with his Spanish teacher well. Maybe having an ESL teacher who supported him provided protection against the impact of the discrimination and bullying he dealt with. A study showed that teacher involvement may protect students from the association between race-based bullying and some unhealthy behaviors, such as smoking.[30]

Language Barriers

Over forty-one million people in the United States spoke Spanish at home in 2019.[31] Despite the overwhelming presence of Spanish speakers in the United States, schools continue to lag behind in making their faculty and staff representative of the students they serve.[32] Some of my interviewees complained about the language barriers they faced at school. Justice, despite being in ESL classes, could not understand her teachers.

> Well, I began school in second grade. And obviously, I didn't understand very much and so this one time kind of stuck with me. One time, I was kind of goofing around with one of the students there. And I guess my teacher wanted us to concentrate and now I know what she meant. She said leave them alone, but at the time I didn't know what she was talking

about, so I just stared at her because I didn't understand. And this class I think was a little bit of ESL, but it was mostly English, and so I kind of just had to figure out what people were talking about based on their actions and that was that.

Justice was enrolled in ESL classes but despite this, the teacher gave her instructions in English that she could not understand. This inability or unwillingness of an ESL teacher to translate instructions for a second grader to ease her adaptation to school is distressing, given the literature that shows the many benefits associated with bilingual instruction.[33]

José also reported experiencing language barriers in his predominantly White school. His school required that he restart first grade. Despite this, José had a hard time adjusting in school because his shortcoming was likely not academic but rather the product of language barriers. He explained, "I remember signing up for school. The first time was a little odd since there was that language barrier and I had to restart the first grade, which didn't set me back too far . . . It was rough at times because they also weren't used to having someone who only spoke Spanish."

José told me a story relayed elsewhere about a time when he copied his assignment from a classmate because he could not understand what he was supposed to do. Despite the school's efforts to communicate with him, José felt his schooling was "odd" because of language barriers.

Zoe also experienced language barriers and felt uncomfortable with the White faculty of her school. She recalled,

So, basically, you would go to regular English courses, but the instructors didn't even know Spanish themselves so it's one of those things either way they would still be speaking to you in English. And yeah, I don't know, I thought that was kind of silly . . . but teachers, I think, were the hardest thing for me. I don't know if it is an identity piece of it, but in Georgia you would see more African American professors than anything. And here you see mainly White professors and I think that was very uncomfortable for me.

Zoe was unable to understand her teachers who continued to talk to her in English. This likely hindered her academic success and school adaptation process.[34] She was aware that not having role models of color also affected her identity. As mentioned above, the availability of gender- or race-matched role models can have a strong positive effect on the development of adolescents' identity.[35]

Teachers' Gender and Ethnic/Racial Match

The disconnect between a largely Anglo teaching force and increasingly diverse and multilingual students has prejudicial effects on the education of diverse youth.[36] Some students in the Chicago area appreciated the racial match between them and their teachers. Angel, for instance, said,

> [The interaction with teachers] was positive. When I was in West Lawn, I had teachers who were people of color. I believe my . . . third grade teacher was Middle Eastern; she was a Palestinian. My fourth grade teacher was a male. My ESL specialist, ESL teacher, she was White, but she was really nice and understanding. She really cared for us. And then in fifth grade, though, is when we moved out from Chicago to the suburbs outside of Chicago and there, things were a little bit different because in the suburbs, right outside of Chicago was more predominantly White.

Having teachers of color and one male teacher was important for Angel, and he did not enjoy moving to the suburbs where students and teachers were predominantly White. Andrés concurred.

> My school had a lot of minorities. African Americans, Puerto Ricans, Mexicans and just other Latin countries and stuff like that. So it wasn't too hard; we kind of grew up in the same culture. Yeah, a lot of the faculty were either Hispanic, Latin or African American. They just knew who we were basically, so I didn't feel like a minority at all.

Having teachers of color helped Andrés not feel "like a minority." The ethnic, gender, or racial match between students and teachers helps students perform better academically.[37] Also, evidence suggests that the teacher-child racial-ethnic match is linked to teachers' differential perceptions of the social and academic behaviors of children in their classrooms.[38]

Mistreatment and Discrimination

Several of my interviewees complained about their negative experiences with teachers and staff that qualified as discrimination. Immigrant students experience discrimination in the form of xenophobia, nativism, and racial microaggressions both outside and inside of school.[39] Experiencing different forms of discrimination has the potential to negatively affect mental health, self-esteem, engagement, and academic performance.[40] Laura described her experience with the school librarian:

> If there is something I do remember, it wasn't from the kids but from faculty. I remember I was in fifth grade and was talking Spanish with one of my friends. And I do remember the librarian telling us to shut up. I remember her saying, this is America, and you can't speak that right now. We were in fifth grade, we were like, "What?" You know, it's like fifth grade, you shouldn't have a faculty member telling you that but . . .

Despite attending a school with a dual language immersion program, Laura's librarian enforced her "English only" policy in the library. Estela faced a similar experience in Phoenix, but unlike Laura's, her school was not ethnically or linguistically diverse. Estela explained,

> Ah well, the teachers, in the community where I was at in Phoenix, I wouldn't say I felt discriminated, but I felt like an outcast. Teachers were not very helpful. Even our ESL classes weren't very helpful to be honest . . . I did really feel a little like an outcast with the teachers . . . Ah yeah, it was a little difficult. I didn't speak English . . . I did feel a little weird. I did feel a little discriminated. The teachers didn't want you to speak Spanish and it was a little hard to blend in the beginning because I didn't know the language.

Estela's teachers were probably trying to make sure Estela learned English. Nonetheless, these messages exposed negative attitudes associated with the use of the Spanish language and the linguistic power and belonging of the English language in the school context.[41] I wonder if Laura and Estela respected the linguistic boundaries constructed in their schools. I also wonder if these experiences hurt their self-esteem and ethnic pride.

Other teachers did not overtly discriminate against my participants, but still made students feel unwelcome. Benita attended a school with no Spanish-speaking teachers. Schools that are well-integrated with little segregation usually inspire feelings of safety, interethnic group cohesion, and trust in teachers' fairness among all students.[42]

> Yeah. So it was very hard because the teachers would get frustrated. I would get frustrated, so I cried. And I was like, "Mom, I hate it here. I don't like it here. I just want to leave and stuff." So it took me a couple of years to adapt. My first and second grade teachers got really frustrated. They got really frustrated that I wasn't spending a lot of time in my classroom since they pulled me out because they couldn't work with me.

Maybe the teachers' frustration was not intentional. Nonetheless, research shows that rudeness demotivates students in the learning process.[43] Expressions of frustration on the part of teachers demotivated Benita to the point that she did not want to continue to attend school.

The Role of Teachers According to Polish Youth

Only two of the Polish interviewees provided judgments about the role of their teachers in their education. Both of their experiences were highly positive. Ali thought her teachers were wonderful. She explained,

> And my teachers were just wonderful. They basically made other kids be friendly to me and help me out and say, you know: "Please, sit with her, please help her as much as you can." I still remember my fourth grade teacher to this day because she helped me so much . . . Teachers were helpful. Yeah, definitely. In the ESL program support team, the teachers were very helpful. You know, they're the ones that help you get acculturated to the English language and the culture. They helped me understand

how everything works and the American school. So that program was very helpful.

Ali's teachers were likely the strongest advocates of any of my interviewees: They "made" other kids become friends with her, help her. They also taught her the language, and about the culture and the American school. Research shows that supportive teachers can have a major impact on children's acculturative outcomes.[44]

Mateusz's teachers were also supportive. He stated,

> Yeah, so teachers were great. I mean, like I said, I went to a bilingual program, at a school in Chicago. So obviously, like I said, my class had mostly Polish kids. So, there were a lot of kids in my situation, and my teacher herself was a Polish person, she was an immigrant. So I think she was more, you know, willing to understand my situation.

Mateusz's immigrant teachers were able to empathize with Mateusz's situation and treated him, as he said later, "not different from any other kid." Much has been said about the disconnect between the largely White teaching force and its mismatch with an increasingly diverse youth population.[45] It is important to note that Mateusz did not comment on his teacher's race but rather her immigrant background. This should be a cautionary tale about narrow understandings of *ethnicity* that treat it as racial only. If we are to serve students of all backgrounds, ideas of ethnicity should be broadened to incorporate not only race but also national origin and/or immigrant background.

The Role of Counselors

School counselors are educators who have crucial roles in fostering academic, socioemotional, and career development.[46] One of my interview questions asked participants about their interactions with counselors. The findings are, in my view, alarming. Thirty percent of my interviewees stated their counselors were helpful to them in the process of completing high school and applying for college, while 70 percent stated they were not. Two of the Polish interviewees provided information about their school counselors and apparently only Ali's was helpful in the college application process.

Helpful Counselors

A minority of my interviewees had good experiences with counselors. Juliana and Jessica were among them. Juliana said, "They used to help me a lot to decide what to take and the best possible way to do, like, classes and everything." In turn, Jessica stated, "Yeah, kind of. I would reach out to them, and they would explain to me about scholarships and everything. It is that what helped me."

Juliana's counselor helped her in selecting the right classes for graduation and college readiness. Like other low-income students, perhaps Jessica lacked other sources of information and assistance to guide her through high school.[47] Jessica's counselor assisted her with the college application process and the quest for scholarships. Unlike other youth of immigrant background, she felt she received considerable guidance regarding postsecondary school.[48] As part of the literature predicted, it is clear that these two interviewees' counselors provided helpful information and resources.[49]

Hector was very enthusiastic about the counselor he had in high school and explained,

> Honestly, I can say that I had one of the best counselors in high school. I remember her so vividly. She was so terribly nice to me, and she helped me out with everything. I think the first time I ever truly opened up about being undocumented was to my counselor because I could tell that she really wanted to help me. I heard stories about my friends having the worst counselors and I felt very grateful for the one that I had.
>
> Right around junior year in high school when I started thinking about where to go to college, I really wanted to become a teacher. That was like my one goal. I was just turning a new page. I started getting better grades and started to feel more comfortable, you know, in my own skin. I got really close to her in my junior and senior year, because she actually helped me set up for this program that my school offered, which allowed you to teach your senior year. You would go to a different classroom for four weeks and teach from kindergarten to eighth graders.

So, she gave me the resources that I needed. She introduced me to the scholarship called the Golden Apple. And it's a, I guess, you could say a very prestigious scholarship . . . I'm grateful that I was lucky enough to actually get the scholarship, but they took the scholarship away because of my undocumented status at the time. So I ended up not pursuing that, but it was because of my counselor that I even got the opportunity to go that far. She really understood where I was coming from. If there was a question that she didn't know, I felt like she had the right contacts and the right resources. She contacted me with a lot of resources. One was a lawyer that dealt with undocumented students and undocumented people. So she was an awesome person to have, honestly.

Hector had a great experience with his high school counselor despite the difficulties he faced. As the literature shows, undocumented students face many challenges in their access to higher education and many counselors are well-positioned to help them.[50] It was sad the Golden Apple Scholarship of Illinois was taken away from him for being undocumented. To this day, this scholarship is only awarded to US citizens or eligible residents.[51]

Like Hector's counselor, Andreíta's counselors did not have all the answers but worked hard to get the necessary resources.

The earliest that I remember a school counselor would probably be in high school. I don't think I had anything like that in middle school or elementary school. I would say, probably at the end of sophomore year of high school, I started talking to my counselor because we had to set up some type of meeting to talk about what we wanted to do . . . That was the only time I remember reaching out to a counselor and that was actually the first time I had to share my identity with them. Ever since I got here, they were like, "Don't tell anyone." I was like, "Okay."

So that was the only time I had to tell someone because they kind of needed to know in order to help, but it still didn't matter because they didn't know how to help. But she was very patient and very persistent in trying to find information for me. But then what was also really sad is that she left, she retired. So, I was like, "Okay, bye."

And then I was off to another counselor who was just like her but tried even harder. She knew the need that I had and wanted to give me the best information, which at that time, wasn't very clear information because everyone was saying so many different things like about funding: "File the FAFSA, do it, don't do it." . . . But she was just very patient and walked me through everything. But that's the only thing I know about counselors.

Like Hector, Andreíta opened up for the first time about being undocumented with her counselor. Even though her counselors lacked information about undocumented students' access to higher education (undocumented students, for instance, cannot apply for FAFSA), they worked hard to find the necessary resources and helped her navigate her way through the college application process.[52]

Estela also thought her counselor was helpful in pushing her to finish school and in applying for college. She explained,

> Also, junior year, all my friends were applying for colleges, and I had to work to, you know, I had to start working to pay even community college. I could only do one class or two. Financially, I couldn't afford it and it is a little harder because we don't get financial assistance. But it was hard because I was in the softball team and cross-country, but I couldn't apply to many things because they required a social security number . . . And she [the counselor] didn't give up on me. I'm very blessed because if it wasn't for her, I would've not finished high school.
>
> And yeah, I think high school was the worst during my experience just because I did like school and I did give up on a lot of my dreams at the time because I couldn't pursue them, you know without a social security . . . She [the counselor] helped me get into my community college. She also helped me get into my church that actually . . . helped me pay for my books through community college and sometimes they would pay a class or two. For me, yeah, she was very helpful. And again, to this day I will remember her because she found little ways to help me out.

Research shows how the limited options after high school are very stressful for undocumented Latino/a youth.[53] Estela told me she missed school for a whole semester and the counselor made special arrangements for her to be homeschooled so that she would not drop out. The same counselor helped her apply to college and find a scholarship. Like other helpful counselors, Estela's worked hard to assist her during the college access process.[54]

Unhelpful Counselors

Seventy percent of the counselors were not helpful, either because they did not have the right information or had a biased view about what undocumented students should do after high school. It is worth reminding the reader that Illinois is a state "welcoming" of undocumented students. The 2003 Acevedo Act (Public Act 93–0007) allowed undocumented students who reside in the state of Illinois, who attended an Illinois high school for at least three years, and/or graduated with a high school diploma or equivalent in the state, to receive in-state tuition.[55] Further, the 2011 Illinois Dream Act (SB2185) made scholarships, college savings, and prepaid tuition programs available to undocumented students who graduate from Illinois high schools and mandated counselors be trained to assist undocumented students in gaining access to higher education.[56] Finally, the Rise Act (HB 2691) of 2019 allowed undocumented (and transgender) students who do not qualify for federal financial aid because of their lack of legal status to receive state financial aid.[57]

Despite the 2011 Illinois Dream Act mandate, some counselors gave incorrect information to my interviewees. This was the case for Marcos and Zoe. Marcos reported,

> "You cannot go to public college" [the counselor said] and you know, and I'm like, "Why can't I get scholarship?" So, it was a big shock for me, it was a very low blow kind of thing. "Well, I recommend you just go to community college to start off and see if you can get scholarships there later or something."

Zoe, in turn, said,

> But I think counselors and teachers lacking information, not knowing how to help us rather than getting good information probably made it

worse. They sent us to a website for scholarships, but they all required residency or citizenship, and I was like, "Well, I guess I'm not going to school." And I think in the second half of senior year I was like, "I don't want to do this." So I went from "There is a future for me" to "Well, I'm going to work at a factory." Yeah, I think I was depressed for the next couple of months after that. I had just given up, I was like, "There's no hope."

These examples show that counselors lacked information. Marcos's counselor was wrong because in Illinois he could attend any public school and pay in-state tuition.[58] Similarly, Zoe's counselor did not provide information about funding options for undocumented students. As previous research showed, some high school counselors misinformed undocumented students and discouraged them from attending college.[59]

Unlike most other participants, Benita attended high school in Georgia. She thought her counselors had no resources or simply did not care. She explained,

Oh, my high school, they didn't know. So when I was applying for college, they had no resources for DACA students. Nothing . . . Like they didn't even ask me if I wanted to go or anything. They didn't care. All they care is for students to graduate because my high school was predominantly undocumented with DACA . . . They didn't know how to work with you. It was kind of like the main point for them to make you graduate, that's it. That was the point. After that, they were done with you. They didn't really care.

Benita's counselors did not have resources for undocumented students who wanted to attend college in a school where most students were DACA recipients. The context of reception, which includes the state policies applicable to undocumented students and the prevailing attitudes about immigration, probably did not help.[60] Georgia bans undocumented students from attending the top public universities and charges out-of-state tuition in other state universities.[61] Not surprisingly, the counselors were probably trained to discourage undocumented students from attending college.

Laura also had negative experiences in a diverse high school in a rural town in Illinois. She recalled,

I don't think we were a priority for them. I was in the top 10 percent of the girls in the area and they gave me a scholarship packet. They said, "You know, for some of these scholarships you need to be a US citizen," and I said, "Does that really matter?" and when they figured out I was not a citizen they took the scholarship packet from my hands and said, "Oh, sorry." At that point I started crying in their office and I don't think they knew what to do with me. They would just like push us aside and you had to fight for yourself kind of thing.

Laura's counselors were pretty insensitive about her reaction when told she could not apply for a scholarship, even though socioemotional support is part of their job description.[62] Laura felt she was pushed aside and forced to fend for herself. She got help from her sister and some history teachers to achieve her college dream.

Finally, I believe Angel's counselor's bias against undocumented students was so significant, it can be classified as racist. Angel reported,

And then when I did meet with a counselor, she was like the worst! She was the least supporting person in the whole school. At that time, I thought I wanted to be a veterinarian and part of the process of meeting with her was doing some research of the things I was interested in. And when I met with her, my mom came with me.

I told her, "These are the schools where I want to apply to, and this is what I want to study and everything." And at the end of it, she said, "Uh, that's not going to work out because you're illegal so I would suggest you to go immediately to the workforce right out of high school. You're not going to be able to be a vet, you can't get a license and you can't pay for school." And then she gave me a list of like, the title said, "Recommended Jobs for Illegal Immigrants." . . . It was bogus.

Not to belittle the profession but it was like a very . . . I don't know where she got the list, but it was like a very generalized list of the jobs that undocumented workers can do, like waiting tables, shoemaking, landscaping and other stuff. But that's when it hit me, and I left out of there crying and really frustrated.

Angel's counselor was right that being a veterinarian would be difficult because of the licensing requirements of some professions and occupations. In general, Congress prohibits undocumented immigrants from obtaining a government-issued professional license unless the state has specific laws authorizing it.[63] But the counselor should not have discouraged Angel from attending college altogether. Further, the list of jobs for undocumented individuals the counselor handed Angel was so stereotypical it can be classified as racist. And Angel is not alone: One study found that numerous undocumented students experienced discrimination and prejudice from high school and college faculty and staff, due to either ignorance or personal bias.[64] This counselor's actions probably had an impact on Angel's well-being and mental health.

The Role of Guidance Counselors According to Polish Youth

Only Ali and Peter provided information directly or indirectly related to their guidance counselors. Importantly, Peter, who obtained an associate's degree, mistakenly thought he could not study in college due to his lack of documents.[65] It is unclear whether he ever reached out to his school counselors or not. In any event, school counselors should provide information about college admissions broadly to students, including information that applies to undocumented ones. This is the only way to guarantee that students fearful of disclosing their undocumented status get the relevant information.

Ali believed her guidance counselors were "a little bit" helpful. She explained:

> A little bit? Yes, they were there, the counselor I had was aware of my situation. And I definitely picked the school that wasn't the most expensive school. I had other schools I wanted to go to, but this was a happy medium where I could get the education I wanted, but then I could pay for it on my own as well, without those government loans that I wasn't able to get.

Apparently, Ali was not thrilled with her school counselors but at least they provided the right information for her to pick a school that she could afford.[66] As mentioned elsewhere, undocumented and DACA students cannot apply for federal financial aid.[67]

Conclusion

This book argues that the incorporation of DACA recipients follows a roller-coaster pattern. This chapter explored the relationships the undocumented youth forged with their teachers and counselors. Experiences with teachers and mentors likely impact who children are, what they believe of themselves, how they think, and how they learn.[68] Most DACA recipients thought their teachers were supportive and helpful, corroborating findings from the previous chapter that overall, *Plyler v. Doe* still grants some inclusion in public schools. Some teachers were essential in motivating and inspiring my interviewees to pursue their college dream. Others went out of their way to communicate with them, in some cases, despite language barriers. Interviewees who received instruction in English and Spanish valued these experiences and their own linguistic identity.[69] This instruction probably protected students who were targets of mockery and discrimination by their classmates.[70] Notably, Polish DACA recipients gave their teachers rave reviews. Further, Ali probably had the most supportive teachers of all. These teachers went out of their way to encourage other children to befriend Ali and helped her during her first few months in American schools. Finally, participants were very appreciative of teachers who matched their gender and ethnic identity. Even one of my Polish interviewees noted that having an immigrant teacher aided his adaptation. These role models possibly improved their academic performance[71] and helped them develop a sense of gender and ethnic pride.[72]

Less than one-third of my participants had bad experiences with their teachers. One of them complained teachers refused to speak to her in Spanish in her ESL class. Paralleling a national trend, other teachers were unprepared to serve the linguistically and ethnically diverse students enrolled in their district.[73] In these cases, participants described their experiences as odd and uncomfortable. In the most serious cases, participants had experiences that can be classified as mistreatment and discrimination, including librarians and teachers enforcing

English-only policies and teachers becoming impatient and frustrated with the schoolchildren. These experiences likely affected their mental health, self-esteem, engagement, and academic performance.[74] None of my Polish interviewees reported these experiences, providing support for the possibility that White undocumented youth may have an easier time incorporating into American society.[75]

The experiences students had with guidance counselors were concerning. It seems that the somewhat smooth incorporation of the early years of schooling deteriorates as the undocumented youth come of age, even in a state where undocumented students pay in-state tuition and have access to state funding.[76] Thirty percent of the counselors fulfilled their role of providing academic advice, encouragement, and guidance for college access. Due to the lack of legally mandated training and preparation, some counselors had to search for information and resources to assist the undocumented youth.[77] Seventy percent of the counselors, however, either lacked the resources to help undocumented students, the disposition to do it, or both.[78] Some counselors provided incorrect information. Others seemed insensitive and uncaring toward undocumented students. In the most extreme case, one counselor discouraged a bright student from attending college and gave him a list of stereotypical jobs for undocumented immigrants. Despite these experiences, 70 percent of the undocumented youth interviewed for this project completed at least a college degree. This speaks to the resilience of immigrant youth.[79] It is worth mentioning that Polish interviewees did not report horrific experiences with their guidance counselors. This observation's generalizability is low given the small sample of Polish students.

4

No Future in Sight

Discovering Immigration Status

Andreíta obtained a master's degree in design activism and her dream is to teach designers about personal values and to build their sense of responsibility on social issues. Her family is from Guatemala and when her parents originally migrated to the United States, she stayed with her grandparents in Guatemala for two years. She joined her parents at the age of five, when she came to the United States by plane with her uncle and met her parents close to O'Hare airport in Chicago.

Andreíta cried a lot when she started school because she was unable to communicate with teachers and classmates. The family lived in a small town in Illinois and her school lacked an ESL program for English learners. Despite this, she had a teacher who, after doing research, managed to teach her English. This teacher worked with Andreíta for seven years until she had a good command of the English language. She met her first friend when she was in third grade and was thrilled to have somebody to play with.

Andreíta always knew she was undocumented because her family was open about it. But she was also coached not to tell anyone about the family's status. The family was cautious and instructed Andreíta to never leave the house without her documents, "just in case" something were to happen. She understood the implications of her immigration status when applying for colleges and realized that without financial aid it was going to be tough to afford college. DACA gave her peace of mind and eventually the opportunity to work in her field of study. The termination of DACA did not surprise her, but the results of the 2016 elections that made Donald Trump president were devastating for her.

Andreíta hit rock bottom in 2016, after both the election results and her father's stage 4 cancer diagnosis. She lost motivation for school, struggled with daily activities, and was even scared to go outside the house. She later attended a Catholic retreat at her school that taught her to place her expectations in God and not in human beings. Last time I spoke with Andreíta she was completing her master's degree.

Different factors in the host society interact with the process of immigrant incorporation. Sociologists and anthropologists refer to this dynamic as the context of reception.[1] The context of reception includes the stance of the host government and of employers, the characteristics of pre-existing ethnic communities, and discrimination by the host society.[2] For undocumented youth, their legal status constrains virtually every aspect of their incorporation.[3] Of particular interest for this study are the laws and regulations that rule the admission of foreign citizens. As Andreíta's story shows, the lives of undocumented youth are shaped in relation to the laws that award and take away rights from them, determining their experiences of inclusion and exclusion. Andreíta always knew she was undocumented but truly understood its implications when she began applying for college.

This chapter analyzes the ways undocumented youth in this study found out they were undocumented and the impact of this discovery on their lives, expectations, and identity. It shows that, after partial inclusion during the early school years, the undocumented youth hit a low point when discovering they were undocumented or when understanding the implications of such a realization. The literature characterizes the experiences of these youth as "liminal" or "in between."[4]

Legal Incorporation

Legal incorporation refers to the place immigrants are located on the immigration status continuum.[5] Undocumented students are exposed to an array of economic, legal, and emotional barriers that are almost never encountered by their citizen peers due to their immigration status.[6] The process of legal incorporation is mostly determined by the opportunities and constraints available in the host society, such as the rules for admission and naturalization of foreign citizens. The legal incorporation of immigrants can follow a progression that includes the obtainment of a work visa (going from undocumented to documented), a permanent residency permit (green card), and citizenship. During the period under analysis, however, undocumented youth followed different stages related to their legal incorporation, including (a) *unawareness of legal status and/or its implications*, (b) *discovery of illegality and deportability*, (c) *deferred (suspended) deportability*, and (d) *threat of deportability*. These changes in documentation status can challenge immigrants' perception of themselves and the world.[7]

Even though contemporary theories of immigrant incorporation try to account for the role of context of reception in contextualizing and shaping immigrants' lives, they fail to fully address the significance of legal status and its role in affecting the pathway to incorporation.[8] This study attempts to address this shortcoming. Youth who could have benefited from the Dream Act are challenged by the volatility of their external environment.[9] The second stage undocumented youth go through is the discovery of their undocumented status. In most cases, they learn they are undocumented and/or understand its implications when they attempt to move through the rites of passage associated with their age.[10] Although some of my participants, especially those who came to the country at an older age and through painful crossings, always knew they were undocumented, most interviewees either found out they were undocumented or only fully understood its implications in their teenage years, when trying to take driver's education classes, looking for a job, and/or applying for college. The Polish interviewees, however, tended to know they were undocumented from an early age.

The discovery of their undocumented status prompts reactions of confusion, anger, frustration, and despair, followed by a period of paralyzing shock.[11] Participants in my sample obtained DACA in 2012 or soon after. For most participants, DACA provided an array of opportunities to obtain driver's licenses and better jobs, and to attend college. These opportunities usually were accompanied by a stronger sense of belonging and stability. The sense of stability, however, was taken away when the Trump administration announced the termination of DACA in September 2017.[12] After this announcement, the youth in my sample reported feeling fear, anger, anxiety, and an increased sense of uncertainty. Even though, after multiple challenges, the program stayed in place, this study considers the important impact of the attempt to terminate DACA.

Illegality is both a juridical and a sociopolitical condition that impacts immigrants' everyday lives.[13] Being undocumented contributes to subjective understandings of the world and to identity.[14] Several works have analyzed the impact of the lack of documents on the lives of immigrants.[15] To my knowledge, however, no previous work has analyzed the impact of several immigration status changes, both actual and perceived (discovery of illegality, acquisition of DACA, fear of losing DACA when the termination of the program was announced in 2017), on the lives of undocumented immigrant youth.

Construction of Illegality

"Illegality" is a juridical status defined in relation to the state, and as such, a political identity.[16] By "migrant illegality" authors refer to the effects laws have on migrants' day-to-day lives, revealing the ways in which undocumented persons experience inclusion and exclusion and how these experiences can change over time.[17] Overall, these works study how legal status is also socially constructed.[18] Nicholas de Genova[19] examines the paradox that while no other country produced more immigration to the United States than Mexico, major US immigration law changes since 1965 have created increasingly severe restrictions on the "legal" migration of Mexicans to the United States. According to the author, the newly created border after the annexation of half of Mexico went virtually unregulated and movement through it was largely unimpeded.[20] During the latter decades of the nineteenth century, the Southwest mining, railroad, ranching, and agricultural economies depended heavily on the recruitment of Mexican labor.

Between 1910 and 1930, one-tenth of the Mexican population relocated north of the border, partly related to political upheavals in Mexico, but mostly due to labor demand. Since its creation in 1924, the Border Patrol assumed its distinctive role as a police force for the repression of Mexican workers in the United States. During the Great Depression, 415,000 Mexican migrants and their US-born children were deported and another 85,000 were repatriated.[21] Due to unmet labor demands, the Bracero Program (1942–1964) reversed the previous policy and imported millions of Mexican workers. Some have estimated that four undocumented migrants entered the country for every documented bracero.[22] Prior to 1965, there were no quantitative restrictions on migration from Mexico.[23] While the 1965 law was celebrated as liberal, it imposed a numerical restriction on immigration from the Western Hemisphere for the first time. Originally allowing 120,000 individuals, in 1976 this cap was changed to 20,000 specifically applicable to Mexican immigration. The Bracero Program had created a migration flow, so the Mexican nationals who were already migrating had no choice but to become undocumented. In turn, the cap contributed to creating the flow of undocumented immigrants to the United States.

The policies established in 1965 are still essentially in place today.[24] Noncitizens can be admitted lawfully to the United States in two ways: under a permanent (or immigrant) status or a nonpermanent (or nonimmigrant) one. Foreigners who can be admitted as lawful permanent residents include relatives of US citizens and lawful permanent residents, and workers with specific job skills.[25] Lawful permanent residency is also available for persons with extraordinary abilities, outstanding professors and researchers, and those who may benefit the national interest. The second path is temporary admission, which is granted to foreign citizens who seek entry to the United States for a limited time and for a certain purpose, such as tourism, diplomacy, temporary work, or study.

If the person does not have a relative in the United States but has skills and a college degree, this person can apply for a green card and later citizenship only if their employer is willing to file the paperwork and, in most cases, pay for the legal fees.[26] In this case, the petitioner also needs to prove that there was no other resident or citizen willing to take the job (labor certification).[27] If the person lacks a college degree but has either exceptional skills or $1 million to invest, they can become a resident and later a citizen. Among persons with exceptional skills are those with "extraordinary abilities" and those who qualify for a "national interest waiver." These two categories have demanding requirements, and it is therefore evident that getting a green card without having a relative or a college degree is extremely difficult. These strict immigration policies have contributed to the high number of undocumented immigrants, estimated at 10.5 million.[28]

Discovery of Lack of Immigration Status

DACA recipients came to the country as children and, unlike their parents, they are often ignorant of their immigration status and/or its implications through most of their childhood. At some point, they find out about their status or understand its implications. *Plyler v. Doe* granted the right to a K-12 education to undocumented students.[29] The transition to adulthood involves exiting the K-12 legally protected years and entering into adult roles that require legal status as a basis for participation. This transition has great implications for identity formation, friendship patterns, aspirations and expectations, and social and economic mobility. In sum, public schooling and US immigration laws collide to produce a shift in the experiences and meanings of illegal status for undocumented youth at the onset of their transition to adulthood.[30]

Different studies conceptualize the "coming of age" of undocumented youth in high school and its consequences for immigrant incorporation, describing a transition to illegality consisting of three stages: "discovery," "learning to be illegal," and "coping."[31] One study showed that at a young age, undocumented youth were unaware of their legal status.[32] When they became aware, they initially could not grasp the implications of their lack of documents. As they grew up, the undocumented youth progressively experienced more situations where their undocumented status set them apart from others. In this way, they navigate "illegality" when they undertake the numerous daily practices that require them to belong in a place they do not have a legal right to be.[33] According to some authors, these experiences create a sense of liminality.[34] The family's mixed or unauthorized status complicates the normative stages of development in multiple ways.[35]

Typically, the life course is punctuated by religious, social, and institutional ritual practices—baptisms, bar/bat mitzvahs, quinceañeras, graduations, marriages, retirements—thus marking entries into new domains of life. A classic work from the field of anthropology terms these transitions as rites of passage, which confer new roles, rights, and obligations.[36] Before entry into the new roles, individuals reside in a space of temporal liminality.[37] Liminality is the transitional moment between spheres of belonging when social actors no longer belong to the group they are leaving behind and do not yet fully belong in their new social sphere. Liminal entities are betwixt and between the positions assigned and arrayed by law, custom, convention, and ceremony. The moment of liminality is characterized by heightened danger and ambiguity.

Another study set out to deconstruct the illegal-legal binary that, its author asserts, characterizes much of the scholarship.[38] This article analyzed the results of forty-two interviews with 1.5-generation Brazilian immigrants and found that participants described four categories of legal membership: undocumented, liminal legality, lawful permanent resident, and citizen. Liminal legality is an in-between status that provides a social security number and a work permit but does not guarantee eventual citizenship. Using sociological stratification theory, the author shows that there is a tendency in sociology to the reification of binaries followed by a deconstruction of those binaries.[39] Whereas in this research the concept of liminality was used to describe the experiences of DACA recipients,[40] in the previous case it was used to describe the experiences of young people without DACA.[41] I believe these situations are different. Before DACA, students had some inclusion in schools but were unable to get a driver's license and work. DACA is a legal creation that offers a work permit and a protection from deportation, but it does not grant immigration status.[42] Its existence and parameters are therefore defined by law. For the sake of clarity, this research uses the terms undocumented and DACA.

Discovery of Immigration Status in My Sample

The undocumented status awakens youth to the reality that they are barred from integrating legally, educationally, and economically into US society.[43] As unauthorized youth pass into older adolescence and emerging adulthood, their awareness is sharpened as they increasingly experience blocked access to expected normative rites of passage, identities, and ways of being. My interview included questions about the discovery of the participants' immigration status. These questions asked, *When did you find out you were undocumented and under what circumstances? How did this affect the perception of who you were? How about your dreams?* The literature argues that prior to discovering they are undocumented, undocumented youth establish school-based relationships with peers and adults that provide key sources of support and identity formation.[44] With some exceptions,[45] the literature locates the discovery of the undocumented status in late adolescence/early adulthood.[46] My findings, however, indicate that most of my interviewees always knew they were undocumented. Specifically, more than 50 percent of the respondents indicated they had always known they were undocumented. For comparison, Roberto Gonzales found that only 19 percent of his participants knew they were undocumented when they were children.[47] Approximately 26 percent of my respondents indicated they found out they were undocumented in high school, 13 percent in middle school, 6 percent in elementary school, and 3 percent little by little. So combined, some 69 percent of my respondents knew they were undocumented before their late adolescence.

Independently of when participants found out they were undocumented, 68 percent of them stated they understood the practical implications of this discovery in their late adolescence and early adulthood. Participants also explained the circumstances or occasion of their discovery of their undocumented status. The largest group of participants, 38 percent, found out they were undocumented or understood the implications of their lack of status when planning or applying for college, 29 percent when trying to work, and 21 percent when trying to get their driver's license or signing up for driver's education at school. Smaller percentages, close to 4 percent, reported finding out they were undocumented when trying to enlist in the marines, when their parents got deported, and when trying to sign up for a school trip.

Those Who Always Knew They Were Undocumented: The Crossing

Some of those who always knew they were undocumented were older when they immigrated and remembered crossing the border without inspection. Cynthia, for instance, who came to the United States when she was twelve years old, explained, "I knew we were coming illegally. Obviously, when crossing the border, I knew it. We were hiding from Border Patrol when crossing and I was conscious of what was going on." Mary, in turn, told me, "I think I always knew. Just by crossing the border, I came in when I was a little older so . . . yeah, just by crossing the border."

Cynthia and Mary had a clear understanding of the meaning of the border: Borders create a sharp division between here and there, inside and outside, us and them.[48] According to Nicolas de Genova, the Border Spectacle signifies the hegemony of the body of immigration law that produces the "national state" and predicates the regime of migrant "legality" and "illegality."[49] Moreover, Cynthia rightly perceived that the threats of detection, apprehension, detention, and deportation contribute to produce the border and immigrant illegality.[50] It was her memory of the border crossing combined with the hiding and fear that contributed to her understanding of her undocumented status.[51]

Other Cases

Marcos also knew he was undocumented. He explained, "My parents were like, 'you are not going to be able to do these things, you are not going to be able to get a license, you are not going to be able to travel.' So it was always in the back of my mind." Juliana, similarly, recalled, "I have always known. But I never knew what exactly it meant until I was fifteen. My parents told me I couldn't get a driver's license. It was just, it was weird. I would see all my friends get their permit and I had to wait." Both Marcos and Juliana always knew they were undocumented but got a better grasp of the implications of their status later in life. Their awareness was not complete until then.

The literature shows that most students from undocumented families are coached to lie about their status.[52] This was also the case among my interviewees. Zoe, for instance, said,

> I've always known, it was no big secret. It's just one of those things, "You are undocumented, don't tell nobody," kind of like that, you know. Like when people would ask, "Where were you born?" "In Mexico," I would say but immediately change the conversation, like to avoid the whole citizenship question, I guess.

Positive emotional well-being is fostered through the development of meaningful relationships.[53] Hugo, mentioned in chapter 3, explained how lying about his status functioned like a stigma that prevented him from developing meaningful relationships with other schoolchildren. Likely, the concealment of her immigration status had an impact on Zoe, as well.

Andreíta's family not only asked her to lie about her status but also trained her about how to be safe to avoid detention and potential deportation.

I always knew [I was undocumented]. Mainly because my family, like my parents and me, it's just the three of us. We did everything together and they were always open about it. They always said, "Just don't tell anyone." There were things that we would do that, I guess you can call rituals almost . . . If we were going to go anywhere, to the movies, to the grocery store, to school, whatever, they always had to know certain things, like where our identifications were. And there was no way we could leave the house without them, just in case.

Andreíta's family was smart to make sure she had her identification each time she left the house in case she was confronted by law enforcement officials. Zaide's family also told their children from a young age they were undocumented and prepared them for their eventual deportation. She said,

I can't remember exactly the time, but it may have been when I started to understand, maybe around eight. It was mostly through my parents. My mom tried to tell me to be careful. I remember her trying to explain the situation they were in, and like trying to put it out there for me also. Like, she'd kind of give me advice and tell me what the plan was in case they [my parents] got deported so I wouldn't be scared. But at that point, whenever they started giving me these talks, I did find myself like stressed out, I guess you can say, and scared for sure. After finding that out and understanding I was like scared kind of every day. I was like, "What if I don't see my parents today or this week?"

Zaide's mom talked to her when she was eight years old, explaining the situation her parents were in and the plan in case they were deported. Zaide was stressed out and scared every day after finding out; she lived her and her family's illegality every day.[54]

Delayed Understanding of Implications

The literature argues that after finding out they are undocumented, undocumented youth come to understand their situation more fully as they progressively experience more situations where their undocumented status sets them apart from others, creating a sense of liminality.[55] The undocumented youth purportedly enter a limbo or liminal space, which cannot be accounted for by binary legal statuses (legal versus illegal) because immigration laws and policies produce grey areas of legality that are temporary.[56] My research shows that as the undocumented youth find out about their lack of documents and understand its implications, they enter a space of exclusion, comparable to that experienced by their undocumented parents.

Luna always knew she was undocumented, but she felt this was "normal" until high school. She told me,

> Well, I always knew that I was born in Mexico because my parents . . . never hid that from me. They told me I was born in a different country. I would tell people as if it was normal. But I remember in fourth grade, every student was required to give a presentation about themselves and their background. So, I told my whole class that I was born in Mexico and that I came to the United States when I was around nine years old. I saw it as normal because they asked, "Where are you from?" and I was like, "Oh I was born in Mexico." And the teacher was like, "Oh that's interesting." And it felt normal, but when I got to high school, I realized that if you want to apply for colleges and if you want to apply for loans or scholarships, you needed a social security or citizenship or you need residency. And that's when I realized that being undocumented was a big deal. Like, it hit me in high school when I started looking at the scholarships and applying for colleges.

Luna thought being undocumented was "normal" and not a "big deal" until she realized the implications that her status would have for her college applications. Even if she always knew she was undocumented, she became aware of the implications of her illegality later in life.[57] Similarly, Alejandro also always suspected he had no documents and told me, "I suspected it. It's like a feeling that penetrated your mind. And I didn't take it badly until later. It started affecting me more as I grew up." Like Luna, Alejandro's lack of documents did not become an issue until later in life. Their transition into adulthood was accompanied by a realization of the restricted rights that set them apart from their peers.[58]

Several other students understood what being undocumented meant later in life. Ana's parents, for instance, were deported when she was in fifth grade. She said,

> The first realization was in fifth grade when my parents got deported; it was kind of an eye-opening moment. But I didn't really understand it until sophomore, junior year when I was applying for college. I think it took me until college to fully grasp everything. You know the deportation of my parents, that affected me in other ways that I didn't even realize until college.

Ana lost her parents to deportation and was raised by her aunt and uncle. This deportation, which deprived her of her parents, opened her eyes to a life of exclusion which manifested even more clearly in the period when she was applying for college.

Other participants also became aware of their lack of rights and the extent of their exclusion when applying to college. Angel, for instance, explained,

> I'm not sure if I essentially always knew, but it was high school when I guess is the time when most folks remember or a time when it hits them the hardest, essentially, and it was because of the college applications . . . the beginning of my senior year of high school. I didn't think much of it, but my parents always taught me since I was young, "Oh, you're going to go to college." That was something that they would always tell me, and I didn't really question how I was going to college. I didn't see, like, my status as a barrier until I had met with my counselor. We had a requirement for graduation to apply to three different colleges/three universities.

Zoe said something similar:

> In senior year, it was one of those things, it became more real because it was my last year of high school and everybody is getting ready to go to college, you know. And my parents were low income, so they couldn't help me financially to pay for school. And, you know, it was like, "I'm going to find a way."

Angel met with his counselor and was given a list of "Jobs for Illegals" when he explained he didn't have documents, an experience that negatively affected him psychologically. In contrast, Zoe continued with a more positive attitude. Despite these differences, these undocumented youth felt a clear sense of exclusion when applying for college.

Impact of Discovering Undocumented Status

One study showed that as undocumented youth understand their illegality, they become frustrated, self-conscious, and develop a heightened sense of awareness.[59] They also became more sensitive to prevailing negative discourses about immigration.[60] Another study showed that undocumented students feel fearful, embarrassed, ashamed, and physically, socially, or morally inferior.[61] These works describe the feelings of most of my respondents. Three respondents, however, stated that the impact was either positive or neutral. Marcos stated that being undocumented was beneficial precisely because it heightened his awareness. He told me,

> This is going to sound weird, but I appreciate the fact that I'm not a legal citizen because it has made me think of my actions. It has made me double think about dumb things that I could have done. It has kept me on my toes, it has opened me up to different things that people take for granted. You know, you have all these kids who were born here, and I know some of them are not going to school, and I'm like, "OMG, I would like kill to have that paper, I would kill to do this." They don't care, they take for granted what they have because it was handed to them.

Not having the privilege of a green card or citizenship made Marcos more careful about his actions and taught him not to take things for granted. He was surely exaggerating when he said, "I would kill to have that paper," but he nonetheless felt he had to fight harder to achieve things in life since opportunities were not handed to him.

Jessica and Andrés explained that discovering they were undocumented did not make them feel inferior. Jessica said,

> I think my parents like told me like little by little. And then I also have like foreign friends who were undocumented, so I don't feel any like weird or anything in the fact that like my parents were there, like, to support

me. I never felt, like people with papers were better than me or anything like that.

Andrés, in turn, asserted, "No, it didn't affect me personally being undocumented. I don't feel bad or inferior to everybody. I just thought, 'I just can't travel.' But I still continue doing my best in school to do better, to like better myself."

It is clear that these participants were aware that the discovery of their undocumented status was supposed to have a negative impact. Jessica said she never thought that people with papers were better than her. Andrés reported not feeling bad or inferior. I wonder if these participants truly felt fine about their immigration status or if these responses were the product of some defense mechanism. I believe that for Jessica this was probably the case. During most of the interview her answers were somewhat defensive, letting me know she was not treated poorly or discriminated against. I felt she thought I was expecting her to discuss only negative experiences with me.

Practical Implications

More than one-fourth of my participants and all the Polish interviewees endured the consequences of their illegality when doors closed for them in their late adolescence. As unauthorized youth pass into late adolescence and early adulthood, they experience blocked access to expected normative rites of passage, such as getting a driver's license, applying for college, and working, among others. A feeling of belonging ("I'm an American because I speak the language, share values, etc.) is met with a symbolic slap in the face ("you are an illegal and cannot belong").[62] Estela, for instance, found out about her status when trying to sign up for driver's education. She told me,

A lot of my friends during my sophomore year were getting their driver's licenses. I couldn't get it. I didn't really understand it at first because I did sign up for the class for driving lessons at school. And then I got called in, there's like a form I remember they gave us. I did fill it out and it did ask for my social security, I remember. I didn't know what it was, to be honest. I was 16 or 15 at the time . . . Obviously, that part wasn't filled out and then

I got called into a room and then the teachers were all confused and then they were like, "You don't have a social?" I was like, "No." I didn't really know and even at home no one really explained it to me. And then they were like, "You just need to go to the social security office and get one." And they didn't understand, I didn't even understand what was going on.

Estela did not know she did not have a social security number until she tried to sign up for driver's education class. Her parents had gone back to Mexico and her aunt raised her and her sisters. When Estela went home crying after the driver's education incident, her older siblings explained the situation to her. In Estela's own words, this realization "was hard" for her.

Ismael started making sense of what it meant to be undocumented when he was looking for jobs and thinking about his driver's license. He explained,

I remember growing up knowing that we were from Mexico, we were immigrants, but was never told the differences. And I think it wasn't until middle school or high school that it started making sense to me being undocumented. That's when it made more sense to me, when I was looking for jobs and started thinking about a driver's license. More so in high school is when I realized I wasn't going to be able to take driver's ed or be able to apply to a job because I didn't have a social security number. That's when I realized that being undocumented and being an immigrant like myself was going to be very difficult.

Ismael understood his status when doors started closing for him. To be sure, he knew he was an immigrant from Mexico because his parents were open about it with him, but only when attempting the typical rites of passage in his late adolescence did he understand that being an undocumented immigrant "was going to be very difficult."[63]

Marcos understood his situation when he was applying for a job and when he had to turn down a great job opportunity because of his lack of a social security number. He explained,

So, the day I was going to start that job, I got a call from the human resource department saying that I was terminated because there was an issue with my social security and I was like, "What?" and I knew already. And they were like, "Oh, you know, you can't fix it by yourself." I'm like, "You know, I'm talking to my mom, we're going to fix it by ourselves, I'll just get back to you when it's fixed." I knew I had lost that job. That was one time.

And the time I was working at the grocery store . . . fast forward a year later, I was eighteen still and I was still in high school. I am at a grocery store and making $7.50 an hour, you know? And I meet this amazing lady with whom I had an amazing conversation and who was actually one of the directors of a state agency. She's, like, "You seem really nice, I'm going to offer you a job, I don't know if you want to take it, but, you know? You can start as an intern, get this much amount of money, we could pay for your school." . . . And I was like, "OMG." And she was like, "So, what do you think?" I was like, "Honestly, I'm happy here." She was like, "Really?"

It is not clear if Marcos had used somebody else's social security number or a fake one to apply for jobs.[64] It is clear, however, that he understood right away what was going on when human resources called him. He also seemed very disappointed to turn down a great job opportunity that would have included support to attend college but couldn't risk the heightened scrutiny of working for a state agency. In Marcos's case, the transition to adulthood involved exiting the legally protected status of K-12 student and entering into adult roles that require legal status as a basis for participation.[65]

Several other students understood the ramifications of their status when applying for college. Andreíta, for instance, told me,

Probably applying to college and then again, the process of already being accepted into college and enrolling. And then getting the results from scholarships. During my senior year, I applied to four scholarships. And I only got two so that was a huge brick wall that I hit because I was like, "There is no way we are going to pay for this." And even just applying, which was so hard to do because nobody knew what was safe to do, like what type of information to give, what type of information not to give. And it was like walking on nails because you didn't want to mess up. But it was something that you had to do no matter what.

Similarly, Benita explained,

> I always knew I was undocumented; I always knew I didn't have papers, yeah. But I just never knew it was going to be an issue. I didn't know because I was in school. I didn't know about the laws and stuff until applying to college. That is when it started getting hard and then I didn't apply to DACA right away. Because I didn't need it until I knew I was going to start applying for colleges, which I needed my social security.

Andreíta and Benita always knew they were undocumented but became aware of the implications when applying for college. When applying, Andreíta lacked reliable information on how to do it and what information to provide, and Benita was unaware of the laws and policies applicable to undocumented students trying to access higher education.[66] After applying, Andreíta became aware she and her family would not be able to afford her college education with just two scholarships. Benita, in turn, understood she was exiting the legally protected status of K-12 student, and that her undocumented status would prevent her from full participation in adult activities.[67]

Unlike Andreíta and Benita, Ernesto knew the rules for undocumented students applying for college in Illinois. Apparently, however, schools ignored this rule.

> I was going into my senior year; it was the summer of 2012 . . . And I had actually started applying to colleges and I had to google what to put in the portion where it asked me to put my social security number. I think it was all zeros. And I would get contacted by colleges asking me why I did that, and I didn't want to answer those calls just because I was scared to open up about that. And then get my parents into a sticky situation.

In Illinois, Public Act 93 of 2003 allowed undocumented students to pay in-state tuition if they attended high school in the state.[68] Ernesto did research and found that students had to enter all zeros in lieu of their social security number. It is regrettable that universities did not know about this rule. As the previous chapter showed, most high school guidance counselors across Illinois were unable to assist undocumented youth with college applications, partly because of their ignorance of rules and regulations.

Finally, one student learned about the implications of his undocumented status when trying to travel. Andrés explained,

> But I found out that I couldn't go to Scotland even though I was accepted to go to Scotland. My parents were, "No, you can't leave the country. I know it would be great and everything, but you just can't." I was like, "Damn! I can't go to Scotland or travel and whatnot." And then my parents were still scared to send me to Washington. That is another place to where People to People send students. And they said, "No! We can't send you there." I think part of me thinks that my mom was also scared to lose me, to let me go and whatnot. But I also thought, "Oh I don't have papers to travel." So that's what my limitation was.

Andrés apparently tried to travel to Scotland with the international student travel agency People to People. Going to Scotland would have been difficult because, as a DACA recipient, he could not have returned to the United States unless he secured a permit from the US Citizenship and Immigration Services called advanced parole.[69] Even with this permit, leaving the country, for DACA recipients, is to risk that they may not be allowed to return.[70]

Major Psychological Impact

More than 50 percent of my interviewees reported that finding out they were undocumented had a negative mental, emotional, or psychological impact on them.[71] Adding undocumented status to an already concerning mix of factors, such as poverty and financial insecurity, creates increased vulnerability.[72] As undocumented youth understand their illegality, they become frustrated, self-conscious, and develop a heightened sense of awareness.[73] They also become more sensitive to prevailing negative discourses about immigration.[74] Some youth develop a sense of non-belonging which some authors term liminality.[75] Another study found that coming of age undocumented entailed intense feelings of anxiety, confusion, frustration, and stress.[76] Still another study detailed how undocumented students had feelings of inferiority, embarrassment, shame, fear, psychological trauma, and depression.[77]

Participants described feelings of confusion, distress, discouragement and hopelessness, frustration, insecurity, stress, and anxiety. Some participants were confused when discovering they were undocumented. Ernesto, for example, explained he had difficulty grasping the situation. He told me,

> Well, my mom basically told us that we didn't have seguro and papeles [social security number and documents in Spanish] and all that stuff. So, I was wondering what that really meant. I mean, I understood what it meant because my mom couldn't get her driver's license, but I didn't understand why. I didn't understand why because I was a little kid. I understood that there was something that we have done that was basically wasn't the correct process or something like that.

Ernesto found out he was undocumented at a young age, and he could not understand why he and his mom ended up in the situation they were in. He did understand they had done something wrong, that they had not followed the correct legal process. Ernesto's family, like every other DACA recipient's family I interviewed, had not followed immigration rules. Immigration laws create a new axis of stratification that, like other forms of stratification, significantly shape life chances and future prospects.[78]

Other interviewees combined feelings of confusion with distress and discouragement. Melody, for instance, explained,

> I think I was twelve. I was in middle school when I found out that I was undocumented. Even at the time I don't think I quite truly understood what that meant. But my parents, I think once we started talking more about traveling around the world, my parents were, like, "Yeah maybe someday." And then eventually they just told us our situation and it was just really discouraging because it felt like a lot of the opportunities that I could have taken were just restricted. It was upsetting but, at the same time, confusing because when you're young you don't really understand,

okay, "What does being documented really mean? Why am I undocumented?" you know. Just all these questions that kind of run through your head, not really understanding the answers to any of these questions.

Melody was confused about what it meant to be undocumented and why she and her family were in that situation. She was also upset and discouraged about the lack of opportunities that being undocumented entailed. Melody considered going back to her native Peru to attend college, but she stayed in the United States to study accounting.

Several participants were extremely discouraged and felt hopeless. Mary, for instance, always wanted to be a teacher, but her high school teacher informed her that her dream was not realistic. Justice wanted to join the marines and realized she could not. This is what Mary told me:

> Since the beginning they [my teachers] were like, "Oh you're going to be a great teacher" or whatever. I had a lot of friends, and they were like, "You just need your social security number." "I don't have one." "Oh, you can't go to college. I mean, you can but you're not going to be able to work." So, I think that's when it hit me and I was, like, so all my dreams of becoming a teacher and helping kids were kind of just garbage because I really can't do anything.

In turn, Justice said,

> So, I don't recall exactly when I learned of it, but I remember that after high school, I wanted to join the marines and be enlisted. But you needed to be a citizen at the time, which I was not . . . I think it was actually really depressing because, at the time, I really wanted to go and do whatever I could at the time. Yeah, it brought down my self-esteem because I thought that I was gonna do it. And then even now, you can't be a police officer in most locations. In most jurisdictions, without having some type of either US citizenship or some type of residency, you cannot do it.

Mary had the dream of becoming a teacher and helping children, but she felt this dream was destroyed. Justice had the dream of becoming a marine, and not having this opportunity brought down her self-esteem.

Learning they had no documents stripped Mary and Justice of their dreams and left them hopeless.

Other participants, like Brianna, Marcos, and Estela, upon learning that they were undocumented questioned the purpose of their efforts. Brianna explained,

> I'm sorry, I felt very frustrated. Yeah, so everyone you know is getting their license. Getting a job. And I said, I wanted to take driver's ed. And my mom, she's like, "You cannot get your license," and I just asked her, "Why not?" She was, like, "You're not from here so you don't have a social security number and without that number, you cannot get your license." I was like, "Okay." I think I just blew it off like, okay, fine, whatever. But everyone started getting jobs and doing other stuff. And again, I told my mom I want to get a job. "Well, you can't." And that's when they sat me down and told me . . . After that, I thought, "Why am I even going to school?" I didn't know what to do. I knew that I wasn't from here, but I never really understood it.

Similarly, Marcos said,

> "I'm going to school but for what? To get a degree if I'm not going to be able to work after I get a degree?" My first year, I did really bad because I didn't care. It was more like, "Why are you doing this? Like, what's the point of going to school if you are going to end up working at a restaurant, if you are going to do this, something that doesn't require a degree?"

Estela, in turn, told me,

> Especially because I was mainly raised here and I was like, "Okay, I can go back home but am I going to have the same school opportunities?" It was just hard . . . To this day, it's hard to explain to people about my situation because I don't feel like they could understand, but I was really disappointed . . . It did affect me in every single way. Emotionally and mentally because I gave up on school. I was just not going to school anymore.

Brianna and Marcos tried to grasp the limitations of their undocumented status. Brianna did not know what to do and "blew it off," and

Marcos just gave up. Estela considered going back home but also just gave up. These youth were working hard to achieve their goals but realized they would not be able to get a driver's license or a professional job after graduation from college. This realization made them lose their motivation to move forward in life.[79]

Dealing with the implications of their undocumented status also created discomfort in the undocumented youths' relationships with their peers. This was the case for Daniel and Hector.

Daniel recounted,

> Yeah, that was my initial response and it made me feel weird not having the privilege to drive. I hated the idea of always hitting my friends up to be like, "Hey, you want to drive me over to this location? Do you want to pick me up?" because I kind of don't have the freedom to drive myself where I want to go. But once in a while, my friend would ask, "Hey, if you can't drive, is it because you don't have the right paperwork or something?" and I kind of just brushed it off and it kind of made me insecure and kind of nervous that they asked questions like that. So, it kind of ruined my self-confidence in a way; I couldn't do what other people could.

Similarly, Hector told me,

> And that gave me so much anxiety because all of my friends like, in any conversation, you know . . . People would ask me, "When are you going to get your first job?" and I would be, like, "You know, not now, I'm too busy, you know, being involved with all these things," even though I wasn't. So, that's when it kind of first hit me and put me in a predicament, where I didn't even know who I was because for the longest time, I was not letting people really know me. And then now, I'm in a stage where as you get older, you kind of want to be noticed or you want to be cared for, you want to have your own friends, and you want to, you know, grow close together with these friends, but I put myself in a weird spot where I kind of want to tell people, but still felt like I couldn't. And that made me question who I was. It wasn't until I met my best friend who was also undocumented.

Daniel and Hector had to dodge their friends' questions, lie, and make excuses for why they were not getting driver's licenses or jobs. This affected Daniel and Hector in different ways. Daniel's sense of self-esteem and self-confidence were hurt for not being able to do what his peers were able to do. Hector felt isolated and could not get close to anyone and be himself until he met his best friend, who was also undocumented.

Discovery of Lack of Documents: Identity and Belonging

Being undocumented has a negative impact on identity formation for youth.[80] Two of my participants reflected on how their discovery of their undocumented status made them question their sense of identity and belonging. Mary said,

> Discovering I was undocumented affected me a lot. I think the way it affected the most was . . . I gave up on . . . I just gave up. It really sucked. I couldn't understand why I was in this situation. I couldn't understand my mother's reasons. I think at some point I kind of blamed my mom . . . It was scary. I didn't even know where I belonged.

Alondra explained,

> I realized I was undocumented when I wanted to work in the summer harvesting corn. They have a program for children to make some money, but you need a good social security number. And this is how in eighth grade I realized I didn't have a social security number. It was scary . . . I feel I was born here because they brought me when I was six months old, and I have never known another place. And I thought "What am I going to do?"

Mary did not know where she belonged, and Alondra felt doors were closing for her in the only country she knew. These participants were faced with conflicting spheres of belonging: Thanks to *Plyler v. Doe*, they had a sense of belonging in public schools but were later faced with exclusion when denied participation in rites of passage typical of their age, such as getting jobs and driver's licenses. In this way, a social hierarchy anchored in legality is established as a social position that grants (or denies) immigrants access to goods, benefits, and rights in society.[81] The literature refers to liminality as the transitional moment between spheres of belonging when social actors no longer belong to the group they are leaving behind and do not yet fully belong in their new social sphere.[82] I see this as a space of exclusion or outsiderness.[83]

Today's undocumented youth and young adults are coming of age amid a political backlash and rising anti-immigrant sentiment that has produced a hostile climate.[84] Some of my participants seemed to internalize racial stereotypes and stigmas about undocumented immigrants once they knew they had no documents. Laura is a case in point. She was discriminated against throughout her schooling by school staff who forbade her from speaking Spanish and classmates who called her wetback and beaner. Once Laura understood her situation better, racial slurs cut a little deeper.

> Yeah, so at thirteen it was just like, "Oh, I can't work," so that's all I really took from my mom explaining to me that I wasn't from this country. Like "Oh, I can't take a summer job. I can't work." But I wasn't of age to work here anyway so it really didn't affect me. Ah, but like I said, after learning that you are not from this country, the racist slurs start hitting you a little deeper. So, you're like, "Okay, they're talking about me." So those friends that were supposed to be your friends and hearing them say like racist things, that hurt a little bit more too.

Daniel recalled,

> And that was the breaking point to kind of understand I was undocumented and, yeah, because I needed papers to get the permit and I couldn't. All of my friends were getting theirs and they were asking why I didn't get mine. It was kind of hard because there was the stigma of being illegal, undocumented, and all of that stuff. I didn't tell anyone that I was undocumented.

Laura had suffered discrimination throughout her schooling, but the racist slurs she was subjected to hurt more after she knew she was undocumented. Daniel felt the stigma of being illegal and undocumented after learning he had no papers, and he kept this information to himself. In this way, undocumented youth move from a space of belonging in K-12 education to the most extreme place of exclusion when they internalize racism. The concept of internalized racism goes beyond the internalization of stereotypes imposed by the White majority about people of color to include the internalization of the beliefs, values, and worldviews inherent in White supremacy that can potentially result in negative self or racial group perceptions.[85]

Finally, Zoe felt the full weight of what being undocumented meant when a librarian was teaching her and her classmates how to apply for FAFSA. She recalled,

> One time, I think it was a librarian and she was going to teach us about FAFSA. She took us to a computer lab to apply for it. And me, not wanting to tell people I was undocumented, because I already knew I couldn't apply for it . . . So she got upset at me, really upset at me because I didn't want to do it. She started making comments like, "Oh well, this is for your own good, this is for your future." And I was like, "No, I'm fine, I don't want to do it." It's not that I didn't want to do it, I just couldn't do it. So, I think it was just little things like that. Maybe they weren't sensitive to people who may not look like them and things like that, so it was an issue for me . . . I don't want to feel like I did in my senior year, like I was nothing. It literally felt that way.

Zoe's librarian worked at a school with a diverse body of students and a substantial share of undocumented students. As Zoe rightly points out, the librarian should have been more sensitive to the needs of students and considered the possibility that maybe some of them did not have social security numbers. Maybe the most extreme way of being excluded is by disappearing altogether, by becoming nothing.

Polish Interviewees

My Polish interviewees found out early in life that they were undocumented, although they understood the implications only later. Mateusz found out on the plane when his family was moving to the United States. He told me,

I forgot how it came about. But my parents let something slip about not having legal status. And I, like, was super surprised. And I was like, "What? We are gonna be illegal?" I yelled this on a plane. And I remember my parents getting, like, super embarrassed, because people heard me yell out. So that's when I found out.

But like I said, when we first moved here, and I was nine years old, in my mind, I always felt like, by the time it would matter, you know, I felt like at the time I was eighteen, something would pass. So that was always, my thinking is like, "Oh, by the time I'm older, this is not going to be an issue." So I didn't really start worrying about it until [I was] about fourteen or fifteen. Or when the DREAM Act, you know, kept failing in Congress, and when my friends started to get their driver's licenses and jobs, and I wasn't able to do that.

So that's really when it became real, and caused me a lot of anxiety and shame. For a long time. I was very embarrassed of my status and the fact is that it made me feel inferior. Not good enough, I guess. In some ways. I know it's not necessarily my fault that I ended up here, but it's always been hanging over my head. Oh, my status. So yeah.

Mateusz was shocked at first when he found out he would be undocumented in the United States. Later in life, when his friends went through the typical adolescent rites of passage and got jobs and driver's licenses, his lack of papers felt more real. This made him feel ashamed, anxious, and morally inferior.[86] During a period when most adolescents go through experiences of increased responsibilities and transformation,[87] my respondents hit rock bottom when they realized the extent of the impact their lack of documents would have on their lives.

Ali's experience was remarkably similar. Ali traveled from Canada to the United States because her family was unable to obtain a visa to come directly to the United States. This experience made her aware of their lack of documents. Ali told me,

Yeah, my parents were always very open with us about our status and things we can do or cannot do here because of that. So I'd say closer to getting into middle school, and then especially high school, my friends were going through milestones like getting a driver's license, right, and I caught it.

So it started to be very real, especially to getting a job at sixteen. All my peers started to work and make some money. I couldn't really work being undocumented, not having a social security number. So it really started to affect me, I think, in high school. And that's when I began getting very frustrated with the way that worked. I was like, "This is my home. This is all I know. "You know? I feel like an American, but I'm not." So I think that became very real at that point.

Knowing does not always equal understanding. Like many of the Latino/a interviewees, Ali understood the implications of her lack of documents only later in life.[88]

Conclusion

This book argues that the incorporation of DACA recipients follows a roller-coaster pattern. This chapter showed that DACA recipients hit a low point when finding out they were undocumented and/or understanding the implications during their adolescence. Participants found out they were undocumented under different circumstances and at different points in their lives. Compared to previous research,[89] my participants found out they were undocumented at a younger age and most of them always knew they were undocumented. However, independently of when they found out they were undocumented, most of them truly understood the implications of their undocumented status only during their late adolescence.[90] Most participants found out about their status or understood its implications when applying and planning for college, trying to work, or trying to get a driver's license.[91]

Some participants vividly remember the crossing and the implications of coming to the United States through an unauthorized entry. Some participants who knew they were undocumented at an early age were asked to lie about it. In some cases, this lie prevented them from building meaningful relationships. Other families had plans in place for potential arrest and deportation. Although these plans seem reasonable from an adult point of view, they caused some children to feel stressed out, scared, and aware of their illegality in everyday practices.[92]

The literature argues that as youth become aware of their immigration status and its consequences, they enter a space of liminality.[93] My findings, however, imply that when finding out they are undocumented these youth enter a space of exclusion and outsiderness, comparable to that experienced by their undocumented parents.[94]

More than one-quarter of my respondents felt the practical implications of their undocumented status when they experienced blocked access to expected rites of passage, such as getting a driver's license, applying for college, working, and planning school activities. More than half of my participants, however, reported experiencing a major psychological impact when discovering their undocumented status or becoming aware of its implications.[95] Participants reported feelings of confusion, distress, discouragement, frustration, insecurity, stress, and anxiety. The discovery of their status made some participants question their identity and sense of belonging. In the most extreme case, the discovery of his immigration status made a participant feel like he was nothing. The next chapter reviews the experiences of my interviewees after acquiring DACA. It shows that despite its limitations, DACA had a positive impact on my respondents' quality of life, psychological well-being, and identity.

5

Deferred Action

Renewed Hope under DACA

Daniel graduated with a business degree from a private college in Illinois in 2018. He and his mom emigrated from the People's Republic of China to Hungary before coming to the United States when he was four years old. At the time, Daniel's dad was already living in the United States, together with his sister, and working for a Chinese company. His dad was able to get him and his mom a visa that later expired because, according to Daniel, the lawyer messed up.

School was difficult at first because Daniel spoke mostly Hungarian and a little Mandarin Chinese, but other children at his school spoke Cantonese Chinese. Once Daniel learned English and Cantonese, however, he was able to communicate with children in the schools he attended. Daniel's life was also marked by his hearing loss, which was diagnosed when he was seven. His hearing loss always made him feel different, despite the broad support provided by the schools he attended.

Daniel was fourteen when he learned that he was undocumented, because he kept pushing his mom to get a driver's license until she finally explained the situation to him. Daniel understood better what it meant to be undocumented at seventeen, when his mom was deported and he and his sister stayed alone in the United States. Getting DACA helped Daniel get a decent-paying sales job after graduating from high school. The announcement of the termination of DACA made Daniel feel defeated and like giving up.

One important turning point in Daniel's life was becoming the president of the DACA club in his high school. Occupying this position helped Daniel develop his leadership and public speaking skills. After this, Daniel became open about his status. I met Daniel when he shared his experience as a DACA recipient on a panel. Last time I spoke with Daniel he had a good job in sales.

As Daniel's story shows, his life was shaped and constrained in essential ways by his immigration status.[1] First, he could not get his driver's license. Later, his mom got deported and Daniel had to fend for himself at a young age. Still later, he felt like giving up when the rescission of DACA was announced. This chapter reviews the impact of the acquisition of DACA on my participants. It pays particular attention to the practical, psychological, and cultural implications of this new status. It further argues that, despite DACA's limitations, its impact was positive and represented a high point in the roller-coaster incorporation of my participants.

DACA Recipients

A profuse body of literature has shed light on the circumstances of the undocumented individuals who came to the country as children.[2] A more specialized body of literature has analyzed the impact of the acquisition of DACA on the lives of these youth.[3] Some of it has used sociological methods to analyze the economic and social impact of the acquisition of DACA.[4] Other works have delved into the impact of DACA on mental health and well-being.[5] Finally, several authors have analyzed the limitations that come with the acquisition of DACA.[6]

The acquisition of DACA has socioeconomic benefits for its recipients.[7] Two studies using the National UnDACAmented Research Project–NURP (N=2,684) showed that DACA recipients increased their social and economic integration in the United States.[8] First, it allowed 60 percent of recipients to obtain a new job, 45 percent of them to increase their earnings, and one-fifth of them to obtain an internship in their field of study.[9] DACA also improved recipients' financial integration, allowing half of them to obtain their first bank account and one-third of them their first credit card. Importantly, more than half of them obtained driver's licenses, which likely expanded educational, employment, and other opportunities. Finally, 21 percent of DACA recipients obtained health insurance.[10]

The other study using NURP found similar results.[11] For instance, DACA increased social mobility among beneficiaries, by widening educational opportunities, opening work and career paths, supporting families and communities, improving health and well-being, and opening access to travel.[12] Another study corroborated these findings and showed that the large majority of those who were not working were enrolled in school and that DACA enabled them to pursue career opportunities they lacked access to before.[13] Finally, another study found that DACA recipients were optimistic about the changes in their lives due to DACA and reported that the major benefits of their DACA acquisition were financial stability (58%), increased opportunities (30%), access to education (20%), getting a driver's license (14%), and reduced fear or greater freedom (10%).[14]

Several studies have addressed the impact of DACA on its beneficiaries' mental health and well-being.[15] DACA can increase the social integration of its recipients by increasing their access to resources, providing them with greater autonomy and a greater sense of belonging.[16] Access to a driver's license, social security number, and work permit allowed them to engage in normal travel and employment activities, which was beneficial to their mental health and well-being.[17] DACA recipients are also more comfortable disclosing their immigration status.[18] Finally, DACA also increased recipients' social support and increased family responsibilities.[19] Another study drawing on a cross-sectional survey of DACA recipients (N=487) found that participants seemed positive about their life changes after receiving DACA, citing financial stability, access to education and resources, and reduced fear/greater freedom.[20] These findings indicated that DACA had a legitimizing effect on recipients, improving their sense of security in their future and sense of self.[21]

Several studies have addressed the limitations of DACA as a temporary and limited solution to the undocumented youths' situation.[22] According to one study, even though DACA protects its beneficiaries from social exclusion, it does not translate into social inclusion.[23] For instance, social and economic gains due to DACA are limited and conditioned by state context.[24] The author argues that this liminal legality creates a double bind for DACA beneficiaries, a form of legal violence, which simultaneously facilitates and obstructs social inclusion.[25] For instance, while DACA makes social mobility more possible, it blocks DACA youth from pursuing their career and educational goals, which are determined by state rules. Also, DACA accelerates the transition to adulthood, while the identity of DACA recipients remains anchored to their ambiguous legal status.[26] Another study found similar results about post-college opportunities.[27] It showed that although DACA facilitates access to a wider variety of professional development opportunities in college, the absence of a permanent status poses barriers. Both DACA recipients and their undocumented peers reported persistent feelings of uncertainty that constrain their career planning.[28]

Impact of DACA: My Sample

My interview included open questions about the impact of DACA on participants. These questions asked, *What was the impact of your acquisition of DACA status on your life? How did this new status affect how you thought about yourself and others?* Respondents discussed the different types of impact they experienced. I classified the themes that came up during the interviews as practical and psychological implications of DACA, decreased fear of police and law enforcement, and impact on sense of identity and belonging (figure 5.1). All my participants, including the Polish ones, discussed the positive practical implications of obtaining DACA, like getting driver's licenses, jobs, and being able to study.[29] Sixty-five percent of them discussed psychological implications of obtaining DACA, like being excited, happy, relieved, and motivated to study and work harder.[30] Twenty-nine percent said that obtaining DACA would help them lose their fears of police and law enforcement.[31] Thirty-two percent said obtaining DACA affected their sense of self and belonging.[32] Finally, 19 percent of my participants described some limitations of DACA, such as the lack of access to FAFSA, the lack of a path to residency or citizenship, the limitations for travel, and the impossibility of extending the benefits to their parents.[33]

Practical Implications of Obtaining DACA

After receiving DACA, beneficiaries experienced greater access to different institutions in the United States, which enabled them to better achieve their potential. Consequently, DACA recipients gained an

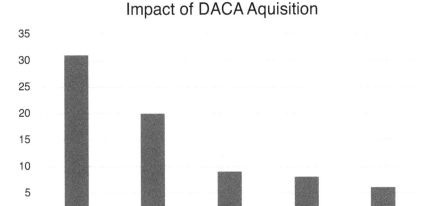

Figure 5.1. Impact of DACA Acquisition among Participants

increased integration into society and overcame some forms of exclusion they previously faced.[34] Overall, they were able to access adult roles.[35] All of the participants commented on the practical implications of DACA on their lives. The main benefit of the acquisition of DACA was the ability to get driver's licenses, better jobs, and increased access to higher education and credit. Hector summarized most of these benefits:

> I knew that it would give us the opportunity to have a social security number, and I knew with the social security number I could pretty much do a lot of things that I wanted. Working, getting a driver's license, getting credit and all that stuff. After the Dream Act DACA was like the next best thing. I remember telling my mom about it and I remember telling my friend who was also undocumented about it. Like, we actually have a shot at doing something. I remember this being my sophomore year in high school.
>
> Before this, I started having conversations about wanting to become a teacher. So, knowing that there was going to be an option even though there were going to be restrictions on it, even though the only thing I could do was work, it was a step in the right direction for a lot of people

in my shoes who didn't even have an option. They would have a say on whether they wanted to be here or not.

Thanks to DACA, Hector had access to jobs, a driver's license, and credit. He could also become a teacher. To be sure, he was aware of the limitations of DACA when compared to the DREAM Act, but was nonetheless appreciative of the benefits of DACA and called it "the next best thing" after the DREAM Act. Further, by giving DACA recipients increased opportunities, Hector felt he and the group of youth who came to the country as children had a say in their situation for the first time.

Access to Jobs

Since its inception, DACA has increased recipients' integration into the workplace and the community.[36] By providing beneficiaries with temporary work permits, DACA enabled them to access better paying jobs and jobs in their areas of interest.[37] By 2016, DACA beneficiaries showed increased labor participation and decreased rates of unemployment.[38] Most DACA recipients (73%) continued to be concentrated in blue-collar occupations, such as food service and restaurants, retail, clerical, maintenance or housekeeping, manufacturing/shipping, health services, and construction,[39] but more DACA recipients found jobs in white-collar occupations when compared with their undocumented counterparts.[40]

Many of my respondents saw an improvement in their job opportunities. Andrea, for example, explained how she went from working at McDonald's to working at the post office.

> I worked for more than five years at McDonald's. They paid me very little, and managers were very rude and treated Hispanic employees very poorly. They think that because we don't have papers, we have to do whatever they say. We had no health insurance, nothing. We had no hope, nothing. But then, thanks for DACA, I got a much better job [at the post office]. I could learn more English, overcome my shyness, and make a lot more money. And have benefits like vacation, holidays, and sick leave. And it was very different, it changed my life.

Andrea had a bad experience working at McDonald's, where she made little money, had no benefits, and was treated poorly. But thanks to DACA, she was able to get a much better paying job with benefits at the post pffice. Many other DACA recipients saw similar improvements in their jobs.[41] José, for instance, went from working as a janitor to working at a movie theater. He explained,

> Well, I had one unofficial job prior to DACA. I was paid in cash to do janitor services. But then I got my first official job three months after I received DACA. That was a really kind of proud moment though it was at a movie theater. It was above the table kind of job and my parents really sort of helped me see how important it was to receive a W-2 for that kind of job. And then I was able to have that job experience.

José was able to go from working as a janitor and getting paid under the table to working for a movie theater and this made him proud. As his and Andrea's stories show, DACA allowed my participants to get better paying and formal jobs.[42]

Combining Work and Education

DACA recipients took advantage of the increased job opportunities that enabled them to access higher education.[43] Thousands of DACA beneficiaries were balancing work and school in 2016, suggesting that they need to work to be able to study.[44] My participants were no exception. When DACA came about, they were able to get better jobs, which allowed them to afford an education. As Alexis noted,

> DACA did help me continue my studies and be able to get a job. If I didn't have DACA now . . . , I don't think I would've lasted this long, you know. Or going to school. I probably would have just got a 9–5 regular job, you know. That is one of the big impacts that DACA helped me and made me feel a little bit freer, you know, here in the US.

José, in turn, told me, "When I started XX University, I was able to get a job and in a few months another job. Without those jobs I wouldn't have been able to afford . . . even with the generous scholarship that I received at XX University. So, it is really the jobs that helped bridge that gap." Angel concurred,

> So, at the beginning, we were really happy and overall, DACA has given me the opportunity to go to school and facing the fact that I can work legally in the United States. I have a driver's license. And giving me a driver's license or a state ID, that form of documentation has helped me like, a lot. With DACA, I have been able to work and help pay for school. So, DACA has essentially allowed me to do all that.

As Alexis's, José's, and Angel's experiences show, having a job allowed these DACA recipients to pay for their education.[45] Alexis and José openly admit that they would not have been able to afford an education without DACA. Overall, having a job turned my participants' career aspirations into a more tangible possibility.[46]

Estela chose an occupation that requires a license. In 2019, at least ten states—California, Florida, Illinois, Minnesota, Nebraska, Nevada, South Dakota, Utah, West Virginia, and Wyoming—allowed DACA recipients to obtain certain professional licenses.[47] Other states, due to citizenship or residency requirements for professional licenses, do not allow DACA recipients to get professional licenses, given DACA is not a path to residency or citizenship. Thanks to the rules in Illinois, Estela was able to become a Certified Nurse Assistant (CNA), which allowed her to continue her studies. She told me,

> I had a daughter at that time already and I had to maintain a job and . . . I started working in the healthcare industry and I was able to get my CNA certification. So this gave me like, a chance to keep moving up. I was able to start taking my other classes that I needed for internships and things like that.

Estela was a mother by the time she obtained DACA. Becoming a CNA allowed her to support her family and continue to take classes. Research shows that 68 percent of DACA recipients completing certification or licensing programs saw immediate salary increases and 76 percent of those at least doubled their income.[48]

For those enrolled in college, DACA opened access to internships and employment opportunities that help students prepare for their chosen careers.[49] A 2020 California survey among DACA recipients at four-year universities showed that 38 percent of respondents had participated in one or more professional experiences.[50] Some participants seemed to appreciate this opportunity. Andreíta, for example, explained,

> I was not really interested in driving so I didn't really care if they gave me a driver's license. A social security number was a bit more helpful in getting work in college because I did all sorts of volunteering work in high school, so I didn't really need . . . I mean, I could have most definitely needed a job, who doesn't need money?
>
> But I never . . . I never had the pressure to get a job. My parents just worked so hard that they just had money and we didn't need to be worried about anything. But it definitely gave me the opportunity to get work in college that was related to my major, so it gave me experience into what I wanted to do. So for that, I am grateful. It makes sense, having the opportunity in college because I never wanted to work in a dining hall and wash dishes when I could very much go get experience in my field of study.

Maybe because she was an only child, Andreíta's parents had enough to support her and pay for her studies. She nonetheless took advantage of the opportunities afforded to her by DACA and held jobs relevant to her career.

Access to Four-Year Colleges

While DACA did not override exclusion from federal financial aid that undocumented students face, it enabled beneficiaries to access new educational opportunities.[51] For many undocumented young persons, DACA facilitated access to four-year colleges.[52] DACA students who received four-year college degrees were more likely to obtain new jobs, increase their earnings, and obtain paid internships in their fields of study.[53] Some of my participants enjoyed these benefits. Cynthia was able to start her studies at a four-year college. She explained,

DACA gave me hope that I could do something more than a simple job and do a degree that would lead to a career. It opened the possibility to dream bigger, more than just a community college. At that time, I had the opportunity to enroll at National Lewis University. And I could apply because I had DACA, without the immigration status being a problem.

Thanks to DACA, Cynthia had the opportunity to dream bigger and plan a career. To pursue her dreams, she enrolled in a four-year university after being enrolled in a community college.

Psychological Implications

DACA has proven effective at increasing a sense of belonging, self-esteem, and social support.[54] DACA afforded its recipients a greater sense of autonomy, better mental health, increased well-being,[55] and increased positivity about their life change.[56] Several participants expressed feeling excited and happy about DACA and some of them discussed their sense of relief due to DACA's benefits. In addition, seven participants described feeling motivated after DACA to study and work harder.

Hector, like several other participants, was very excited about DACA: He was "blown away." He told me,

Honestly, DACA was something that blew me away. I was really happy. I remember hearing the news about DACA . . . it was something that got me really excited . . . I wanted to do so many things around high school. I didn't have the best life at home; there were things with my dad that were happening and all I could think about was "I want to help my mom, I want to help her succeed." I want to give her everything, but I couldn't do it if I didn't work. So knowing that this was coming just around the corner, I was excited.

When our applications were finally open . . . I remember getting everything that I needed; I had to go to like my old elementary schools to get proper documentation because I needed to prove that I was here before . . . The process was expensive, but I knew that it was gonna be worth it. And when I finally got it and I finally got my first job . . . I was so ready to work my entire life ever since I was thinking about it, so now that I got the opportunity, like I just kind of went crazy with it.

Apparently, Hector and his mom were having trouble with his father. Therefore Hector was eager to work to be able to help his mom succeed, so when he got his first job he was excited.

Other participants were also excited, happy, and hopeful when DACA came about. Ana, realizing the DREAM Act would probably never pass, was optimistic about the opportunities DACA offered. She said, "Definitely, it [DACA] is very exciting. And my family was one of the least hesitant. We were like, 'Okay we are going to take advantage of this opportunity because we don't know if the Dream Act is ever going to pass.'"

Laura, in turn, was happy and relieved she would not have to struggle as much as her siblings did. She explained, "Yeah, I was happy. It was a relief for me because I knew I didn't have to struggle as much as my brother and sister did. So, they had to go for quite some time without having a license or, hmm, without being able to drive a car just because they didn't have the proper ID's."

Zoe, too, found hope when DACA allowed her to get a job at Burger King. She told me,

> When I heard [about DACA] I was in the living room with my mom, I just wanted to cry in tears, like "OMG, maybe there is something." But when I started school, I didn't have DACA and at that time I had found a job that was paying under the table, so I barely had enough money to pay for three courses. So the next year, once I had DACA, I found a minimum wage job at Burger King and people were like, "Why do you work, why do you care so much about Burger King?" and to me it was like the best thing ever . . . DACA gave me some kind of hope.

Ana, Laura, and Zoe, like many DACA recipients, were positive about the life changes brought about by DACA.[57] These opportunities likely gave recipients increased well-being,[58] peace of mind,[59] and hope.[60]

Like Laura, Lucio was relieved after getting DACA, and he felt like a "normal person." He told me,

> After getting DACA it was like a huge relief for me. I could drive like a normal person. If I get in an accident . . . if something happens, I can legally go to authorities and seek help the right way. I would call the police to come here and do a proper investigation. And I have insurance so if I hit you, I can pay for your car. It became easier to move around and it was easier to integrate because I was struggling to become part of the economic and political system.

Lucio was relieved and felt protected if something were to happen to him, like a car accident, because he had car insurance. Coinciding with previous findings, he also felt a greater sense of freedom because in such case he would be able to go to the police.[61] Finally, he felt a sense of belonging, that he was finally a "normal" person, who could become part of the economic and political systems.[62]

Previous research shows how DACA's increased opportunities for integration into society helped some recipients find the motivation to study and work harder.[63] DACA seems to have increased investment among adolescents, increasing both school attendance and graduation rates, and to a degree, college attendance.[64] Psychologists classify motivation as intrinsic or extrinsic.[65] The original idea was that intrinsic and extrinsic motivation were antagonistic. According to this conception, extrinsic motivation referred to behaviors performed in the absence of self-determination, whereas intrinsic motivation referred to behaviors performed in its presence.[66] Other studies, however, showed that extrinsic rewards can complement or increase intrinsic motivation rather than decrease it.[67] In other words, people can be self-determined even when they are offered extrinsic motivators.[68]

The situation of undocumented students is unique because even after getting a college education they can end up working under-the-table, blue-collar jobs due to their lack of a work permit. In most cases, if a student has positive expectations for a career outcome, these are likely to be an important source of motivation for engaging in their program of study.[69] DACA's work permit, at least temporarily, puts students on equal footing with their work-able counterparts and can motivate them to study and work harder. This was true for many of my participants. Some of them, like Marcos, realized they could go back to college. He explained,

So, when I acquired DACA, I was actually able to get a job at College of DuPage in their restaurant and it was an amazing job. There were a lot of cool things about it. And you know, it was amazing. And I was like "OMG, my life changed."

And that's when I decided to go back to school. And actually, take school seriously. I'm like, "Marcos, don't just take 2–3 classes." And because I didn't take school seriously back in 2008, I was in academic probation . . . I was like, "Okay, I can do this." I got a good job. I was working for the government, pretty much for the government because College of DuPage is a public community college. So it's a government institution. So, I had a good job, good paying and everything. And ever since then, like, you know, I moved restaurants, I'm still in school, I'm almost going to graduate, next year.

Marcos lacked motivation when he enrolled in college for the first time. Having access to a better job changed his life and motivated him to go back to school and be a better student.

Andrés and Estela also found motivation in the opportunities afforded by DACA. Andrés set himself a goal for the first time and told me,

Oh, it [DACA] opened up so many opportunities for me to start trying to figure out where I was going and what I wanted to do. It gave me this motivation, so I was like, "Alright. You gotta get your things together and start motivating yourself to where you want to be." Because I went to a high school that was mostly college prep and they started talking to us about college during freshman year . . . I was like, "Oh, this is going to be great." So I was really excited.

Estela found the courage to do what she always wanted to do.

I feel that it [DACA] gave me more courage to continue on, you know, . . . I always wanted to go to college and my family would tell me there was no point for it. I've always been a determined person and I feel like it [DACA] gave me more determination on what my goals were because when I started college, we didn't have DACA yet. So, I'm glad I didn't give up and I think it gave me more courage and more determination to keep going on what I'm doing.

DACA motivated Andrés and Estela to continue with their studies. Before DACA, their opportunities were restricted by the lack of a work permit and by uncertainty. For the first time, Andrés was able to ask himself where he wanted to go and what he wanted to do. Knowing where he wanted to go, and knowing it was possible, motivated him to plan for college. Estela, in turn, always wanted to go to college but found more courage and determination once she got DACA. As these comments show, DACA pushed participants to dream about the future and work toward their goals.[70]

Fear of Police and Law Enforcement

Entering the country without inspection is a criminal misdemeanor, but living in the United States without lawful status is a violation of civil law.[71] Despite this, undocumented immigration is criminalized. Previous research shows that young immigrants and their families are afraid of driving because being pulled over for a traffic violation can potentially lead to the detention-to-deportation pipeline.[72] This is especially true after cooperation between the federal government and state and local police increased in recent years, through the agreements called 287(g) that allow the federal government to cooperate with local authorities to enforce immigration law.[73] Having DACA has also been shown to decrease this fear.[74]

Nine of my participants reported that DACA decreased their fear of being pulled over by the police. Many of them drove without a driver's license before they had DACA. Their experiences with the police are outlined in another chapter. Suffice it to say, most of my participants learned to fear the police because of the potential consequences of an arrest. Lucio summarized his worst fears:

> It [DACA] changed things a lot. Getting DACA, I could get a license so I didn't have to be fearful of getting stopped; I was a little bit calmer . . . they [the police] can come at you really hard. Some are nice but sometimes you get like the hard ones. They take you away. And you know they lock you up and then you're scared that you might be separated from your family. You get out, you're lucky.

Lucio described the fear of getting dragged into the detention-to-deportation pipeline.[75] He knew about other people getting pulled over by the police and ending up deported and separated from their families. Having a driver's license allowed Lucio to drive without fearing getting pulled over.[76]

Several participants agreed with Lucio, including Brianna, Marcos, and Estela. Brianna, for instance, told me, "So when I finally got my permit it was bittersweet, because it was some freedom. Not complete freedom, but now I could drive without overlooking my back to see if police officers were behind me; I felt a little calmer. So yeah." Marcos, in turn, explained, "It changed things a lot, getting DACA I could get a license and I didn't have to be fearful of getting stopped, I was a bit calmer. It was a huge relief for me." Finally, Estela said,

> So, it really gave me hope, like, a lot of hope and I could drive freely and not be scared. I still remember when I started driving with my driver's license. It was so weird. I was still driving so afraid, but then I would remember, "Oh no wait, I do have my driver's license." It really opened up a lot of doors for me.

Brianna, Marcos, and Estela were used to driving without a license and fearing they would be pulled over by the police. They felt less fearful, freer, calmer, relieved, and hopeful they could drive with a license and without fearing they would be pulled over by the police.

Implications for Identity and Sense of Belonging

In sociology, the concepts of belonging and identity are sometimes used interchangeably to reflect the subjective sense of being part of a social group.[77] The concept of belonging is linked to the context of reception and the forms of exclusions connected to immigrant integration, such as the intersection of race, class, gender, and legal status.[78] The concept of belonging may reflect both how an individual perceives themselves and how this individual is perceived by others. In this chapter, the concept of belonging is analyzed from the perspective of the individual and refers to the feeling of being part of American society. The concept of belonging is sometimes associated with feeling at home.[79] Research shows that DACA increases the sense of belonging among recipients.[80]

Eight participants in this research alluded to how DACA influenced their sense of identity and belonging in American society. In some cases, having DACA made participants feel like everyone else. This finding is consistent with the literature that shows that undocumented youth feel different for not having papers, even in cases when parents worked hard to make them feel "normal."[81] These youth are deprived of typical rites of passage and must make excuses when they can't get a driver's license or a job.[82] These exclusions contribute to undocumented youths' outsiderness. As these rites of passage became a reality thanks to DACA, my participants felt an increased sense of belonging. Benita is a case in point. She explained how she felt: "I felt like everybody else . . . I could apply . . . I got a job. I felt like a normal person without getting financial aid. But at least I was able to get my driver's license. I was able to go to school. I was able to work full-time." Benita, after obtaining DACA, was able to feel like a "normal person" without financial aid, when she was finally able to legally drive, to go to school, and to work.

Melody and Ernesto concurred. Melody recalled,

And I just remember once the papers finally got back, I was like, "Yes, now I can, I can go and get a job. I can save up. I can go to school. I can finally get a license and drive around." I remember all my friends had their licenses at sixteen, seventeen, and I didn't get one until I was twenty. And they would always tell me "Oh, why?" And they would just make fun that I just didn't know how to drive. I would just tell them, "Oh, I just didn't have enough opportunity to practice driving and this and that." But I remember being able to get my license, an ID, and finally getting a job.

Ernesto described,

Oh yeah. It changed everything for me, honestly. It was just a different feeling . . . it's just something that people don't think about it . . . it's just the ability to drive, the ability to work. The ability to not be scared of getting pulled over and go to jail. Like, if I get pulled over and they run my driver's license and see that I am someone who's following the law, just driving his car. Just that simple. I'm just driving this car, following the law, going to work.

This research shows that having DACA, even with its temporariness and limitations, eases these feelings of outsiderness. As my participants were able to get driver's licenses and jobs, they felt part of American society, like everyone else, and like an average American.[83] These findings point to the transformative impact of immigration status on my respondents' sense of self.[84]

Other participants made more explicit references to their sense of belonging in the United States.[85] Interestingly, three of the five respondents who preferred to conduct the interview in Spanish were in this group. These respondents alluded to the fact that they came to the United States at an early age and already felt part of the United States. Alondra, for instance, told me,

> I thought, "What am I gonna do?" I came here when I was six months old and know no other place . . . I then got DACA in 2015 when I was fifteen years old and started high school. It was exactly during my freshman year. It was then when I started working and had the opportunity to buy my own stuff without asking my parents for money.

Cynthia explained,

> Getting DACA helped me feel more secure here in the United States. Despite having been raised in Mexico, I can't imagine my life there, I can't imagine what my life would be like there. The country I know professionally is this one. I don't know Mexico. Having DACA gave me a bit more stability in the United States.

Finally, Nathaniel said,

> I got very emotional, and it gave me the opportunity to do the things I wanted to do, like getting my driver's license and a job. I finally felt part of a country from which I already felt part of without being equal to everyone else.

Alondra, Cynthia, and Nathaniel made similar remarks. Alondra and Cynthia mentioned not knowing another country and described the impact DACA had on their lives in the United States. Nathaniel, in turn, mentioned feeling part of the United States even before DACA. These comments imply that the respondents believed they deserved the opportunities afforded to them by DACA because they knew no other country and/or already felt part of the United States.

One last participant also made a case about deservedness. Making use of the so-called DREAMER narrative,[86] Hector defended the right of DACA recipients to relief when he referred to the lack of blame on the part of the young individuals who were brought to the country as children. He explained, "That is something that is easily forgotten, especially with students/people my age that came in at a really young age. You know, getting blamed for something that didn't even have an input. So, I thought about it as almost like a blessing, or something that I had been hoping for."

To make a case for deservedness, Hector adopted the DREAMer narrative used by the undocumented youth movement to defend the right of the immigrants who came to the United States as young children, and went on to become high school valedictorians, Ivy League college students, and military members, to stay in the United States.[87] Although this narrative became divisive for the immigration reform movement, it nonetheless was very effective in bringing the undocumented youth movement to the forefront of American politics.[88] In this particular case, Hector seemed to imply that the opportunities afforded to him by DACA were things he and other young immigrants deserved, given their lack of input in the decision to migrate.

Limitations

Finally, a group of six participants described some limitations of DACA.[89] Previous studies addressed these limitations as perceived by its beneficiaries. One study explored how the liminal legality caused by DACA creates a double bind for DACA beneficiaries, a form of legal violence which simultaneously facilitates and obstructs social inclusion.[90] Another study explored the uncertainty and anxiety associated with having to renew one's legal protections, the potential lapse of benefits, the cost associated with the renewal, and the possibility that the program could end at any time.[91] According to these studies, even though DACA facilitates economic inclusion, it does not offer access to federal financial aid,[92] offers no path to citizenship or a more permanent status,[93] does not solve the licensing issues for students who want to pursue careers requiring licensing in states that forbid it to DACA recipients, such as South Carolina,[94] retains limitations to travel,[95] and does not protect the parents.[96]

My participants discussed most of these limitations: the lack of FAFSA, a path to citizenship, opportunities to travel, and opportunities for these youths' parents. Cynthia discussed her difficulties covering college expenses and lamented that DACA did not grant access to FAFSA. She said,

> I imagine that because of my English and because DACA was so new they only gave me 30 percent of the scholarship. I had to cover the rest without access to FAFSA . . . FAFSA was not part of the plan. They gave us a social security number, but we didn't have access to those tools, to that kind of aid.

Even though undocumented youth have the right to a K-12 education, they lack access to federal student aid.[97] It is up to the states to grant access to state aid and scholarships, including in-state tuition for public colleges and universities. Illinois granted in-state tuition to undocumented students who attend public colleges and universities in 2003,[98] and access to state financial aid and scholarships in 2019.[99] At the time Cynthia was studying, however, she had no access to state financial aid and struggled to afford college due to the lack of access to federal financial aid.

Unlike the DREAM Act first introduced in 2001, DACA does not provide a path to citizenship or another type of permanent status.[100] Ana referred to this limitation when she said, "Yeah, I was very hopeful. I was excited. I think we were hoping it would be some sort of Dream Act so that there would be a path to citizenship but, unfortunately, it wasn't."

Apparently, Ana expected DACA to grant a path to citizenship and was disappointed when it did not. Without a path to citizenship or permanent status, DACA recipients face constant uncertainty about their future and are required to renew their work permit every two years. They also face limitations when it comes to careers that require a license.[101]

DACA recipients could originally travel abroad with a special permit called advance parole.[102] Out of 800,000 DACA recipients, only 22,000 applied for advance parole to travel outside the United States before this benefit was rescinded by the Trump administration.[103] The USCIS is currently accepting applications for advance parole. At the time of the interview, however, this special permit to travel was suspended. Juliana stated, "Well, it gave me an opportunity to work and go to school. But there's also a limit to it which makes me kind of upset. Because I really liked learning about cultures, and I've always wanted to travel. But because of it, I can't travel outside."

Finally, Ernesto was disappointed that DACA does not benefit recipients' parents. He told me, "My first job was at this local restaurant called Los 3 Burritos. I was a cashier and I felt like I had a purpose. I had the right to do something that my parents didn't, and it sucks because I wish that it would have extended to my parents, but at the same time there's so much I can do."

Getting a job at a Mexican restaurant gave Ernesto a sense of purpose. Despite this, he lamented that DACA did not benefit his parents. Comprehensive immigration reform has proven challenging in recent years.[104] Comprehensive immigration reform refers to omnibus legislation that attempts to address the following issues: demand for high- and low-skilled labor, the legal status of the millions of undocumented immigrants living in the country, border security, and interior enforcement.[105] The last time legislators came close to significant immigration reform was in 2013, when the Democrat-led Senate passed a comprehensive reform bill that would have provided a path to citizenship for undocumented immigrants and tough border security provisions.[106] Congress is currently debating the Build Back Better Bill, which would give a work permit and protection from deportation to undocumented immigrants who have been in the country since 2011. It has been approved in the House of Representatives.

Polish Interviewees

The impact of the acquisition of DACA on my Polish interviewees mirrored that of their non-White counterparts. Polish interviewees were quick to identify the practical advantages of obtaining DACA to get

driver's licenses, access to better jobs, and college. Ali mostly emphasized the practical implications of DACA. She told me,

> Yeah, so that came out around the time that I was graduating high school
> and wanting to go to college. So freshman year of college is when I ap-
> plied for DACA, when it first came out. And I did it for my brother as
> well. So I helped him receive that. But it felt very positive. And that it was,
> you know, something that was going to help all of us in a way where we
> can get an education, get a job, start being, you know, part of the com-
> munity. And it was such a wonderful thing that came out at the time, I
> was so grateful to be a part of that.
>
> So once I received that, I started working right away to pay for my col-
> lege education on my own with a little bit of my dad's help, but we weren't
> allowed to take out any government loans, anything like that. So we had
> no help either. So I think the kids that were a part of DACA were very
> hard working, because we had such limited resources that we had to
> make everything happen on our own. So it came at a perfect time because
> I wanted to get a college education. So I was able to do that . . . I went to
> public school.

Ali prepared the applications for herself and her brother and was appreciative of the opportunities DACA created for education[107] and work.[108]
But she also felt having DACA gave her the opportunity to start being a
member of the community.[109]

Mateusz was likewise enthusiastic about DACA and provided exten-
sive comments on its positive impact.

> So I think DACA was 2012, which is when it was introduced by President
> Obama and I applied for it right away, as soon as it became available. I
> know there was like an event. I remember it was held at Navy Pier. For
> people who are eligible. It was like an informational event that I went to.
> I got a chance to meet representative Gutierrez and Dick Durbin, shake
> their hands. So I, I've always been very on top of this stuff, you know. I'm
> visiting forums about the Dream Act and just following its development
> in just like I said, it's something that has been a huge source of anxiety.
> That day was probably the best day of my life up to this point, because it
> opened up so many doors, you know?

I was at, I was a sophomore in college when that happened. So you know, prior to that point, I did not have a social security card, which obviously means I couldn't pay taxes, I couldn't get a job legally, I couldn't get a driver's license, none of that stuff. And I was going to school. So the question was, like, you know, what would I do if I graduate and not have a social security card, not have an ability to work? So I don't know. I mean, I don't know if I'd still be here. I don't know if I'd be working construction. Like a lot of people. I have absolutely no idea what would have happened. But the fact that it did pass, and it passed before I graduated, it literally made everything that has happened since possible, you know, moving to DC, getting a job, now going to school here, none of this.

It's crazy, because it's just a little tiny piece of paper, that social security card makes all the difference in the world, you know, for me and so many other people. I just remember once I got like, when I went to the Social Security Administration, and they printed me the card, and I got it, I was just, I was so happy. Like, really, it's hard to explain, it was just like an explosion in my heart.

And it's sort of how I feel now, when I think about oh, if, if, if something does pass, if I become documented and I can actually visit my grandma in Poland. That's, yeah, I'm sure it's gonna be the best day of my life. But up to that point, when I got that call, and I got my social security card when I got my driver's license, you know, and stuff became possible. It was definitely a huge, huge change in my life, a huge turning point.

Coinciding with previous findings, Mateusz was actively involved in the DREAMer movement and attended an event in Chicago where DACA applicants could file their applications.[110] He described the day he applied for DACA as the "best day of his life" because of the number of opportunities it opened up for him. Further, Mateusz thought he would not be in DC attending school and working if it weren't for "this tiny piece of paper." Showing emotions previously recorded in the literature, he was so thrilled, he felt an explosion in his heart.[111]

Conclusion

DACA was neither a perfect nor a permanent solution, though it gave its recipients relief from deportation and a work permit. Despite this, every one of my interviewees appreciated its practical advantages. In comparison with the previous stage, when my participants discovered they were undocumented and/or first understood its implications, DACA represented a high point in their lives. DACA had practical and psychological implications, removed the fear of police and law enforcement agents, and influenced their identity and sense of belonging.

DACA impacted students' ability to get driver's licenses, find jobs, and continue their education, impacting students' socioeconomic incorporation into US society.[112] DACA improved participants' job opportunities, allowing them to get better paying jobs, sometimes with benefits, or jobs in their professional areas of specialization.[113] Thanks to its work authorization, even in the absence of federal financial aid, DACA allowed many participants to afford higher education and to access professions requiring licensing.[114] Finally, DACA allowed some participants to move from community colleges to four-year institutions.[115]

DACA also benefited students psychologically, and embracing the opportunities afforded by DACA made participants excited, happy, and hopeful.[116] Importantly, DACA motivated several students who had lost motivation after discovering they were undocumented, inspiring them to study and work hard, and to continue their education. Among my participants, DACA seems to have increased school attendance, graduation rates, and college attendance.[117]

Many participants had driven without a license before DACA. Most of them obtained driver's licenses after DACA, and they expressed decreased fear of getting pulled over by the police and being mistreated and/or dragged into the detention-to-deportation pipeline.[118] Participants expressed feeling less fearful, freer, calmer, and more hopeful when driving with their newly acquired licenses.

Research shows that having DACA increases the sense of belonging among recipients.[119] DACA influenced identity and sense of belonging for several participants, making them feel normal, like everyone else, and part of American society. Some participants explained that DACA made them feel more established and secure, which was a relief considering they knew "no other country." Finally, one participant stated that DACA was what he deserved because individuals in his situation came to the country at an early age and were therefore not to blame for their immigration status.

Finally, a group of interviewees described some restrictions associated with DACA.[120] My participants discussed many of the limitations of DACA discussed in the literature, including the lack of access to FAFSA,[121] no path to citizenship,[122] lack of opportunities to travel,[123] and lack of opportunities for these youths' parents.[124]

6

Deportable Again

Navigating Policy Shifts

Justice's dream is to become a US Marine or a police officer. She came to the United States at the age of seven with her mother and siblings. The family decided to come to reunite with her father, who was working in the United States and traveling back and forth. Upon arrival, Justice, her mom, and siblings stayed for a few days with a person her mom knew. Justice remembers the neighbors tried to interact with her and her family, but since Justice and her family did not understand English, they just stared at them.

Justice started school in second grade. Despite being placed in ESL classes, she had a hard time understanding her teacher who spoke English to her. She was able to make friends easily in her ESL classes, however, because many children were Latino/a and spoke Spanish. After her parents separated, Justice went through a period of "acting up" in school. After switching schools twice, she ended up at an "all-White" school. Her counselor in this school made assumptions about her and asked whether she would have graduated from her previous, predominantly Latino/a school, or dropped out pregnant if she had stayed. Being fifteen at the time, the thought of dropping out of school or interacting with boys "in that manner" had never crossed Justice's mind.

Justice found out she was undocumented when trying to enlist in the marines. On this occasion, she was asked if she was a citizen and she said she was in the process of getting citizenship. But once they determined she was undocumented, they turned her down. Not being able to realize her dream of becoming a marine was depressing for Justice and brought down her self-esteem. She was thrilled when DACA came about, and she could finally get an ID and a decent job. When the termination of DACA was announced, however, Justice thought she would end up working dead-end jobs again and wouldn't be able to pursue her alternative dream of becoming a police officer.

Justice believes diverse schools crowded with students should be able to provide mental health support and a space for children to talk about their problems. She also wishes she could trade spots with other citizen-youth who take their opportunities for granted, do the bare minimum in class, and do not attend college. Observing this type of behavior makes Justice frustrated. After completing college, she moved to Florida. She may attend law school someday.

As Justice's story shows, her life was full of ups and downs. She could not join the marines because of her lack of documents, which was a blow to her self-esteem. Later, she was able to obtain DACA and get better jobs. But the announcement of the termination of DACA threatened to put an end to what she had and to her alternative dream of becoming a police officer. The lives of most DACA recipients follow a similar up and down pattern, frequently triggered by perceived or real changes to their immigration status.

This book argues that the volatility DACA recipients experienced resembles a roller coaster. Thanks to *Plyler v. Doe*, DACA recipients gained a sense of inclusion and belonging in public schools, although this sense of belonging was uneven among my participants. Later, however, they faced exclusion when prevented from participating in rites of passage typical of their age, and they generally experienced a negative psychological impact.[1] This partly changed when they acquired DACA and participants were able to get driver's licenses, work, and attend college.[2] Most felt excited, happy, and hopeful.[3] Further, they experienced an increased sense of belonging.[4] The announcement of the termination of DACA, however, threatened to throw DACA recipients back into a space of exclusion. This chapter, after reviewing the announcement of the termination of DACA and its many court challenges and the recent memo from the Biden administration to strengthen DACA,[5] assesses the impact of the announcement of the termination of DACA by the Trump administration on September 5, 2017, on the lives of the DACA recipients featured in this study.

The Rescission of DACA and Its Impact

The literature on the impact of the rescission announcement and subsequent legal battle is scant. One study analyzing qualitative data from a sample of sixty-five DACA recipients in California found that the uncertainty around the program had a negative impact on 83 percent of recipients' sense of belonging in American society.[6] The main factors contributing to this decreased sense of belonging were the participants' greater sense of exclusion in American society coupled with their feelings of vulnerability. The negative portrayal of immigrants, especially of Latino/a origin in the media contributed to DACA recipients' sense of exclusion. In turn, the announcement of DACA's rescission confirmed DACA recipients' feeling of continued legal vulnerability. Further, one-third of participants reported they regretted applying for DACA, because providing all their personal information to the government could make them more likely to be deported.[7]

Another study analyzed the areas of life in which DACA recipients felt uncertainty after the announcement of the rescission.[8] In this study participants were asked to list the areas in which they were facing uncertainty. The most common were employment and career opportunities, followed by education. Other areas of uncertainty included mental health, deportation, family/relationships, friendships, romantic relationships, mobility, and safety. Other themes discussed in this study were coping with the uncertainty, including disconnectedness and avoidance of stressful thoughts, and strategies of resistance and resilience exhibited by DACA recipients on their college campuses.[9]

Because the emotions triggered in participants by the fear of losing DACA resemble the emotions experienced in the original discovery/realization of their lack of documents, in this section I also draw on literature regarding the latter. Research shows that as undocumented youth understand their illegality, they become frustrated, self-conscious, and feel a heightened sense of awareness.[10] Some youth develop a sense of non-belonging that some authors term liminality.[11] Also, coming of age undocumented entails intense feelings of anxiety, confusion, frustration, and stress.[12] Finally, undocumented students often experience feelings of inferiority, embarrassment, shame, fear, psychological trauma, and depression.[13]

Nathaniel's trajectory exemplifies this process of changing levels of inclusion/exclusion. When he understood the implications of being undocumented, Nathaniel said,

> I clearly remember when I discovered I was undocumented when I was fifteen. Well, I knew I was undocumented before, but I ignored the implications because it didn't affect me until I was fifteen when I had to take

driver's ed. All the students started getting their driver's licenses. I passed the class but then realized I couldn't get my license. This was when it hit me. I realized I was undocumented and had more limitations than my classmates. I would see them travel, and I didn't have that opportunity. And that's when I understood that I'm in a country that is not mine and many doors are closed for me.

He commented about getting DACA,

Oh my gosh. When I heard about DACA, I couldn't believe it. I thought, "I can't believe it." I had graduated from high school when I got DACA and was thinking of getting a fake social security number to be able to work. I was still self-employed, but I wanted to have the opportunities everyone else had. Then they announced they were going to give DACA to those who, like me, had arrived in the United States at an early age. I was four when I got here. I got very emotional, and it gave me the opportunity to do the things I wanted to do, like getting my driver's license and a job. I finally felt part of a country from which I already felt part of without being equal to everyone else.

Nathaniel then reflected on the announcement of the termination of DACA.

I felt very frustrated because I had started college and felt doors would close again. I was feeling up on a cloud, not in the shadows as I felt before [I had DACA], when I had to be hiding, living a life that was not mine. I didn't want to lose all this because DACA had changed my life.

Nathaniel's realization of the implications of being undocumented made him feel he was in a country that was not his own. Getting DACA helped him finally feel part of the country; however, he felt this sense of belonging would be gone if he lost DACA.

Impact of the Rescission of DACA on My Participants

Participants in my sample were asked during the interview: *What was the impact of the termination of the DACA program in September 2017 on your life? How did this change affect the way you thought about yourself and others?* Nine themes emerged from their answers, with most participants discussing more than one theme (figure 6.1). Fifty-two percent of my participants reported that the announcement of the termination of DACA caused fear and related feelings; 45 percent expressed other feelings, such as frustration, anxiety, defeat, sadness, devastation, and hopelessness; 24 percent reported an awareness of the lack of opportunities; and 24 percent expressed a feeling of injustice and unfairness. In turn, equal percentages (15%) of my participants discussed three themes: how the announcement impacted their sense of belonging in American society; the sense of worthlessness of the amount of time and effort they had invested in furthering their college careers and professional lives; and the impact of the announcement not only on them but also on other DACA recipients. Finally, 36 percent told stories of resilience, such as ideas for alternative plans and determination to continue fighting.

Psychological Impact: Fear

Confirming previous studies, more than half of my participants expressed emotions of fear and panic after the announcement of the termination of DACA.[14] Some participants felt vulnerable and became aware of the fragility and temporariness of DACA or what the literature has called "transitory legality."[15] Laura, for instance, explained,

> But having someone decide that you are not worthy of being here even after all the hard work, even after going to school, after paying taxes, and everything. You know, doing what the average American does and being told that you are not worthy of being here, that you don't deserve to be here after all, is scary because a man in an office or a few people in an office have the right to decide.

Angel agreed with Laura about DACA's fragility.

> But I think that the way it [the announcement of DACA's termination] impacted me the most was thinking how fragile the system is and how easily it can be taken away. And how vulnerable we are left without it. Because, let's say, if DACA was taken away from those who have it, they [the

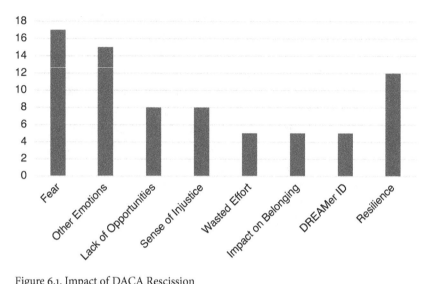

Figure 6.1. Impact of DACA Rescission

government] have all our information: they know where we live, where we work, like, all of it. So that's, like, a very scary process and was part of the risk that we were taking.

Laura felt having one or a few persons deciding that after all their hard work a group of individuals was not worthy of being in the country was scary. Angel reflected on the fragility of DACA. Further, confirming previous studies,[16] he felt vulnerable because the government had all his information, and this information could potentially be used to deport him. Interestingly, he thought that taking away DACA criminalized the undocumented youth who benefited from it even more.

Melody also worried about the potential detention-to-deportation pipeline to the point that it made her paranoid. She stated, "Especially now that they had information about, you know, who the DACA recipients were and that we are undocumented. Where we live and about our parents. So that kind of made us a little bit paranoid." Like Angel, Melody worried about her own deportability and that of her parents. Research shows that DACA-registered youth tend to worry more about the deportability of their parents than their own.[17]

Some participants noted that not having DACA would make them fearful of the police (again). As explained before, many of the participants in my study had negative experiences with the police, most of them while driving without a license before they obtained DACA. Research shows that race consistently shapes individual perceptions of the police.[18] The literature's findings on immigrants' trust in the police are mixed. One study found that Latinos' and Asians' perceptions of the police are somewhere between those of Whites and Blacks.[19] Theodore and Habans, on the other hand, found that both documented and undocumented immigration statuses were associated with negative attitudes toward police.[20] Still another study concluded that Latinos/as are generally more mistrusting of law enforcement than Whites and African Americans, and that Spanish-speaking and undocumented Hispanics/Latinos are more likely to have experienced, or have concerns about, inequitable treatment by law enforcement.[21]

Two of my interviewees were worried that they would once again fear encounters with law enforcement. Marcos, for instance, remembered, "It was scary. It was going back to, like, before DACA when I would drive, I would see a cop behind me, and I would shake. I was scared all the time because I knew that I would be like going back to before I had DACA." Zoe agreed.

Yeah, I mean I don't think I ever . . . I mean, I did drive without a license for a while, and I was scared. I mean, I think even until this day driving with a license, I am still terrified. You know, I get in really panic mode. I'll probably start driving even slower, but yeah, I think that definitely that stuff still has an impact on me. You know? . . . I mean it is still scary, don't get me wrong.

As these comments show, some of my participants' experiences of driving without a license before they had DACA were traumatic, and they dreaded the possibility of driving without a license and being at risk for deportation once again. This finding corroborates my contention that the incorporation of DACA recipients, with its ups and downs, follows a roller-coaster pattern.

Finally, one participant compared the lack of safety following the loss of DACA with White nationalist attacks on Latinos. The interviews for this study took place during the Trump administration. Racism against Latinos/as is not new but Trump's rise to power was built in part on Latino racialization and openly discriminatory views about other groups.[22] Research shows that a resurgence of overt racism and White nationalist violence targeting Latinos paralleled the political ascendance of Trump. Marcos stated,

> So, you know, you are not one of these viral videos of those getting attacked by a White person. You're not, you know? Even though you have that safety of DACA, you don't anymore because of the way things are right now. It's like, scary, yeah. You have DACA but that doesn't mean anything anymore. It just means you can work; it doesn't give you that security that it did when it first came out.

Marcos thought the precariousness of DACA was not as bad as being attacked by a group of White nationalists, but he lamented the few securities that DACA afforded during the Trump administration. In his own words, "DACA didn't mean anything anymore."

Psychological Impact: Frustration, Anxiety, Defeat, Sadness, Devastation, and Hopelessness

Forty-five percent of my participants expressed emotions such as frustration, anxiety, defeat, sadness, devastation, and hopelessness. These emotions mirrored those that DACA recipients experienced when they first discovered/realized they were undocumented.[23] Zoe felt frustrated: Having DACA, to her, felt like a never-ending roller coaster. She explained,

> And then I'm like . . . it's frustrating, you know. Not knowing where your life is going to head from one day to another. Not too long ago, when they were recommending DACA recipients to do the renewal though mine expires in 2020, you know? . . . I remember just crying . . . I'm like, "Here we go again." It's just a never-ending roller coaster; that's how it feels, you know? So, the worst aspect of it I guess is feeling like someone's playing with your life. That's how it feels like, I guess.

Zoe referred to the uncertainty she felt living with DACA,[24] and her frustration when the Trump administration allowed DACA recipients to renew only once more before terminating the program.[25] To her, it felt like a never-ending roller coaster. Zoe's comparison to a roller coaster likely referred to the ups and downs in her life, especially those related to her immigration status, like discovering she was undocumented and understanding the implications, acquiring DACA, and then risking losing it. According to her, this roller coaster was intentionally caused by somebody playing with DACA recipients' lives.

One participant mentioned how the anxiety that she originally felt while knowing she had no documents[26] had taken over again. Anxiety may involve a visceral fear, which is accompanied by a physical response controlled by the autonomic nervous system.[27] It may also entail worry or a feeling of uncertainty.[28] These emotional and cognitive feelings are frequently intertwined.[29] Hector explained,

> You know, all the anxiety that I had managed to overcome, you know, took over again. Even now in the current state that we're in, it's really hard for me to not be able to work again. Or even the most extreme case, you know, when your high anxiety in your brain goes to the most bizarre places, like, you know, what if I get deported?

Hector worried that he wouldn't be able to work again or that he might even be deported. In his case he seemed to experience both fear and worry. These emotions mirrored the ones participants felt when they originally learned they were undocumented.

Other participants felt defeated. The original realization that they had no documents made some participants lose their motivation to move forward in life.[30] Daniel's and Hector's comments exemplified this loss of motivation. Daniel reported,

> Yeah. I got really discouraged by that; I kind of felt defeated. I kind of felt like giving up and didn't want to finish school anymore. I kind of just wanted to drop out and just wanted to move back to China. It teared down the confidence in a lot of people because the deportation protection was terminated.

Hector concurred:

> Or, it felt like it [DACA] was gonna be gone. I felt defeated. I felt like all the work that I put in and the effort was just kind of wasted at that point. I went back to not knowing what I'm going to do now, you know? Because I'm not married. I'm not with anybody and had no route at the time to, like, you know, get papers.

Daniel felt like giving up and Hector did not know what to do next. Daniel even considered moving back to China. Hector felt all the work and effort he put in was wasted. Overall, both participants felt defeated and uncertain about the future.

Other participants felt devastated and hopeless.[31] Ana, for instance, felt devastated but was more worried about her brother's future than hers. She explained,

> I was very devastated, but I think I was more devastated for my brother because I've been fortunate enough to get a master's degree education here in the United States. So, if for whatever reason I needed to leave, I have my education. But he has not finished his undergraduate yet. So, if he had to leave, for example to Mexico and start all over, . . . I think that scared me more than my own future.

Ana thought that if she had to leave the United States at least she would have her master's degree. But she worried about her brother, who had not finished his undergraduate degree at the time. As this comment shows, Ana was not only an accomplished DACA recipient but also a caring sister.

Benita also felt devastated, or in her words, "smashed into pieces." She explained,

> I cried. I cried because it [DACA] was the only thing that got me to school. It was the only thing I had, to go to school, and they [the Trump administration] took that away. I felt like they smashed me in pieces. It was like being deported, and I should not be deported. I had no status . . . it was rough. Me and my mom called the lawyer right away. We tried everything. We looked for second opinion or stuff like that. It was a rough

time for us. I was in school in the middle of sophomore year when that happened. No, it was my junior year when that happened. So, it was hard because once it got terminated, my DACA expired.

Benita was devastated by the termination of DACA; it felt "like being deported." DACA had helped Benita achieve her dream of attending college. She and her mom looked for alternative ways for Benita to get her papers but failed. Benita's DACA unfortunately expired after the termination. Her state of mind was back to the moment when she realized the implications of being undocumented. The last time I spoke with her, she had not been able to renew it.

Mary's hopes and dreams were crushed after the announcement of DACA's termination because she wouldn't be able to achieve her dream of becoming a bilingual director. She explained,

> So, when President Trump announced that he was terminating DACA, I think all my hopes and dreams were crushed just because, as I said before, I have a goal. I have a dream to become a bilingual director. But if DACA is taken away I can't work. I won't have access to an actual legal status. So, when he said that, I started thinking, what am I going to do? It's really hard for someone that has lived here most of their lives and doesn't have something like a piece a paper that is pretty much all you need. Just that little piece of paper that other people take for granted. And we need it; it is kind of our life support.
>
> Yeah, I feel like all of my dreams collapsed. I found myself every single day googling DACA. Like, you just live in constant fear because you don't know what's going to happen and you don't know how that's going to affect you.

Mary worried that without DACA she would be unable to work and achieve her dream so her "dreams collapsed." She referred to having documents as "that little piece of paper that other people take for granted." Apparently, she believed people who have documents failed to appreciate the opportunities they have. Because of DACA's termination, Mary lived in constant fear.

Lack of Opportunities

Twenty-four percent of my participants discussed the lack of opportunities that losing DACA would entail, like not being able to attend school and losing jobs.[32] Nathaniel and Abraham discussed the impact on their college education. Nathaniel said, "I felt very frustrated because I had started college, and I felt like doors would close for me again." Abraham, in turn, stated,

> Yeah. Well, when I heard that, I was still in school in Illinois. So, I was like, "I don't think I'll be able to finish school because I'm going to go back to out-of-state tuition, and you know that was going to be very expensive." They were going to take away scholarships and stuff like that. I didn't really want to think about it much because I didn't want to worry about it during school, you know. I just wanted to focus on school while it was still on the news.

DACA likely made it possible for Nathaniel and Daniel to attend college. Like other youth in a similar situation, they felt the complications of not having DACA, such as loss of scholarships and jobs, would jeopardize their college education.[33] As a result, they believed they would go back to having limited college opportunities.

Finally, Marcos noted the disadvantages he would encounter in the labor market by not having DACA. He explained,

> It was like, "Oh I might lose my job now. I might have to go back to working for that mom and dad place and make the same amount of money and have talent go to waste because I am not learning anything." It was scary. I'm like, "OMG." Luckily my DACA expiration date was this year because I had just renewed it. And now I was able to renew it again. And I got super excited. I'm like, "Yay, I'm not going to lose my job; I'm not. I don't need to be scared yet, you know?" Even though it is still very scary.

Marcos feared he would lose his job and go back to working in that "mom and dad place." If forced to do this, he would earn less money than in his current job and his "talent [would] go to waste." He was not alone. Seventy-two percent of DACA recipients who participated in a survey in Colorado in 2018 said it was unlikely or very unlikely they could keep their current job.[34] Luckily, Marcos had just renewed his DACA. The lack of job opportunities that would follow my participants' loss of DACA would resemble the lack of opportunities they faced before getting DACA.

Sense of Injustice

Some participants discussed the unfairness of losing DACA. Laura, quoted above, felt this sense of injustice when she referred to a man in an office having the right to decide you are not worthy of being here. Zoe echoed this belief:

> You know, just because I look at those people in power, and I think sometimes it goes to that whole identity thing. None of them can relate to me when they don't share my culture, share my traditions; they don't, you know? Even the experience of maybe having family that are immigrants. They don't have that; they probably can't relate to me, and I think these people are the ones making all these rules for us.

Zoe hinted at the lack of diversity of President Trump's Cabinet and the lack of connection in that the decisions about immigrants' fates were being made by people unable to relate to her and her situation. Trump's Cabinet had very few women and members of underrepresented groups.[35] In 2017, his Cabinet was already shaping up to have a smaller percentage of women and non-Whites than the first Cabinets of former Presidents Barack Obama, George W. Bush, Bill Clinton, and George Bush.[36] Zoe was troubled that a group of White persons whom she thought could not relate to her and her situation orchestrated DACA's rescission, including Attorney General Sessions, Acting DHS Secretary Elaine Duke, DHS Secretary Kirstjen Nielsen, DHS Acting Secretary Chad Wolf, and President Trump himself.[37]

José agreed with Laura and Zoe that it was terrifying to have other people make decisions about his life. He stated,

> But it was really . . . it brought a lot of fear because once you have these opportunities, this sort of safety, it feels terrifying to know that

it is as easily taken away. To potentially have to go back to trying to find a job under the table. To potentially no longer being able to have liberty of driving. It was really kind of terrifying to just kind of sit there and wait while other people decided what you were going to do with your life.

José was terrified by the fragility of DACA and how easily he could lose all the opportunities it had afforded him. Like other participants, the loss of DACA would put him right back to the circumstances he had before DACA, when he held under-the-table jobs and could not legally drive.

Wasted Effort

Fifteen percent of my participants reflected on the effort they had expended to get where they were and lamented that their efforts could go to waste. Hector, Juliana, and Laura were among them. Hector stated, "Ah, like everything I had worked for four years with DACA was kind of pointless." While Juliana explained, "Well, it's pretty scary. If it [DACA] is terminated, I can't continue working, and my college is basically worthless. Because I need a work permit to work. And if I get a college degree, I can't work." Laura, in turn, said, "Everything that I worked for can be gone instantly."

All three participants agreed that their efforts could be wasted if DACA were permanently removed. Hector and Juliana thought their four years of college would be pointless or worthless, presumably because they would not be able to work in their professions. Laura simply said everything she had worked for would be gone instantly. As these comments show, the potential loss of DACA represented a big low in the lives of my participants.

Sense of Belonging

Being undocumented has a negative impact on identity formation of youth.[38] Several participants expressed that the realization that they were undocumented had a negative impact on their sense of belonging.[39] Mary, for instance, did not know where she belonged; Nathaniel, mentioned earlier, understood that he was in a country that was not his own, and Alondra felt doors were shutting for her in the only country she knew. When asked about the impact of the announcement of the termination of DACA on his life, Marcos offered a general reflection about the Trump administration. He felt it set us back to 1970. He explained,

> Even though this whole administration has pretty much set us back, taking our community and set us back to 1970. You know that's how it feels now, it's not okay to speak our language anymore. It's not okay to . . . it's like I have to prove [something] to the Americans, and I'm American. I have to prove to them that I speak the language, that I can roll with the punches, and that I am American . . . and leave my heritage behind, but that I'm not Mexican kind of thing. And it's kind of hard because that's not who I am.

Marcos felt the Trump administration denied a space of inclusion for DACA recipients. In order to fit into this society that made no room for DREAMers, he felt he had to deny his heritage and language, he had to prove he could speak the language, and roll with the punches. Overall, he felt he had to prove he was American. Consistent with previous research, Marcos felt a decreased sense of belonging in American society during this period.[40]

Research shows that a theme among undocumented youth is that since they came to the country at an early age, their country of origin is foreign to them.[41] At the same time, they are socialized as outsiders in the only country they have ever known.[42] These themes came up during many of my interviews, including Hector's, both when discussing DACA recipients' original realization of their lack of documents and the termination of DACA. He explained, "What am I going to do then? Like, I've been here since I was four. I don't recall anything in Mexico particularly like, you know, like this is primarily my home. When DACA got taken away, I would say I felt anxious and, overall, just scared, honestly." Because Hector came to the United States at an early age and considers the United States to be his home, he probably could not picture himself back in Mexico, a country he does not remember. The potential termination of DACA, therefore, made him anxious and scared.

DREAMer ID

The term "Dreamer" was originally employed by immigrants' rights advocates and activists as a strategy to humanize and garner empathy for the undocumented youth, in reference to the DREAM Act originally introduced in Congress in 2001.[43] Leading advocacy groups "highlighted immigrants who came to the United States as young children and went on to become high school valedictorians, Ivy League college students, and military members."[44] Because of the valuable contributions of this group of youth, the DREAMers narrative goes, they deserve special consideration. Some of my participants referred to the DREAMers' accomplishments and contributions to the American society. Nathaniel, for instance, explained,

> I think we [DREAMers] have a lot to offer to this nation. I have friends who are doctors, nurses, and now with COVID-19 they are much needed. They contribute a lot to this nation. And now they are closing the doors for them, and I think this is unfair . . . I think DREAMers have made positive contributions to this nation, and I don't see a reason why they would take DACA away.

To justify the deservedness of DACA recipients for their permits, Nathaniel highlighted DREAMers' contributions to the United States, especially in healthcare professions and occupations. Further, he emphasized the importance of their contributions during the COVID-19 pandemic. Over 200,000 DACA recipients have been working in occupations at the forefront of the COVID-19 response in health care, education, and food services.[45] Several bills in recent years have considered giving special permits to essential workers, including the most recent effort in the fall of 2021 to include immigration provisions in the reconciliation bill that was shot down by the parliamentarian, who determined that these provisions were not primarily related to the budget.[46]

Zaide made similar remarks. Even though she referred to DACA recipients and not DREAMers, she also discussed the accomplishments and contributions of these young undocumented individuals. Zaide stated,

> Yeah, so whenever they announced that DACA was terminating, it was very emotional. Like, I don't support them to end it . . . if they do end it, what would happen next? I feel like a lot of DACA recipients are generally pursuing their dreams, their careers, and working hard to contribute to the economy and to fields such as health care. So, I felt like if they terminate DACA, it puts me in a place of, like, what happens next? Is all the hard work going down the drain? Now we have to, like, go back to Mexico and start over?

The announcement of the termination of DACA was very emotional for Zaide and made her uncertain about the future. But when referring to deservedness, she did not speak about herself but about DREAMers in general: those DACA recipients pursuing their dreams, their careers, and contributing to the economy and important fields, such as healthcare. If DACA were terminated, all the hard work would go down the drain.

Making Alternative Plans: Resilience

The stories of the DACA recipients I interviewed also spoke about their adaptability, ability to make alternative plans, and determination to keep fighting. As reviewed before, some participants were depressed and felt like giving up, but others showed adaptability and an ability to overcome adversity and make alternative plans.[47] This was the case for Lucio, who considered working with somebody else's social security number. He explained, "When they announced they were going to terminate DACA, I thought about working with different papers, but if you get caught you get in trouble." Probably because of his parents' experience, Lucio knew that individuals without documents in the United States often work with a social security number that either is made up or belongs to somebody else.[48] Even though he knew this was a risky option, he considered working "with different papers."

Some participants, like Justice, considered returning to their countries of origin. She recounted,

It [the announcement of DACA's termination] didn't make me scared necessarily. It just made me think, wow, what would I do? What would happen? And I honestly don't know if it would happen; I would probably have to look . . . I mean there would be nothing for me to do here. I wouldn't work a regular job, and I don't want to work where they pay cash . . . Those are usually kind of dead-end jobs. And so I'd rather not work those . . . I would have to try to travel down south and find something else to do. I would probably have to give up my dream of becoming a police officer for sure.

Unlike Lucio, Justice ruled out working the kind of jobs that she called "dead-end," the type of jobs one can get without documents. For this reason, she considered traveling down South, presumably to Mexico, her country of origin, and finding something else to do.

A couple of my participants were in serious romantic relationships with American citizens at the time of the announcement of DACA's termination. Ismael got married.

It [the announcement of DACA's termination] didn't affect me that much. I was already planning long term what I was going to do if I wasn't going to be able to renew DACA and continue working. So, at the time, I was dating my current wife. We had been dating for five years, and we started discussing the possibility of getting married . . . In February of 2018, we got married, and July of 2018, we submitted my application [for residency].

Marrying an American citizen is the fastest route to a green card and eventual citizenship.[49] Ismael had been in a relationship for five years when the termination of DACA was announced, and was already engaged. So, in his case, setting a date to get married and applying for residency made sense.

Ernesto was also in a long-term relationship with an American citizen and considered getting married but decided against it. He explained,

I am . . . I have a girlfriend that I've been serious with for a year; I can get engaged, I can get married and get all that stuff, but him [President Trump] ending DACA really put me in a corner. Like, I am still obviously single, I'm not engaged, I'm not married because I don't feel like that road is appropriate until I'm for sure that I want to marry the girl I'm with.

I don't want to go through something that I am not sure about . . . getting married to someone is a life decision and my mom would always get on me to get married young so I could get that out of the way. But I didn't think that was right. I just couldn't do it. I felt that if I'm going to marry someone, it is going to be because I don't see anything else other than the future with the person.

Despite his mom's advice to marry young, Ernesto did not think getting married was the appropriate road to take until he was sure he wanted to spend the rest of his life with his girlfriend. This decision potentially put Ernesto back in the situation he was in before having DACA.

Finally, some participants expressed their desire to keep fighting in general. Even though undocumented populations tend to be fearful of revealing their immigration status, the active stance of the undocumented youth movement is reflected in their slogan "unapologetic and unafraid."[50] Zoe and Abraham seemed to reflect this spirit. Zoe asserted,

It was, "The fight is not over," kind of thing. I'm not going to give up something that was given to me and I worked so hard for. Because, to me, even though DACA is not a way to residency, it has its flaws, they gave us something so small, we took it, and it is going to be like, "Never mind, we are taking it back." I'm stronger than this, and I'm going to keep working.

Abraham similarly expressed a desire to stand up for himself:

But there was this time in my head, it came, like, If they take it away and I get pulled over by a cop and I get arrested for being an immigrant and get charged for it and I get to the detention center. I am just not going to sign my papers of release, you know. I am going to stay there until something happens or I fight my case, you know?

Zoe was determined to keep fighting for what was given to her. Abraham seemed to imply that if he got arrested, he would refuse to leave the detention center as a sign of protest and fight his case. As we see in the next chapter, several of my participants had an active stance in the undocumented youth movement.

Polish Interviewees

Compared to my non-White interviewees, my Polish interviewees seemed less impacted by the announcement of the termination of DACA. Non-White interviewees reported feelings of fear, anxiety, defeat, sadness, devastation, and hopelessness, and a disappointment with the lack of opportunities. They also had strong feelings about the injustice of the situation and the extent to which their efforts on jobs and careers had been wasted. In their comments, many referred to how DREAMers in general were undeserving of the treatment they were given. Mateusz, Peter, and Ali, my Polish interviewees, reacted differently to the announcement. Peter, a political science major, offered a political and somewhat optimistic read of the situation. He told me,

> You know, I mean, obviously, I was very sad. But at the same time, I wasn't, I wasn't as depressed I feel, as some people because I, I, you know, I did political science in college, so I have a pretty good understanding of the political system and the tides. And I know that majority opinion is on this side of DREAMers. And I feel like once you already give us DACA and the work permit, and the work authorization, it would be extremely difficult to take away and it would also be a political loser, even for Republicans. I mean, there's majority support, even among Republicans, to do this, and nobody wants to take away, you know, a chance at an opportunity from kids, especially in the land of opportunity right now.

Peter provided a political analysis about the situation of the DREAMers. Maybe he is right that, eventually, a solution will be given to this group of youth who came to the country as children. After all, public opinion, as he says, has been on the side of the DREAMers.[51] Further, at the time of writing, the Biden administration issued a new memo that attempts to fortify DACA.[52] But a permanent solution with a path to citizenship will have to come from Congress and this seems unlikely to happen in the near future.

Ali's reaction to the announcement of DACA's termination was in line with the rest of my non-White interviewees in that she was sad and referred to the DREAMers and how hard they work to highlight the injustice of the situation. She also made claims of belonging. Ali said,

I actually remember that day, because it was the day of my birthday that they announced that. That's driving to work. And I think my mom called me with the news, which is like, "Oh, my Gosh, go check this out." And I immediately started crying in my car. I was like, "How could they do this?" You know, it was awful. Because, like I said, the kids that are a part of DACA are the most hardworking people. And I couldn't understand why they would decide to do that. So thinking about that, I'm getting teared up, but it was Yeah, it was definitely scary. Because then it's like, what's next? What do we do? Because this is our home.

Ali cried when she heard the news. She had a hard time understanding how the government could do such a thing to such a group of hardworking individuals. Ali got scared and wondered about the future she and other DACA recipients had in the country they call home. It is worth noting, though, that at the time of my interview with her, Ali had been able to apply for a green card through marriage.

Finally, Peter was not affected "as much," as he put it, by the announcement of DACA's termination, because he also was in the process of applying for a green card through marriage. He recalled, "In 2017? That's when I was in the process of getting married, and I was starting on the paperwork. So, at that time, you know, it, I was already kind of having an idea that I'm, that I'm gonna, you know, have a valid status. So. So it didn't really affect me as much."

Peter was lucky he was in the process of getting married when DACA was terminated. It is curious that two of my Polish interviewees were in this situation when, out of the non-White DACA recipients interviewed for this study, only Ismael, of Mexican origin, was able to get a green card through marriage. Intermarriage with natives is often seen as the last step toward assimilation in the host country.[53] In fact, intermarriage and integration are often segmented and vary by country of origin, skin tone, gender, and social class.[54] The intermarriage patterns I observed in my research clearly speak to the easier time that White immigrants, in my case DACA recipients, face when acquiring ultimate incorporation into society.[55]

Conclusion

This chapter reviewed the impact of DACA's rescission announcement during the Trump administration. Participants discussed the negative emotions triggered by the announcement, including fear, frustration, anxiety, a sense of defeat and devastation, and hopelessness. Other participants discussed the decreased college, work, and other opportunities they would face after the termination of DACA, their sense of wasted effort, and a diminished sense of belonging in American society. Others told stories of resilience and determination to keep fighting. Overall, my Polish interviewees seemed less impacted by the announcement of the termination of DACA, but still echoed many of the themes discussed by the non-White interviewees, including the lack of opportunities and the decreased sense of belonging in American society.

In general, the themes that emerged during our discussion of the termination of DACA mirrored those that arose during our discussion of participants' discovery of their undocumented status or realization of its implications. The predominant emotion was fear. Some participants feared that, without DACA's protection, they and their families could become easy targets for deportation because the government now knew their identity and personal information.[56] Others dreaded going back to driving without a license and fearing interactions with the police and potential detention-to-deportation scenarios.

As with the period when they discovered they were undocumented or realized the implications of this status, some participants felt frustrated, anxious, and defeated. Moreover, several of them explicitly referred to having the same emotions they had before having DACA, emotions that they had managed to overcome. Several participants discussed the practical implications of the loss of DACA, such as the inability to continue studying, the loss of jobs, and driving without a license. Others felt a diminished sense of belonging and increased sense of outsiderness in American society.[57] Interestingly, when making the case for the right to inclusion, some participants turned to the

DREAMer ID and referred to the contributions DACA recipients were making to American society.[58]

Polish participants were more likely to get their papers through marriage. In fact, whereas only one non-White respondent was able to get his residency (green card) through marriage, two of three Polish interviewees were able to do the same thing. Segmented patterns of intermarriage based on country of origin and skin color observed among immigrants in general seem to be true for DACA recipients as well.[59]

Despite adversity, several participants showed resilience and determination to overcome the obstacles created by the potential termination of DACA and to keep fighting.[60] Some participants considered different options, including working with falsified papers, going back to their countries of origin, and getting married. Several of them expressed the sentiment "the fight is not over." As the next chapter shows, this inclination to fight for a better life was common among my participants.

7

The Fight Is Not Over

Mobilizing for Change

Angel's dream is to work for a nonprofit that helps working families. He came to the United States from Mexico at the age of seven with his mom and twin brother, because his mom wanted a new start. The family arrived by plane at Chicago's Midway airport with a visitor's visa, and they stayed once that visa expired. Upon arrival, Angel and his family lived in an attic apartment. Their landlord was Latino and he ended up being good friends with the family.

When Angel and his brother started school, they were placed in ESL classes. He was fortunate to attend a diverse school in Chicago, where 60 percent of the students were Latino/a and the rest Polish. Angel identified with Latino/a students and made friends easily. He still keeps in touch with a couple of friends he made back then. Several of his teachers were persons of color and were very helpful to Angel. Things changed, according to Angel, when the family moved to a suburb of Chicago that was predominantly White. While enrolled in his new school, Angel felt "out of place."

Angel always knew he was undocumented but only understood its implications when applying for colleges. His parents always told him, "You are going to go to college," so he always "knew" he would go. His counselor, though, was very discouraging and suggested that instead of going to college Angel should just join the labor force and take a stereotypical job for undocumented immigrants, such as a landscaper or waiter. Right after graduation, DACA came about and Angel was able to get a scholarship, work, and pay for school. After attending a community college for two years he transferred to a major public school in Illinois. The announcement of DACA's termination made Angel aware of how fragile DACA is and how easily it can be taken away.

While at his four-year college, Angel worked for the Latino/a cultural center on campus, finding resources for undocumented students. He was also a member of a college group representing undocumented students. These experiences were influential for his sense of identity and boosted his self-confidence and grades because "folks at the cultural center believed in him." Thanks to his time at the cultural center, Angel felt empowered as a person of color, undocumented, and queer, in his own words. Last time I spoke with him he had graduated with a degree in anthropology and was working full time for a school in Southside Chicago.

Political participation and civic engagement are important indicators of the political incorporation of immigrants.[1] Through participation, people can have input into the political system.[2] Even though voting is a form of participation reserved for citizens, undocumented immigrants can participate in society in meaningful ways. A case in point is the undocumented youth movement (DREAMers), which has been one of the most important such groups in this century.[3] Unable to vote, and like many other undocumented youths, Angel not only chose to join the Latino/a cultural center on his campus, but also dedicated his time to gather resources for the undocumented who were formerly invisible on his campus.

This chapter reviews forms of participation and resistance among my interviewees. It shows that besides immigration reform mobilization and participation in protests, undocumented youth can also resist the immigration system by participating in campus- and community-based organizations and activities, social media platforms, and other daily practices.[4] Further, this chapter argues that driving without a license, a common practice among my non-White interviewees, becomes a form of everyday resistance in a country that allows them to study in K-12 schools but not participate in other important rites of passage.

Political Participation

Noncitizen immigrants can participate in different social and political activities.[5] Active and engaged members of society foster effective governments.[6] The involvement of immigrants in the political arena can also make the political system responsive to their needs.[7] In this sense, political incorporation can be defined as "the extent to which group interests are effectively represented in policy making."[8] Political participation can be defined as an activity that has the intent or effect of influencing government action.[9] This definition includes forms of participation that are voluntary and not for pay.[10]

Upon arrival into a country, immigrants are also presented with several opportunities to participate in different social activities.[11] Schools are one of the first institutions that immigrants encounter. Since the 1982 Supreme Court decision *Plyler v. Doe*, which granted undocumented children the right to a K-12 education, thousands of undocumented children have gone through US public schools. Public schools play three distinct roles in shaping the educational experiences and political and civic engagement of undocumented youth: They act as integrators, as constructors of citizenship, and as facilitators of public and community engagement.[12]

Since the 2006 marches, undocumented youth have been mobilized in unprecedented numbers. Many of these groups were local and started in schools. School-based DREAMers clubs work to educate parents about their undocumented children's rights and options to enroll in higher education and train teachers and counselors on how to better serve and assist the undocumented children.[13] Schools can play a critical role in preparing undocumented students to be their own advocates for change.[14]

College campuses have long been a space for student activism.[15] The state of Illinois grants in-state tuition to undocumented students who attended a state high school for three years.[16] Even though these students still lack access to federal financial aid, they have some inclusion in Illinois colleges and universities. Several of my interviewees were involved in student groups on different campuses: University of Illinois at Urbana-Champaign's I-CAUSE, Illinois Coalition Assisting Undocumented Students' Education;[17] University of Illinois at Chicago's Fearless Undocumented Alliance;[18] Northern Illinois University's Dream Action NIU;[19] and Dominican University's Undocumented and Immigrant Allyance.[20] These student groups actively advocate for undocumented students and share important resources with them.

Citizens and noncitizens alike can have input into the political system in different ways outside of voting, including contacting public officials, working on political campaigns, participating in public meetings, and signing petitions.[21] Contacting public officials was important during the DREAM Act campaign, when the undocumented youth movement mobilized to support the passage of the DREAM Act and wrote letters to public officials.[22] But these campaigns entailed more than just letter writing. By telling their stories (disidentificatory strategy) as undocumented and demanding the passage of the DREAM Act, immigrant youth sought belonging in US society.[23]

Noncitizens can also participate in demonstrations or protests, which are important for democratic countries because they offer a space for public expression of concerns by groups that otherwise are excluded from the political process.[24] Latino protest movements have a rich history in the United States. In the 1960s and 1970s, for instance, many Latinos protested police brutality and limited educational opportunities, and demanded higher wages and greater political rights, building a movement that continues to have an impact in the present.[25] In 2006, thousands of Latinos participated in protests in cities across the country against US House Bill 4437, which would have allowed the government to aggressively track undocumented immigrants and impose penalties on people who assisted them. After this first wave of protests, immigration reform rallies became common and reached areas not previously mobilized.[26]

The mobilization of undocumented youth has been studied extensively.[27] In the early 2000s, immigrant rights organizations led the campaign in support of DREAMers. Designed to appeal to Democrats and Republicans alike, this campaign focused on the merits and respectability of DREAMers.[28] Later on, frustrated with the lack of success of the early campaign and the inability of Congress to approve a path to citizenship, DREAMers moved from a narrative of respectability to one of grassroots and resistance.[29]

As an active participant in immigration reform told me, "A version of the DREAM Act with a path to citizenship for undocumented youth is introduced in Congress virtually every year." The 2010s were no exception. During these years, the undocumented youth movement, led primarily by college students and graduates and accompanied by civic associations, mobilized again to garner support for the DREAM Act.[30] On March 10, 2010, the Undocumented and Unafraid national coming-out day took place in Chicago; students held a march and publicly proclaimed their undocumented status in front of the media.[31] In July 2010, twenty-one members of undocumented youth organizations around the country dressed in caps and gowns and staged an act of civil disobedience in the US Capitol Building in Washington, DC.[32] This was preceded by a smaller act of civil disobedience that took place in Senator McCain's office and constituted an escalation from the previous DREAM Act campaign, which included letter writing, marches, and press conferences.[33]

Except for the yearly rallies across the country on May Day,[34] protests to support immigration reform seem to have decreased. In a way, the undocumented youth movement has changed tactics from direct action to more institutionalized forms of advocacy, through specialized non-profit organizations that advocate for immigrant rights, such as United We Dream.[35] The networks of trust and support built by individuals can have an impact on their incorporation into the host society.[36] Sometimes these networks are crystallized in civic associations. Volunteer organizations can instill civic virtues and skills as members learn how to organize meetings, express their viewpoints, engage in collective decision making, and resolve common problems and concerns.[37] DREAMers emerged as a strong interest group and organized a network of organizations with formal structure.[38] Several other specialized immigrant rights organizations work at the state level, advocating for specific issues such as changing licensing rules that exclude DREAMers from different professions and occupations.

Despite the visibility of the undocumented youth movement, not all undocumented persons are comfortable with public forms of activism because of fear that revealing their undocumented status may lead to their deportation or the deportation of their parents.[39] This was especially true during the Trump administration (2016–2020), characterized by heightened immigration enforcement.[40] Fear, however, does not impede participation in everyday resistance practices.[41] On some occasions, resistance is more active, even violent. More often, according to James C. Scott, resistance takes the form of passive noncompliance, subtle sabotage, evasion, and deception.[42]

Two different types of activities highlighted in this research fit under this category. As was common under the heightened immigration enforcement during the Trump administration that put people at risk of detention and deportation, some of my participants opted for more covert ways to engage in resistance that put them at lower risk of detention-deportation, such as participating in a research project, a class panel, or discussions with coworkers about immigration and DACA. I also argue that driving without a license, which was common among my participants before Illinois allowed undocumented persons to obtain driver's licenses on July 1, 2014,[43] can be seen as a form of daily resistance, of passive noncompliance with state immigration policies.

Immigration Status and Participation: My Sample

The original questionnaire did not include a question about social and political participation, but the topic came up in several of the interviews. For this reason, I added a second set of questions as a follow-up to the original interview. It was important to determine if the undocumented students I interviewed were comfortable revealing their status because openness about it also influences the type of activities undocumented youth can participate in.[44] Corroborating previous findings,[45] undocumented youth's openness about their immigration status was higher after high school than during the high school years (figure 7.1). More specifically, whereas 36 percent of respondents were open about their status during high school, this number for the years after high school was 72 percent. As these numbers show, the undocumented youth became more comfortable with their status as they grew older. Fifty-five percent of my interviewees stated they participated in a group representing undocumented immigrants or DREAMers, and 44 percent stated they did not (figure 7.2). I also asked interviewees if they participated in rallies or had other ways of expressing support for undocumented populations and/or DREAMers. The results showed that 64 percent of my interviewees participated in a rally or another activity in support of undocumented immigrants, and 36 percent did not.

Participants provided examples of the ways in which they participated in social and political activities. I then classified the answers as traditional participation or everyday resistance. Although not every respondent gave an example, the results were interesting. Whereas 58 percent of my interviewees participated in traditional social and political

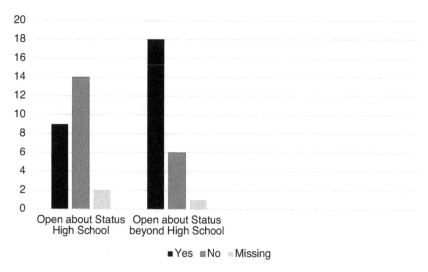

Figure 7.1. Openness about Immigration Status, High School and College

activities, such as groups representing undocumented immigrants or marches, the other 42 percent participated in activities I classify as everyday resistance, such as participating on a panel where DREAMers told their stories, informing their coworkers about DREAMers, or following a group representing Latinos such as United We Dream.

Groups Representing Undocumented Immigrants or DREAMers

Several interviewees participated in groups representing undocumented students both in high school and college. Several of them took leadership roles and created these groups. Benita is a case in point. Benita attended high school in Georgia. Her school lacked resources for undocumented students so Benita created them. She explained,

> I did it myself, I created a club with the DREAMers at my school. We called it The Dreamers' Club. Yeah. And after that, after I got in college, I started mentoring kids in my high school with DACA because they have the same issues. They didn't know, we didn't know we could go to school. I mentored them. One of them got accepted into Harvard. That was my biggest accomplishment. I cried in tears with him . . . I was so happy for

him. Yeah, I did . . . After I left, they created a program called . . . I don't know what it is called exactly The Youth Latino? But it has a bunch of Hispanic students. They take them to college tours and talk to colleges.

Benita attended high school in a state that explicitly prohibits undocumented students from receiving in-state tuition. Not surprisingly, her school lacked resources for undocumented students. Benita created a group for undocumented students so that others in her situation would have more resources than she did. Her activism and mentorship, even after she left the school and the state to attend college in Illinois, allowed a student to get accepted into Harvard.

Daniel was active in groups representing DREAMers both in high school and in college. I met Daniel when he told his story in a panel at a conference that I attended in 2018. He explained that one turning point in his life was when he became the vice president for the DACA club at his school. He commented about this experience, "That was really helpful. It put me into a leadership position. And I had to constantly talk to people and do speeches. I was the leader in helping people do their work. And just be really organized." Daniel was able to grow in his positions as a leader in the DACA club of his high school. He continued to be active in the private university he attended.

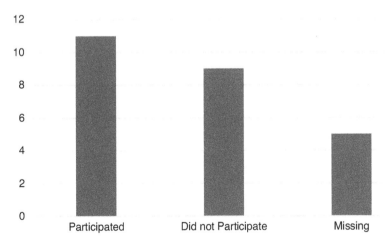

Figure 7.2. Participation in Groups of Undocumented Persons or DREAMers and Marches

[I was] active in high school and in college. [In college] we started having meetings with LASO, the Latino American Student Organization at my school. It was literally one meeting during my sophomore year. It was just one meeting. It got to the point where high school students started gathering with us as a way to support their undocumented identity. It was me and another girl, Jiménez, who kind of just told everyone, "Hey you know what, we should try to come up with something and try to bring people together." It was Eva [last name], the adviser for LASO, who kind of just had an idea of who was undocumented and just got all of us together.

Our first meeting was about ten people, but we didn't have another meeting until the following year. So [Spanish Last name] and a few other people decided to start a club, an undocumented club to help advocate for undocumented students. It wasn't until last year that Andrea [last name] made it a real club with a real adviser and they called it HOPE. And that's when they started really pushing for, you know, the rallies, and pushing for policy change in [university name]. So I think that group is really making a difference in the [university name] community.

Daniel is ethnically Chinese and formed alliances with Latino/a leaders and mentors to create groups of DREAMers in high school and college. Like Brenda and other DREAMers in my sample, admittedly biased because the same DACA recipients who are easy to reach for interviews are those engaged in their communities,[46] Daniel was civically engaged. He and Benita chose a pathway of social responsibility acting as role models and educating others.[47]

Angel and Ana chose similar paths during their college years, both at the same public school. Angel explained,

Because it is really hard to trace them [undocumented students] and there weren't many undocumented students when I was there. There were a few, but there was no way to trace them. I mean, it would be illegal to find a way for the student database to track who is undocumented.

We were able to establish a coalition for undocumented students. We set it up. A few undocumented students that I met, we all met and we set it up. It is still active at [university name] and focuses on undocumented students' rights, solidarity, with majority if not all the students being undocumented. But there are other student groups based out of La Casa that do work without being undocumented. And right now, there are a lot of organizations and fraternities and sororities that do fundraisers for undocumented students. There are undocumented folks in the community that work a lot with these groups as well.

This organizing experience empowered Angel,[48] who, as explained earlier, was told by his school counselor that he could not attend school and should go straight from high school into the labor force to do a manual job. As he later explained to me, this organizing not only benefited students on his college campus but also gave him a sense of self-pride and belonging.

Ana participated in the same group. She expanded on the group's goals, saying,

I was part of a couple short-term grassroots programs in my freshman/sophomore year of college. It wasn't until junior year that one program [name] began to gain momentum on campus with students and faculty/staff. It began with three students and two faculty members and now it's grown into a bigger group. This program aims to bring awareness of our status and create an inclusive climate for undocumented students to voice their concerns. We do various trainings for students and staff/faculty to educate on the topic and create allies in all departments of our campus.

These efforts at this major public school paid off. Undocumented students often lack the same campus support structures and networks available to students who are not undocumented, while facing more stressors and complicated state and campus policies.[49] Groups like the one Angel and Ana participated in bring resources and social support to undocumented students.

Ernesto attended another major public university in Illinois. He tried to remain engaged on his campus, but his student obligations seemed to limit this participation. He told me,

When I went to community college, I was actually a recipient of the Illinois Dream Fund. I won scholarships through them and got scholarships through the Illinois Legislative Latino Caucus Foundation (ILLCF),

I think. And through them I got a lot of contacts with people from UIC. I think her name is Tanya Cabrera. A lot of very helpful people that got me in contact with the Latino resource center here. And to be honest with you, I joined the Latino resource center and I try to give them as much of my time, but obviously it is very hard as a mechanical engineer to do a lot of these events. Just time-wise but at [university he attended], they have helped me so much! I can't even explain to you. I think I've gotten almost $20,000 in scholarships.

Ernesto was not as active as Benita, Angel, and Ana because of lack of time. He was, however, a beneficiary of different advocacy groups at the University of Illinois at Chicago and his own school and received multiple scholarships.

Marches and Rallies

Several interviewees participated in protests and marches. Protesters typically have different degrees of involvement.[50] Some participants were novices in marches and protests while others were die-hard participants. Laura is a committed activist who was open about her immigration status throughout high school, volunteered with several immigrant rights organizations, and participated in a protest in Springfield, Illinois, when she was invited to speak after the announcement of the termination of DACA was made. Paradoxically, she "came out" as a DREAMer soon after the termination of DACA was announced in September 2017. Laura spoke at length about her experience.

> So, ah, when DACA ended, like I said, DACA only gives you a guarantee that you won't be deported for two years and as long as you keep renewing that permit, and as long as you keep being accepted you won't be deported. So you have that sense of safety . . . but having someone decide that you're not worthy of being here even after all your hard work, even after going to school, after paying taxes, and everything. You know, doing what the average American does and being told that you're not worthy of being here or that you don't deserve to be here after all the hard work is scary . . . a man in office or a few people in office have the right to decide.

So, after hearing that, like, you're just scared. Like everything that you have worked for . . . like me, I just thought about my education. I was like, "everything that I have worked for can be gone instantly because someone decides that I'm not worthy of being here or that I'm not American enough to be here even after being here my whole life." And it's scary and it makes you angry because you feel powerless and vulnerable. Like I said, they, once you apply for DACA, they know where you at, where you work, where you go to school, they know that your parents aren't here legally. They know everything about you and they can target you. So if they really wanted to do something, they could come find you and it's scary to know that everything can go away. Everything that you worked so hard for can go away in a matter of minutes because someone decides that you don't belong here anymore.

And that's really scary and my first time actually opening up about being a DACA student was at that rally in Springfield. And like I said, I did it just because I was so tired of people just talking a talk without having information or accurate information about the subject. Like, I would hear people around me talking about it but not really knowing, they were just going with what the news said. Like, what they heard from people around them but within their own circle, with people with their own beliefs. And it was time for them to hear an actual story of a real person going through it. So, when I was asked to do the DACA rally, they explained to me, "only if you're sure." But they made me feel very safe about it, so I decided to go up there and tell my story.

And like I said, I had people message me a lot afterwards and one of those messages was a bad message, but instead most of those messages were "you . . . I switched my stand on the topic because of your story because I was only listening to the news and I didn't have a face to put with the story, but then you told your story so now we know what DACA actually is and what it actually stands for." And a lot of people think that . . . people still think that DACA gives you a path for citizenship or that, you know, you receive, that we receive aid for school or, hmm, welfare benefits, food stamps, health care and all that, but we don't receive any of that. But people still think that, and people don't want to stop thinking that and won't open up their minds to change their point of view, their political point of view. So it keeps going and they keep passing it down.

Laura was open about her immigration status in high school but became more open over time. Laura was frustrated and scared after the announcement of DACA's termination. However, she decided to speak up, to tell her story at a rally because she was tired of the lack of knowledge about DACA exhibited by the people around her. I attended this rally as well. Laura made a heartfelt speech about her personal story and struggles. She was also pleased that she was able to change some minds. Likely, the impact of her story was much stronger than we know.

Abraham attended a retreat where he and other undocumented youth were taught how to become immigrant rights activists, "gladiators," in the words of Lester W. Milbrath.[51] He recalled,

> I remember going to Las Vegas for a retreat to learn about DACA and undocumented people. It was a big group. And we did a rally/march on a super busy Las Vegas intersection. I believe we were there for thirty minutes, one hour. We did that to learn how to express our voices and have our voices heard in a peaceful way.

When asked to expand on this experience, Abraham clarified that the retreat also taught DREAMers about their rights, especially the rights a person has if detained while protesting without documents. He explained,

> [I] remember learning about the rules/laws when you are a DREAMer or even when you get detained and don't have anything to protect you (paperwork). They [the trainers] would always tell us, "Do not sign anything without you being able to understand it." I don't remember if she [the trainer] was a lawyer or an actual police officer but it was this older lady that actually was giving us a lot of information about what to do or say if we ever get detained without paperwork. It was something really interesting because I got to also meet different people from different backgrounds and it's just crazy how many of us are on the same boat and the least people you expect do want to help and want the best for us.

The retreat Abraham attended taught DREAMers how to advocate for themselves through peaceful protest while providing them training about their rights, a bootcamp of sorts. The rally was peaceful, but because it blocked a busy intersection in Las Vegas, protesters were likely at risk of being arrested. Abraham then expanded on this action:

> One thing I do remember is we blocked an intersection when we did a peaceful protest. We had shirts on that said "DREAMers" or "DACA," I believe, and posters. I honestly can't remember what we were chanting but it was like a little saying or a song, I can't remember exactly. But while we were doing that it was exciting and scary at the same time because you never know what can happen even if it's a peaceful protest. But it was over fifty of us, from adults to teenagers. I remember I was still in high school when I went to that. Also, while we were out there blocking the street some people actually got out of their cars and were on our side and that felt amazing, knowing some people do have our backs and want the best for us.

The protest included t-shirts, signs, and chanting. Abraham was moved by the support received from passersby.

Cynthia and Marcos grew up in the Chicago area and participated in rallies and demonstrations in the area related to DACA, the DREAM Act, and immigration reform. Cynthia participated in a demonstration when DACA first came about. According to her, on this occasion, "we all reunified at Navy Pier." On August 16, 2012, during the "DREAM Relief Day," the Illinois Coalition for Immigrant and Refugee Rights went to Navy Pier to do intakes for young immigrants who qualified for DACA.[52] Some politicians attended the event, including Senator Durbin, one of the original co-sponsors of the DREAM Act. "As the crowd kept growing—the immigrant advocacy group put the final estimate at 13,000—organizers began turning people away, explaining that they were able to help only about 7,500 people and process no more than 1,500 applications," an article in the *Chicago Tribune* explained.[53] I wish I had asked Cynthia if she was able to fill out her application on this historic day.

Everyday Resistance Practices

The fear of deportation among undocumented immigrants is well established in social science literature.[54] The Trump administration's heightened immigration enforcement led some at the Southern Poverty Law Center to speak of the "Trump Effect."[55] While interior deportations continued to rise and the future of DACA was unknown during the Trump administration, the deportation threat and the fear associated with it increased. Fear of deportation naturally induces immigrants to conceal their immigration status, including from institutions that would benefit from their trust, such as schools.[56] It also affects the relationship between immigrants and government agencies, such as the police.[57]

Fear of deportation played a major role in precluding certain immigrants from participating in social and political activities.[58] Fear, however, does not prevent involvement in everyday resistance practices.[59] Sometimes resistance is active, even violent, but other times it manifests itself as passive noncompliance, subtle sabotage, evasion, and deception.[60] These daily resistance practices are typically more hidden or disguised, individual, and not politically articulated.[61] "Where institutionalized politics is formal, overt, concerned with systematic, de jure change, everyday resistance is informal, often covert, and concerned largely with immediate, de facto gains."[62] Everyday resistance to slavery in the American South, for example, could only succeed behind the mask of public compliance.[63]

Several types of participation, I argue, fall within passive resistance, including partaking in research or panels, participating in NGOs helping DACA or undocumented immigrants, donating money to an organization supporting DREAMers, helping other immigrants, and discussing issues related to immigration with coworkers. Six of my subjects participated in what I classify as daily forms of resistance (figure 7.4). I also argue that driving without a license, which was common among my participants before Illinois allowed undocumented persons to get driver's licenses on July 1, 2014,[64] can be seen as a form of daily resistance, of passive noncompliance with state immigration policies.

During the 2010s, panels featuring undocumented students sharing their experiences became common in higher education institutions across the United States.[65] These panels were used by schools such as Arizona State University to serve a triple purpose: creating awareness about the hardships facing undocumented immigrants, improving attitudes toward them, and improving educational success of undocumented students by mobilizing the campus community and the resources available to them.[66] Several of my interviewees participated in this type of panel. I met Daniel, a Chinese American DACA recipient, during one such presentation at the 2018 Sharing the Dream Conference hosted by the Illinois Association for College Admission Counseling. On this occasion, a group of six DACA recipients or undocumented students shared their experiences, and the audience asked them questions and offered support and resources. Daniel also participated in this type of panel both in high school and college.

Zoe also participated in panels featuring undocumented students at the community college she attended. She told me,

> Especially like when I was at the community college, I met younger kids who are undocumented, so, you know, I'm definitely older and, you know, we're talking about middle school and even elementary. And when I was working there as a student worker, we would do tours and sometimes, I would do student panels and talk about me being undocumented and how that changed up since I went to school. I still remember the faces of these kids that pretty much told me, "Whoa, I didn't know I could go to school. I didn't know I could have a future." So, to me it's like, just because right now in this moment we don't know what's really going to happen, that kind of thing, I don't want to give up. So I think right now I am just trying to be strong. So maybe that's one of the things that's made me grow. This whole experience made me not want to give up, you know, just keep fighting.

Zoe provided great insight into the panels of undocumented students she participated in. Importantly, these panels were also eye-opening for other undocumented students who did not know they could attend college and "have a future." In addition, they educated the campus community on the plight of undocumented students.

Ernesto did not think of himself as an activist: He never participated in a group representing DREAMers or in a rally or protest. He nonetheless participated in panels featuring undocumented students. Ernesto explained,

> I have done panels at the university that I go to where I sat down at a sociology class with three other students that were part of Dream Action

at NIU. We tried to tell them our . . . I was not trying to get sympathy from these people. I was just explaining to them that I came here when I was five, [that] there's no process for me to take to [get papers] . . . When they ask, "Why don't you become legal?" But it's not that simple, and it is something that they don't understand. And it is something that they don't want to understand. They take the simple rhetoric that the president has put out that we are all "this kind of people." That we're rapists and all that stuff.

Ernesto clearly had a role in educating the campus community about his life as an undocumented student. Even though he tried to be factual about his situation, he still struggled with the widespread stereotypes disseminated by Donald Trump since the announcement of his presidential campaign. The audience could not understand the intricacies of becoming documented in the United States. Despite his participation in such panels, Ernesto did not consider himself an activist. At a later point, he explicitly stated, "I participated in panels of undocumented students in classes; I was open about my status but I'm not an activist."

Ernesto seemed to be making a distinction between participation in traditional activities, such as groups or protests, and taking part in a panel where students shared their experiences as undocumented individuals. According to Ernesto, participation in a panel did not constitute a traditional form of activism. I believe with Ernesto that participation in panels can be considered as everyday resistance, a practice more disguised, individual, and not politically articulated that can create awareness about the situation of undocumented students on college campuses.[67]

Other interviewees expressed similar views about their participation. Nathaniel was not open about his immigration status in high school but became open about it after that. He also participated in a nonprofit that supported undocumented students. Nathaniel mentioned, "I was part of an organization called CASA that helped undocumented high school students further their education by helping them obtain grants and fundraising money."

Likewise, Estela supported United We Dream, a nonprofit advocacy organization at the forefront of the DREAMers movement dedicated to "ensuring that people who are, have been, or will be directly impacted by the immigrant experience are at the forefront of decision-making."[68] Even though Estela was not open about her immigration status during her high school years or later, she followed United We Dream and donated money to them. I argue that this discreet work with nonprofit organizations is another practice of daily resistance.[69]

Other interviewees chose even more private ways to resist. Brianna, Alondra, Hugo, and Mary never disclosed their immigration status during their high school years, and Alondra and Mary continued to conceal their immigration status past high school. Despite their private nature, these youth found ways of quietly advocating for DREAMers and undocumented persons. Brianna, for example, participated in research projects to help DREAMers. Likely, this was the reason most interviewees agreed to answer my questions: to get their voices heard and potentially influence policy. Alondra and Hugo described finding "other" ways to advocate for and help DREAMers which did not involve participation in groups of DREAMers or marches. In turn, Mary reported having discussions with her coworkers about her situation and that of DREAMers in general. Overall, these courageous youth, afraid to be open about their immigration status, found meaningful ways to fight for change.

Driving without a License

Driving without a license can be considered a form of resistance practice. Although the situation is different, I associate these practices with those of slaves' engagement in petty theft or work for an employer without their master's permission, as James C. Scott discusses in his work.[70] Fear does not impede participation in everyday resistance practices.[71] Often, resistance takes the form of passive noncompliance, subtle sabotage, evasion, and deception.[72] Further, for these undocumented youth, driving without a license to go about their daily lives can be considered a practice of daily resistance, of passive noncompliance with Illinois immigration policies, which until July 1, 2014, precluded undocumented individuals from having a driver's license.[73] Interviewees in my sample drove to attend school, go to work, and give rides to siblings and other family members.

Youth are the most surveilled group of Americans.[74] Additionally, minority youth frequently live in neighborhoods disproportionately targeted for proactive policing.[75] Black distrust of the police is well documented.[76] Although the research on Latino/a trust in police is less consistent, immigration status has been a reliable predictor of distrust in police.[77] Understandably, undocumented immigrants who fear deportation tend to be less trusting of the police. Moreover, a recent study found that both legal status and local context influenced trust in the police.[78] Importantly, this study, which included the city of Chicago, addressed the context of reception, the stance of the host government and of employers, the characteristics of preexisting ethnic communities, and discrimination by the host society.[79] Of particular interest in this case is the stance of local government with respect to immigration policies. Specifically, the above-mentioned study showed that in cities more welcoming of immigrants, like Chicago, immigrants exhibited higher levels of trust in the police.[80]

A trend toward devolution of immigration responsibilities to local levels has characterized immigration policy in recent years.[81] This trend has been termed immigration federalism.[82] Between 2005 and 2011, for instance, as many as 370 local governments proposed or implemented policies addressing issues related to undocumented immigration in their communities.[83] In 2017, legislators across the country considered passing a total of 206 immigration bills, a 110 percent increase from the previous year.[84] These policies cover different topics, including education, identification, employment, health, voting, and law enforcement. In 2010, for instance, the state of Arizona passed Senate Bill 1070 and House Bill 2162, partly aimed to require law enforcement officers to determine the immigration status of individuals during lawful stops.[85] The 1996 Illegal Immigration Reform and Immigrants Responsibility Act (IIRIRA) authorized the devolution of immigration policy enforcement.[86] In addition, some local policies regarding immigration are grassroots responses to the presence of immigrants.[87]

The Illinois TRUST Act, which took effect on August 28, 2017, prohibits state and local law enforcement in Illinois from participating in federal immigration enforcement.[88] This law precludes local law enforcement in Illinois from detaining an individual solely based on an immigration arrest warrant, which is a request to detain issued by an immigration agent and is not ordered by a judge.[89] Before 2014, when my interviewees drove without licenses, however, state and local police were able to cooperate with federal immigration authorities, and it is understandable that they feared being deported. Further, this fear would have been justified until President Obama, on November 20, 2014, called for an end to a program called Secure Communities, which allowed local authorities to cooperate with ICE by detaining and deporting immigrants stopped for minor offenses like traffic violations.[90] Under the new rules, local police in some states were no longer asked to routinely detain immigrants without papers when they are stopped for traffic violations.[91]

Driving without a License: My Sample

Participants were asked about their experiences interacting with law enforcement. This question was added to the questionnaire by one of my research assistants, Victor, who was a former DACA recipient and thought such interactions, especially those when driving without a license, had been life-changing. I wish I had the number of students who actually drove without a license. However, the Institutional Review Board that had to approve my research refused to let me ask questions that could "incriminate" the interviewees, so I am able to include only those subjects who volunteered such information. This section reviews the experiences my interviewees had with police and law enforcement while driving without a license. It shows that, despite fear of the police, many undocumented youths in my sample drove without a license before they had DACA and resisted local immigration policies that barred them from driving.

Driving without a License

An important number of my interviewees drove before they had a license. Zoe was one of them. She reported,

I did drive without a license for a while. Hmm, and I was scared. I think even until this day driving with a license, I'm still terrified, I get into panic mode. I look at those people in power and I think it goes to that identity thing. None of them can relate to me when they don't share my culture, share my traditions, even having a family who are immigrants. They can't relate and I think these are the people making all the rules for us.

Zoe never fully overcame the fear of getting caught driving without a license. The literature discusses the extent to which undocumented immigrants fear police because of potential deportation or because of experiences with the police.[92] Zoe's panic is likely partly justified because of fear of falling into the detention-deportation pipeline, but she may have also been fearful of police practices coming from persons who do not share her culture, her traditions, or immigrant background, and who cannot "relate" to her. Despite her fears, Zoe may have had no other option than to resist state immigration policies that precluded her from driving.[93]

Mary had a terrifying experience with police while she was arrested for driving without a license. She recounted,

So, I actually, when I was seventeen and I was actually going to school, I got pulled over and instead of just getting a ticket, you know, like any other person legal here, I was actually taken to the police station and left there until someone came and picked me up. So my brother had to go and pay $100 to get me out. Then I had to go to court and pay the actual ticket. So I think that that was . . . I already knew that I was undocumented but that day was kind of like, "Oh whoa!" I really don't have the legal status to be here, that kind of thing. It was definitely an eye opener.

Mary's experience of being arrested for driving without a license made her more aware of her status in the United States,[94] in particular, of the subordinate relationship undocumented immigrants have with the state that controls them. This situation bears a resemblance to other subordinate relationships Scott addresses,[95] such as those between boss and worker, landlord and tenant, lord and serf, and master and slave. Despite this subordination, Mary likely resisted her subordinate relationship with the state and its immigration policies by driving without a license.

Abraham encountered a police officer who was somewhat understanding when he was stopped for driving without a license, but he was nonetheless upset. He told me,

> The cop was nice, you know? He's like, "I know this whole situation with DACA, you guys have to wait and stuff like that." My friend, who is from here was with me and the cop was like, "Why isn't he driving if he has a license?" I was like, "I don't know, I didn't really think about it." And he was like, "I'll let you go this time but don't be driving without your driver's license. I understand you guys are suffering because you can't do anything, but you also have to follow the rules."
>
> I didn't want to answer him either. I was like, "Yes, sir. I understand." But in my mind, I was like, "I know, I understand I have to follow the rules, but they want us to have a good record, have a job or go to school so that we can be able to apply to DACA, you know? But how do you guys want us to get from school, you know? If we don't have someone available to drive us to school or work every day." So, that was my frustration when I was waiting to get my DACA at the beginning.

Abraham was lucky the police officer let him go. Despite expressing some understanding about DACA beneficiaries and their plight, the officer nonetheless reaffirmed the platitude to respect the law of the land. The law and the idea of legality legitimize the borders of the imagined community of the nation.[96] As Kitty Calavita says about Spain, immigration laws and policies have one conspicuous effect: Instead of controlling immigration they control the immigrant.[97] Restrictive immigration policies fail to deter immigrants from arriving in the country, but they control them once they have arrived.

Daniel also drove without a license until he had DACA, but his experiences with the police were positive. He compared his situation with that of Latino/as and Blacks and said,

> I think because my ethnicity is Asian, Chinese mostly, I think that we deal with police a lot easier. Let's just say that it is easier for me to deal

with police than a Black person or a Hispanic person. Police were always nice to me. They were never a huge dick to me. I remember getting pulled over . . . the first time I got pulled over, I got really nervous. It was after I got my license, so I was able to drive. The third time I got pulled over, I got very nervous and I kind of already admitted that I was speeding. So that was my fault. By then I already knew how to deal with the police. He gave me a ticket but any time after that the police was nice to me.

Daniel was never pulled over when driving without a license, and his experience was positive when he was pulled over after having a license. Unlike previous research showing that some Asian undocumented students share White supremacists' ideas,[98] Daniel exhibited a high awareness and empathy with other non-White undocumented persons and their less positive experiences with the police.

Estela's description of her encounter with police is illustrative of this difference. Estela was in a car accident after she had a valid driver's license, but the police treated her poorly and assumed she had no license. She recounted the incident:

I got into a car accident in a suburb where I had heard people that they were [racial] profiling and stuff and, at the time, I had already my driver's license, but I was still scared. One of the things that I do remember from that incident is that the police officer called and said, "Oh, we have an accident." And he was like, "I'm assuming, this is a no driver's license." And I kept . . . like, "No, I have a driver's license." And he wouldn't speak to me, that was very scary. And finally, I called my boyfriend's parents, they are American. They came and it was . . . it felt terrible. They actually spoke directly just to my boyfriend's parents, but they wouldn't speak to me. And then even they noticed it and that was my only experience with the police once I had a license, and I was still scared. And it was just a car accident.

Research shows that undocumented immigrants resent being treated with suspicion or contempt if they feel there is no basis for doing so.[99] Estela had a driver's license when she had the car accident. The police, however, assumed she had no driver's license and acted as if Estela was not even there, thus dehumanizing her.[100] Her experience contrasts sharply with Daniel's, described above.

Not Driving without a License

Some participants decided not to defy state law and refrained from driving without a license. Andrés feared deportation. He explained,

> My mom always said, "keep your nose clean," basically. "Don't do anything stupid, I don't ever want to see you in handcuffs." I never want to see my mom cry, so I've always been scared to get caught up in different kinds of things. So, I was just like, "Alright, lay your options. What are you going to do? Are you going to be drinking underage or are you going to keep studying? Make your mom cry and see you in handcuffs?" So, I don't want to see my mom cry because she has sacrificed a lot. So I'm like, "I'm just going to keep going, keep studying." But other than that, my parents fear the government, they fear the police and things like that . . . They feel like they would get deported right away if they get a speeding ticket. So, my mom always says, "Keep your nose clean."

For undocumented Latino/a populations, fear of deportation is a daily experience.[101] For these populations, any contact with government authorities produces fear of entering the arrest-to-deportation pipeline.[102] Fear of deportation creates, in the best case, ambivalent attitudes toward the police, and in the worst, intense fear.[103] Understandably, Andrés's parents recommended he stay out of trouble. Thus, Andrés followed the rules.

Like Andrés, Liz decided not to risk driving without a license because she feared police brutality and criminalization. She explained,

> I see videos of police brutality and police asking us for citizenship or they're just incriminating people just based on how they look. I have this image in my head of how police can be intimidating, but when I do encounter police like walking on the street, I know that I haven't done anything wrong so what do I have this fear with me . . . honestly, I have not experienced anything with the police. I've been good, I have a good

record, but it is just that feeling of fear that they have this power over me, but . . . when I really I haven't done anything. It's just fear for no reason.

My findings corroborate previous research showing that undocumented populations' fear of the police is not just related to the fear of deportation, but also for the police's reputation of being overly punitive.[104] For different reasons than Andrés, Liz also decided not to drive without a license.

Polish Interviewees: Attitudes toward Revealing Status and Participation

Two of my Polish interviewees, Peter and Mateusz, were private about their immigration status (I have no information for Ali, the third). At first, Polish subjects were less likely to reveal their status in high school than my non-White interviewees (For non-White interviewees' attitudes, see figure 7.3). Mateusz later changed his mind about revealing his immigration status. He said,

> I was always afraid of people judging me. So yeah, so I didn't, I didn't talk about it openly. For a long time. Even after I graduated college, I moved to DC. And I haven't really been talking about it. But now that I'm, now as I've gotten older, from twenty-six, and so I started to open up about it. So like I said, you know, I'm in the MBA program here at the University of Maryland. And here, I've been very open about it with everybody. So I, I always just get it out there and say it right away. It's sort of like a completely new approach for me where it's sort of no big deal. And it once again, it's not, it's not really an issue because I think people forget, when they don't really, it's not something that they think about often when they have a conversation with me since I'm so, I think, pretty well assimilated. But yeah, so I was definitely very closed about it and very embarrassed about it for a long time. Now I'm open about it.

Mateusz's attitude toward revealing his status corroborates previous findings that the college experience shapes attitudes about their immigration status among undocumented students.[105] More specifically, students seem to move away from emotions such as shock, shame, embarrassment, and fear of deportation that initially lead them employ a

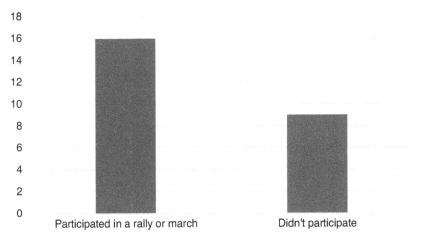

Figure 7.3. Participation in Marches or Rallies

variety of stigma management methods to keep their status secret while accepting its negative societal evaluation.[106] The college experience, however, facilitates the stigma resistance of redefining their identities, making them consider the denial of their full participation in society as an injustice, engaging in social activism, and publicly embracing an undocumented social identity.[107]

Neither of the two Polish interviewees who responded to the questions related to participation were actively involved in open forms of participation. As these findings show, at least two-thirds of my Polish interviewees abstained from participating in groups of DREAMers, marches, or other social or political activities, contrasting with the rates of participation among my non-White interviewees. This finding may corroborate previous research that Polish immigrants tend to participate in informal activities, such as helping neighbors, but not in formal ones, like membership or voluntarism in NGOs.[108]

Finally, neither Mateusz nor Ali drove without a license. It seems they took their parents' advice to "keep their noses clean" very seriously. Ali explained,

Yeah so, especially when we were younger, for my brother and I, my parents were always kind of scared for us, like, "Listen, you guys aren't like your friends. You have to be extra careful, right? Because you're

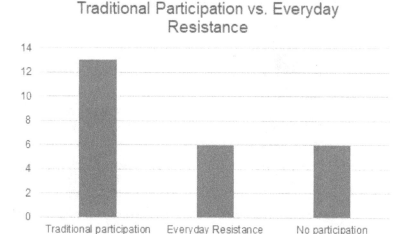

Figure 7.4. Traditional Participation vs. Everyday Resistance

undocumented or you're under this program, or you cannot get into any trouble." . . . They always wanted us to be careful. Even with speeding tickets, you know? You get pulled over and you have this extra sense of anxiety, because you never know what they're gonna ask you, how that might impact your application, your status here.

So we wouldn't ever really get in trouble. But I do remember I got pulled over for a traffic violation and started crying immediately. That fear takes you over. We don't feel as comfortable as our peers do. Where it's no big deal. Right? Every little thing was a big deal coming across any interaction with law enforcement.

Like some of the non-White participants, Polish students received advice from their parents to stay out of trouble. But unlike their non-White peers, my Polish participants did not drive without a license. Both groups of interviewees, however, seemed to share the fear of the police.[109]

Conclusion

This chapter reviewed the ways in which the undocumented youth in this study fought to get their voices heard despite adversity and the ups and downs in their lives. Active and engaged members of society are crucial in fostering effective and responsive government.[110] The undocumented youth movement has been active in advocating for their rights.[111] Overall, my non-White interviewees' behaviors were consistent with this finding: They were open about their immigration status, and participated more in different activities, including passive resistance practices such as driving without a license. Although the number of Polish interviewees was small, my findings suggest that this group seems to be more closed off about their status and less likely to participate in both traditional and passive resistance practices.[112] Further research among White undocumented populations would be useful to determine if this is typical.

This research corroborated previous findings that as students enter higher education, they are more likely to reveal their immigration status.[113] By the time they had finished high school, most of the non-White students and two of the Polish ones in my sample were comfortable revealing their immigration status. Gaining "visibility" has different advantages, including providing an opportunity for educational and other institutions to serve their needs, and being able to identify other persons in the same situation who can share resources and offer support.[114] "Visibility, however, can be a double-edged sword, by making students more vulnerable to be discovered by immigration enforcement agencies and thus enter the arrest-to-deportation pipeline."[115]

Except for the Polish students, my interviewees actively participated in society in different traditional ways, including joining groups representing undocumented students, marches and rallies, and leadership workshops for undocumented students. Further, several of them took leadership positions in support groups for undocumented students, both in high school and college, and "came out" at rallies. Participation in some of these activities also had a positive impact on these undocumented youths' identity and self-esteem.[116]

My non-White interviewees who were private about their immigration status also found ways to participate in everyday resistance practices, including volunteering time to an NGO that supported undocumented students, helping other immigrants, discussing immigration issues with coworkers, and participating in panels of undocumented students in college.[117] The active participation of my interviewees in informal

202 | THE FIGHT IS NOT OVER

activities demonstrates that research that narrowly defines participation will miss important ways in which undocumented youths contribute to their high schools, colleges, and communities.

Finally, undocumented youth also chose to drive without a license, providing yet another example of their active stance in society. Immigration laws and policies, instead of controlling immigration, control the immigrant.[118] Restrictive immigration policies fail to deter immigrants from arriving in the country, but they control them once in the country. However, undocumented immigrants are not merely passive subordinates of modern states, but find ways to resist federal and state immigration laws.[119]

Conclusion

DACA's Status and Prospects for Solutions

At the time of writing, almost twelve years after DACA was first approved, its fate remained unclear. On August 30, 2022, the Biden administration issued a Deferred Action for Childhood Arrivals rule with the intent of preserving and fortifying DACA that was to go into effect on October 31, 2022. This regulation would rescind the Napolitano memo from June 15, 2012, that created DACA, but leave most of the requirements to obtain DACA unchanged.[1] Currently, DACA recipients can continue to submit renewal requests and USCIS (US Citizenship and Immigration Services) will continue to adjudicate DACA renewals per the terms of the Napolitano memo. USCIS will not grant any initial DACA requests or requests from persons whose DACA has been expired for more than one year.[2] Governors of several Republican-controlled states, including Texas, have challenged this new memo in the courts.[3] DACA recipients and eligible individuals will continue to be subject to the ups and downs of shifting legal contexts. In its latest upset, a court in Texas decided that the Biden administration's Final Rule, which attempted to give DACA recipients a firmer legal standing, was unlawful.[4]

As a way of confronting President Joe Biden over his border policies, Texas Governor Greg Abbott began sending willing asylum-seeking migrants to Washington, DC, in April 2022.[5] Later, he expanded his busing operation to include New York City and Chicago.[6] The busing of migrants is part of Operation Lone Star, launched by Governor Abbott in March 2021.[7] Operation Lone Star is a nearly $4 billion initiative that features a multifront effort of Department of Public Safety state troopers and Texas National Guard soldiers at the border in addition to the US Customs and Border Patrol agents already assigned to the area.[8] The operation also includes the use of drones, helicopters, and patrol cars.[9]

While border apprehensions are at a record high, the majority of Americans see the situation at the border as an "invasion."[10] The Border Patrol has apprehended migrants more than 1.8 million times since October 2021, most of whom continue to be expelled under Title 42, a health order that has been implemented since the pandemic.[11] Republicans are more likely to characterize the situation at the border as an invasion. They are also likely to endorse the conspiracy theory called "replacement theory," the false belief that Jews or elites are deliberately replacing White Americans with immigrants and people of color.[12] Within this climate, Congress's inability to pass immigration reform should come as no surprise. At the same time, former President Trump has once again put immigration at the center of his 2024 presidential campaign, promising sweeping raids, mass detention camps, and deportations.[13] In this climate, the fate of DACA recipients and undocumented youth remains uncertain.

The Crossing: Leaving Countries of Origin

This book has argued that DACA recipients follow a *roller-coaster* pattern in their incorporation into US society. DACA recipients grow up unaware of their lack of papers and/or its implications. Thanks to *Plyler v. Doe*, they enjoy a certain level of inclusion in schools, although as we have seen, this inclusion was less than perfect, especially for non-White DACA recipients. Upon coming of age, DACA recipients realize the obstacles and limitations they face because of their lack of papers. Later, DACA gives them protection from deportation and a work permit, but after 2017, the security afforded by these protections is almost nonexistent. Memos, court decisions, and rules have combined to create a climate of uncertainty that, as this book has shown, has had harmful effects on the lives of DREAMers. This book set out to answer the question, What are the consequences of the United States' delaying deportation but also not delivering full integration into American society to a group of undocumented immigrants who arrived in the country as children and are protected by DACA? It also sought to overcome the omission in the traditional research on undocumented youth, which tends to overlook the experiences of White undocumented individuals.[14] In what follows, I offer some concluding remarks. Although my participant sample is small, I hope this research will help to generate new hypotheses and further research.

Overall, I found that the situation of the participants' families prior to coming to the United States was not as bad as I expected and that the decision to migrate was mostly forward-looking; to use a cliché, they were in pursuit of the American dream. The reasons for migration were similar for non-White and Polish interviewees. The American dream is not merely economic. For instance, although one-fourth of my participants reported having moved for economic reasons, another one-fourth moved for reasons that were beyond economic. Also, one- fifth of my interviewees migrated for more personal reasons, to reunite with a relative who was already residing in the United States. This research thus supported the contention that the opportunities for which immigrants migrate involve much more than just jobs and income differentials to include a better future for the children and a more appealing quality of life.[15]

Some families, however, may have reached an extremely low point before migrating due to insecurity. This was the case for the participants from Peru and El Salvador, who stated that they had moved for political reasons such as turmoil and natural disasters.[16] More specifically, the political turmoil followed by insecurity in El Salvador explained the migration of Ana's family to the United States, while Melody's father's political involvement with President Fujimori in Peru led to her family's migration. As a reminder, El Salvador has experienced one of the highest rates of violence in the world and has alarming rates of femicides.[17] Besides political instability and rampant corruption, El Salvador has a serious gang problem. In turn, Peru went through the impeachment of President Fujimori in 2000, and he was removed from power at the end of that year. It is possible that both families had life-threatening experiences before moving to the United States.

Immigration policies and borders are state tools for population demarcation and control.[18] Even though the militarization of the US-Mexico border in recent years has not stopped immigrants from crossing the border without inspection, it has raised the economic and human cost of crossing it.[19] This study's participants' border crossing experiences varied by origin, age, and the time and type of crossing. In contrast to the non-White interviewees, the Polish participants for the most part had non-traumatic crossings. The non-White youth who crossed without inspection through overland travel had the most traumatic experiences, including spending time with coyotes, hiding from the border patrol, accidents, dehydration, and separation from their parents. The ones who came through la Línea by car probably had the second most traumatic experiences, which included lying to authorities, hiding, or both. Finally, the participants who came to the United States with visas and through airports had the best experiences despite some minor problems.

The process of migration can take years and include separation from family members who either move ahead of the family or stay behind in the country of origin. This separation can be temporary or permanent.[20] Numerous participants, non-White and Polish alike, experienced painful family separation. This separation sometimes led to a catch-22 situation in which reunion with parents also meant losing contact with grandparents or other caretakers. For instance, some participants stayed in their home country with grandparents when the parents moved to the United States. When they finally reunited with their parents in the United States, my participants were hurt by the separation from their grandparents. Overall, the migration experience of my interviewees was plagued by trauma, pain, and loss.

Incorporation into Schools

Schools are essential in the cultural incorporation of immigrant youth.[21] This book argues that the process of incorporation of DACA recipients follows a roller-coaster pattern. The arrival and initial interactions in schools were excellent for some and difficult for others. For one, the process of language acquisition was challenging for most of my participants. Sometimes, the process of language acquisition was intertwined with the process of social incorporation, and students who struggled to learn the language also struggled to make friends. Overall, however, compared with later periods, thanks to *Plyler v. Doe*, DACA recipients found spaces of belonging in schools.

Friendships proved vital to the incorporation of immigrant youth in the United States.[22] This study followed Berry's classification of the paths to acculturation as *assimilation, integration, separation,* and *marginalization*.[23] Most participants chose the pathway of separation, followed by integration, marginalization, and assimilation.[24] Importantly, none of the Polish interviewees followed the marginalization path. Further research should be conducted on the integration of White undocumented youth in schools. Overall, this study provided support for the contention that schools, despite their vital role in the socialization of first-generation immigrants, often fall short of their promise to engender a sense of belonging and membership for undocumented students.[25]

Experiences with teachers and mentors likely impacted who children are, what they believe of themselves, how they think, and how they learn.[26] Most DACA recipients thought their teachers were supportive and helpful, although the experiences of my non-White participants differed sharply from Polish interviewee Ali's. She was the participant who received the most support from her teachers, who encouraged other schoolchildren make friends with her. Finally, participants appreciated having teachers who matched their gender and ethnic identity. Even one of my Polish interviewees noted that having an immigrant-background teacher aided his adaptation. These role models possibly improved their academic performance[27] and helped them develop a sense of gender and ethnic pride.[28]

Fewer than one-third of my participants had bad experiences with their teachers. Mirroring a national trend, some teachers were unprepared to serve the linguistically and ethnically diverse students enrolled in their school.[29] In these cases, participants described their experiences as odd and uncomfortable. Some participants experienced outright mistreatment and discrimination, for example including librarians and teachers enforcing English-only policies and teachers becoming impatient and frustrated with the children who were English learners. These experiences likely affected the youths' mental health, self-esteem, engagement, and academic performance.[30] Importantly, none of my Polish interviewees reported these experiences. Although more research should be conducted, White undocumented youth seem to have an easier time incorporating into American society.[31]

The experience with counselors is pivotal because it marks the transition from partial inclusion to partial exclusion in late adolescence.

Experiences with counselors were overwhelmingly unsatisfactory (70%); these important school professionals failed to provide support and information to guide students through their path to college due to lack of information, resources, and sometimes intent to help. This finding is very concerning in a state that has been providing in-state tuition to undocumented students since 2003 and has a state DREAM Act that is supposed to guarantee that school counselors are trained to serve undocumented students.[32] Thirty percent of the counselors fulfilled their role of providing academic advice, encouragement, and guidance for college access. Due to lack of the legally mandated training and preparation, some counselors had to search for information and resources to assist the undocumented youth.[33] It is worth mentioning, again, that Polish interviewees did not report horrific experiences with their guidance counselors.

The "Discovery"

Compared to previous research, my participants found out they were undocumented at a younger age and most of them always knew they were undocumented.[34] However, most understood the implications of their illegality only during their late adolescence.[35] DACA recipients hit a low point when finding out they were undocumented and/or understanding its implications during their adolescence. The literature argues that as youth become aware of their immigration status and its consequences, they enter a space of liminality.[36] My findings, however, suggest that they enter a space of exclusion and outsiderness, similar to that experienced by their undocumented parents.[37] Further research should be conducted on the experience of undocumented youth when they discover they are undocumented.

My respondents felt the practical implications of their undocumented status when they experienced blocked access to expected rites of passage, such as getting a driver's license, applying for college, working, and planning school activities. Importantly, the majority of my participants reported experiencing a major psychological impact when discovering their undocumented status or becoming aware of its implications.[38] Participants reported feelings of confusion, distress, discouragement, frustration, insecurity, stress, and anxiety. The discovery of their status made some participants question their identity and sense of belonging. In the most extreme case, the discovery of his immigration status made a participant feel like he was nothing.

DACA

DACA, which gave its recipients relief from deportation and a work permit, was neither a perfect nor a permanent solution, but in comparison with the previous stage, when my participants discovered they were undocumented and/or understood its implications, DACA represented a high point in their lives. Receiving DACA had a practical and psychological impact on my interviewees, eliminated or reduced their fear of police and law enforcement agents, and influenced their identity and sense of belonging.

Every one of my interviewees appreciated DACA's practical advantages, including the ability to obtain driver's licenses, find jobs, and continue their education. Further, DACA impacted interviewees' socioeconomic incorporation into US society.[39] DACA allowed them to get better paying jobs, sometimes with benefits, or jobs in their professional areas of specialization.[40] DACA allowed many participants to afford higher education and to access professions requiring licensing.[41] Finally, DACA allowed some participants to move from community colleges to four-year institutions.[42]

DACA's benefits made participants feel excited, happy, and hopeful.[43] DACA even motivated several students who had lost motivation after discovering they were undocumented, inspiring them to study and work hard, and to continue their education. Among my participants, DACA seems to have increased school attendance, graduation rates, and college attendance.[44] Research shows DACA increases the sense of belonging among its beneficiaries.[45] DACA influenced identity and sense of belonging for several participants, helping them feel normal, like everyone else, and part of American society.

Much has been written about the restrictions and limitations associated with DACA, including its temporariness, absence of a path to citizenship, and lack of access to federal financial aid (FAFSA).[46] My participants cited many of the limitations of DACA discussed in the literature, including the lack of a path to citizenship[47] and access to FAFSA,[48] the restrictions on travel,[49] and the absence of opportunities for the legalization of these youths' parents.[50]

End of DACA

DACA's rescission announcement during the Trump administration, subsequent court cases, and constant changes highly impacted my participants and represented a low point on the roller coaster. Participants discussed the negative emotions triggered by the announcement, including fear, frustration, anxiety, a sense of defeat and devastation, and hopelessness. Other participants addressed the decreased college, work, and travel opportunities they would face after the termination of DACA, their sense of wasted effort, and a diminished sense of belonging in American society. However, others told stories of resilience and determination to keep fighting.

Although my sample of Polish interviewees was small (N=3), they seemed less impacted by the announcement of the termination of DACA, but still discussed many of the themes addressed by the non-White interviewees, including the lack of opportunities and the decreased sense of belonging in American society. Polish participants were more likely to get their papers through marriage. In fact, whereas one non-White respondent was able to get his residency (green card) through marriage, two of three Polish interviewees were able to do the same thing. Segmented patterns of intermarriage based on country of origin and skin color observed among immigrants in general seem to be true for DACA recipients as well.[51] Further research should be conducted on the intermarriage rates of documented-undocumented individuals.

In general, the themes recorded about the termination of DACA mirrored the themes subjects reported about their initial realization of their lack of documents or its implications. The predominant emotion discussed was fear. Some participants felt frustrated, anxious, and defeated. Moreover, several of them explicitly referred to having the same emotions they had before DACA, emotions that they had managed to overcome. Several interviewees discussed a diminished sense of belonging and an increased feeling of outsiderness in American society.[52]

Interestingly, when making the case for the right to inclusion, some participants turned to the DREAMer ID and referred to the contributions DACA recipients are making to American society.[53] Despite adversity, several participants showed resilience and determination to overcome the obstacles created by potential termination of DACA and to keep fighting.[54] Some participants considered different options, including working with different papers, going back to their countries of origin, and getting married.

The Fight Is Not Over

Undocumented youth in this study fought to get their voices heard despite adversity and the ups and downs in their lives. Overall, my non-White interviewees' behaviors were consistently active in society:[55] They were open about their immigration status and participated more in different activities, including passive resistance practices such as driving without a license. Although my sample of Polish interviewees was small, my findings indicate this group is more closed off about their immigration status and less likely to participate in traditional forms of participation as well as passive resistance practices.[56] It also speaks to the invisibility of non-Latino/a DACA recipients.[57] Further research is needed regarding the social participation of White undocumented youth.

DACA recipients actively participated in society in different traditional ways, including in groups representing undocumented students, marches and rallies, and workshops for undocumented students, and some of them took on leadership positions. Those who were private about their immigration status also found ways to participate in everyday resistance practices, including volunteering time to an NGO that supported undocumented students, helping other immigrants, discussing immigration issues with coworkers, and participating in panels of undocumented students in college. Research that narrowly defines participation will miss important ways in which undocumented youth contribute to their schools, colleges, and communities.

Many undocumented youths chose to drive without a license, providing yet another example of their active stance in society and their ability to fight for better incorporation into society. The ability to obtain a driver's license also has civil rights implications for undocumented immigrants.[58] Only seventeen states and the District of Columbia allow undocumented immigrants to obtain driver's licenses, including California, Colorado, Connecticut, Delaware, Hawaii, Illinois, Maryland, Nevada, New Jersey, New Mexico, New York, Oregon, Rhode Island, Utah, Vermont, Virginia, and Washington, provided the applicant provides certain documentation, such as a foreign birth certificate, foreign passport, or consular card and evidence of current residency in the state.[59] The denial of licenses to undocumented immigrants increases fears of arrest and deportation,[60] limits access to jobs and work hours, and increases immigrant vulnerability to exploitation by unscrupulous employers.[61] More states must allow for undocumented immigrants to obtain a permit to drive for their better incorporation in society.

Despite the active stance of DREAMers, the undocumented youth movement has somewhat lost momentum. Except for the yearly rallies across the country on May Day,[62] protests to support a path to citizenship for DREAMers have been qualitatively and quantitatively transformed. For one thing, the undocumented youth movement has changed tactics from direct action to more institutionalized forms of advocacy at the state level, such as the fight for DACA recipients' access to state licenses, or specialized nonprofit organizations that advocate for immigrant rights on the national scene, such as United We Dream.[63] Also, even though a version of the DREAM Act is introduced every year, the pressure from the undocumented youth movement on legislators to pass a path to citizenship for them has decreased. Without Democratic control of the US House of Representatives and Senate, and/or a depolarization of immigration issues, DREAMers will continue to endure the ups and downs that have characterized their process of incorporation into the United States.

ACKNOWLEDGMENTS

I write this book as a Latina immigrant, a researcher, and an immigrant rights activist. When the termination of Deferred Action for Childhood Arrivals (DACA) was announced by the Trump administration in 2017, I worried that DACA recipients, who were given a month to renew their DACA, wouldn't have $495 for the renewal fees. I thus organized a fundraiser and supported ten students in the Central Illinois region to renew their DACA. As part of their application, DACA recipients provided an essay discussing their life stories and explaining how the scholarship would further their life and career goals. The ups and downs facing these youth and their ability to navigate them intrigued me. A 2018 grant at Western Illinois University allowed me to hire a research assistant and pay a small stipend to participants of the research project that became this book.

This project and my 2016 book, *At the Core and in the Margins: Incorporation of Mexican Immigrants in Two Rural Midwestern Communities*, led me to found a nonprofit to support the successful integration of immigrants in Beardstown and Monmouth, Illinois. I chose the name Western Illinois Dreamers to honor the struggles of the young protagonists of this book and the fact that, in the words of one of my participants, "the real dreamers were the parents."

My activism in defense of undocumented students during the Trump administration facilitated the recruitment of participants through different universities across Illinois. Two DACA recipients helped me with the interviews and transcriptions and connected me with other networks of non-college-track DACA recipients. The interviews were very emotional, and about half of my participants cried during the interviews. Many times, I cried with them.

As I wrote this book in 2021–2022, I followed DACA's legal fluctuations. I borrowed the term roller coaster from one of my participants. Every time I finished updating the last court case, a new one came out.

These pages describe the impact of real and perceived legal changes on the lives of DACA recipients. As you read, remember other less fortunate youth who don't even have DACA. And neither do their parents. If you want to take it even further, stay informed, use inclusive language, educate a friend, and advocate for immigration reform so that we can live in a true nation of immigrants.

***

This book benefited from the help of many individuals, to whom I am indebted for their support. I'm thankful for the funding from Western Illinois University's Research Council. I'm grateful to Marcy Olague-Jamaica for her assistance during the interviews, the transcriptions, and the feedback on the chapters. I'm also indebted to Konrad Sowizral for helping find Polish interviewees and assisting during their interviews and with the transcriptions. I'm appreciative of the support by colleagues and students at different Illinois universities who helped me recruit participants. I also benefited from the insightful feedback provided by anonymous reviewers, and the support of my editor, who was always responsive and insightful.

I couldn't have written this book without the support of my husband and family, who put up with long working hours and emotional days during the interviews and writing process. Finally, I'm grateful to the courageous DACA recipients who trusted me and agreed to be interviewed. I hope they will continue to fight and gain a path to citizenship.

APPENDIX

Table A.1. Selected Characteristics in Sample

Pseudonym	Age	Gender	Country	Age at Arrival	Children	Discovery Status	Interview Language	College Degree
Zaide	26	Female	Mexico	3	No	8 years old	English	Yes
Juliana	19	Female	Mexico	4	No	Always knew	English	Yes
Jessica	19	Female	Mexico	3	No	Little by little	English	Yes
Melody	26	Female	Peru	8	Yes	12 years old	English	No
Justice	24	Female	Mexico	7	No	18 years old	English	Yes
Nathaniel	25	Male	Mexico	3	No	15 years old	Spanish	No
Hector	22	Male	Mexico	4	No	High school	English	No
Alondra	20	Female	Mexico	6 months	No	8th grade	Spanish	Yes
Andrea II	29	Female	Mexico	15	Yes	Always knew	Spanish	No
Cynthia	25	Female	Mexico	12	No	Always knew	English	No
Brianna	29	Female	Mexico	1	No	Always knew	English	No
Jacob	20	Male	Mexico	1	No	13 years old	English	No
Carmen	25	Female	Mexico	6	No	n/a	Spanish	No
Lucio	23	Male	Mexico	8	No	Always knew	English	Yes
Laura	20	Female	Mexico	3	No	13 years old	English	Yes
Marcos	28	Male	Mexico	5	No	n/a	English	Yes
Zoe	25	Female	Mexico	3	No	Always knew	English	Yes
Estela	29	Female	Mexico	5	Yes	Always knew	English	No
Angel	23	Male	Mexico	7	No	Always knew	English	Yes

TABLE A.1. (*cont.*)

Pseudonym	Age	Gender	Country	Age at Arrival	Children	Discovery Status	Interview Language	College Degree
Abraham	25	Male	Mexico	7	No	Senior year	English	Yes
Andrea I	22	Female	Guatemala	5	No	Always knew	English	Yes
Ana	24	Female	Mexico	4	No	5th grade	English	Yes
Benita	21	Female	Mexico	4	No	Always knew	English	Yes
Alejandro	24	Male	Mexico	11	Yes	Always knew	Spanish	No
Daniel	23	Male	China	4	No	15 years old	English	Yes
Liz	19	Female	Mexico	1	No	Always knew	English	Yes
Andrés	21	Male	Mexico	2	No	High school	English	Yes
José	23	Male	Salvador	6	No	Always knew	English	Yes
Ernesto	23	Male	Mexico	5	No	Always knew	English	Yes
Mary	31	Female	Mexico	13	No	Always knew	English	Yes
Ignacio	24	Male	Mexico	13	No	Senior year	English	Yes
Julio	22	Male	Mexico	8	No	Senior year	English	Yes
Ismael	30	Male	Mexico	2	No	Always knew	English	Yes
Ali	30	Female	Poland	9	No	Always knew	English	Yes
Peter	27	Male	Poland	11	No	Always knew	English	Yes
Simon	29	Male	Poland	9	No	Always knew	English	Yes

NOTES

INTRODUCTION

1 US Citizenship and Immigration Services, "Humanitarian or Significant Public Benefit Parole for Individuals Outside the United States," October 23, 2023, www .uscis.gov.

2 Migration Policy Institute, "Profile of the Unauthorized Population: United States," accessed December 3, 2023, www.migrationpolicy.org.

3 Julia Albarracín, *At the Core and in the Margins: Incorporation of Mexican Immigrants in Two Rural Midwestern Communities* (East Lansing: Michigan State University Press, 2016).

4 Shoba Sivaprasad Wadhia, *Banned: Immigration Enforcement in the Time of Trump* (New York: New York University Press, 2021); Immigrant Legal Resource Center, "DACA," 2023, www.ilrc.org/daca.

5 David H. K. Nguyen and Zelideh R. Martinez Hoy, "Jim Crowing Plyler v. Doe: The Resegregation of Undocumented Students in American Higher Education through Discriminatory State Tuition and Fee Legislation," *Cleveland State Law Review* 63 (2014): 355.

6 Ed Kilgore, "Will Democrats Accept Border Concessions to Get Ukraine Aid?" *New York Magazine*, November 29, 2023, https://nymag.com.

7 Kilgore, "Will Democrats?"

8 Kilgore, "Will Democrats?"

9 Kara Cebulko, "Documented, Undocumented, and Liminally Legal: Legal Status during the Transition to Adulthood for 1.5-Generation Brazilian Immigrants," *Sociological Quarterly* 55, no. 1 (December 2014): 143–67, https://doi.org/10.1111/tsq .12045; Roberto G. Gonzales, "Learning to Be Illegal: Undocumented Youth and Shifting Legal Contexts in the Transition to Adulthood," *American Sociological Review* 76, no. 4 (August 2011): 602–19, https://doi.org/10.1177/0003122411411901; Julian Jefferies, "The Production of 'Illegal' Subjects in Massachusetts and High School Enrollment for Undocumented Youth," *Latino Studies* 12, no. 1 (2014): 65–87, https://doi.org/10.1057/lst.2014.5; Amanda Morales, Socorro Herrera, and Kevin Murry, "Navigating the Waves of Social and Political Capriciousness: Inspiring Perspectives from DREAM-Eligible Immigrant Students," *Journal of Hispanic Higher Education* 10, no. 3 (July 2009): 266–83, https://doi.org/10.1177 /1538192708330232; Veronica Derricks and Allison Earl, "Information Targeting Increases the Weight of Stigma: Leveraging Relevance Backfires When People Feel

Judged," *Journal of Experimental Social Psychology* 82 (May 2019): 277–93, https://doi.org/http://dx.doi.org/10.1016/j.jesp.2018.12.003; Carola Suárez-Orozco, Hirokazu Yoshikawa, Robert T. Teranishi, and Marcelo M. Suárez-Orozco, "Growing Up in the Shadows: The Developmental Implications of Unauthorized Status," *Harvard Educational Review* 81, no. 3 (2011): 438–73; Rebecca Maria Torres and Melissa Wicks-Asbun, "Undocumented Students' Narratives of Liminal Citizenship: High Aspirations, Exclusion, and 'In-Between' Identities," *Professional Geographer* 66, no. 2 (2013): 195–204, https://doi.org/10.1080/00330124.2012.735936.

10 Roberto G. Gonzales, *Lives in Limbo: Undocumented and Coming of Age in America* (Berkeley: University of California Press, 2015).

11 Jennifer L. Hochschild and John H. Mollenkopf, *Bringing Outsiders In: Transatlantic Perspectives on Immigrant Political Incorporation* (Ithaca, NY: Cornell University Press, 2009).

12 Albarracín, *At the Core and in the Margins*.

13 Elaine Karmack and Christine Stenglein, "How Many Undocumented Immigrants Are in the United States and Who Are They?" Commentary, November 12, 2019, www.brookings.edu.

14 Aristide R. Zolberg, *A Nation by Design: Immigration Policy in the Fashioning of America* (Cambridge, MA: Harvard University Press, 2009), 1.

15 Kitty Calavita, "The Paradoxes of Race, Class, Identity, and 'Passing': Enforcing the Chinese Exclusion Acts, 1882–1910," *Law & Social Inquiry* 25, no. 1 (2000): 1–40.

16 Mae M. Ngai, *Impossible Subjects: Illegal Aliens and the Making of Modern America* (Princeton, NJ: Princeton University Press, 2004).

17 Margaret Sands Orchowski, *The Law That Changed the Face of America: The Immigration and Nationality Act of 1965* (Lanham, MD: Rowman & Littlefield, 2015).

18 Linda K. Ko and Krista M. Pereira, "'It Turned My World Upside Down': Latino Youths' Perspectives on Immigration," *Journal of Adolescent Research* 25, no. 3 (2010): 465–93.

19 Julia Albarracín, *At the Core and in the Margins*.

20 Ko and Pereira, "'It Turned My World Upside Down.'"

21 Immigrant Legal Resource Center, "DACA."

22 Albarracín, *At the Core and in the Margins*; Shoba Sivaprasad Wadhia, *Beyond Deportation: The Role of Prosecutorial Discretion in Immigration Cases* (New York: New York University Press, 2015).

23 Wadhia, *Beyond Deportation*.

24 Michael A. Olivas, *Perchance to DREAM: A Legal and Political History of the DREAM Act and DACA* (New York: New York University Press, 2020).

25 Loan Thi Dao, "Out and Asian: How Undocu/DACAmented Asian Americans and Pacific Islander Youth Navigate Dual Liminality in the Immigrant Rights Movement," *Societies* 7, no. 17 (2017): 1–15, https://doi.org/10.3390/soc7030017; Torres and Wicks-Asbun, "Undocumented Students' Narratives of Liminal Citizenship"; Benjamin J. Roth, "The Double Bind of DACA: Exploring the Legal

Violence of Liminal Status for Undocumented Youth," *Ethnic and Racial Studies* 42, no. 15 (November 18, 2018): 2548–65, https://doi.org/10.1080/01419870.2018 .1540790.

26 Roth, "The Double Bind of DACA."

27 Cecilia Menjívar and L. J. Abrego, "Legal Violence: Immigration Law and the Lives of Central American Immigrants," *American Journal of Sociology* 117, no. 5 (March 2012): 1380–1421, https://doi.org/10.1086/663575; Roth, "The Double Bind of DACA."

28 Wadhia, *Beyond Deportation.*

29 Olivas, *Perchance to DREAM.*

30 Olivas, *Perchance to DREAM.*

31 Olivas, *Perchance to DREAM.*

32 Wadhia, *Beyond Deportation.*

33 Olivas, *Perchance to DREAM.*

34 Wadhia, *Beyond Deportation.*

35 Roberto G. Gonzales, Veronica Terriquez, and Stephen P. Ruszczyk, "Becoming DACAmented: Assessing the Short-Term Benefits of Deferred Action for Childhood Arrivals (DACA)," *American Behavioral Scientist* 58, no. 14 (2014): 1852–72.

36 Kevin R. Johnson, "Lessons about the Future of Immigration Law from the Rise and Fall of DACA," *Immigrant & Nationality Law Review* 39 (2018): 265.

37 Kevin R. Johnson, "Lessons about the Future of Immigration Law from the Rise and Fall of DACA," *UC Davis Law Review* 52 (2018): 343.

38 Jie Zong, Ariel G. Ruiz Soto, Jeanne Batalova, Julia Gelatt, and Randy Capps, "A Profile of Current DACA Recipients by Education, Industry, and Occupation," Migration Policy Institute Fact Sheets, 2017, www.migrationpolicy.org.

39 Nation World News Desk, "Biden Wants to Strengthen Protection for DACA Recipients," *Nation World News*, September 11, 2022; Department of Homeland Security, "Deferred Action for Childhood Arrivals," Referral Registry, August 30, 2022, www.federalregister.gov; Immigrant Legal Resource Center, "DACA."

40 National Immigration Law Center, "Deferred Action for Childhood Arrivals (DACA) Final Rule Summary," 2022, https://www.nilc.org.

41 Nicholas Fandos, "House Votes to Give Millions of Dreamers and Farmworkers a Path to Citizenship," *New York Times*, March 18, 2021, www.nytimes.com.

42 Fandos, "House Votes."

43 Nation World News Desk, "Biden Wants to Strengthen Protection for DACA Recipients."

44 Shoba Sivaprasad Wadhia, *Banned: Immigration Enforcement in the Time of Trump* (New York: New York University Press, 2021).

45 Julie Hirschfeld Davis and Michael D. Shear, *Border Wars: Inside Trump's Assault on Immigration* (New York: Simon & Schuster, 2020).

46 Olivas, *Perchance to DREAM.*

47 Davis and Shear, *Border Wars.*

48 Olivas, *Perchance to DREAM.*

49 Charles Fendrych, "DHS v. Regents of the University of California: Administrative Law Concerns in Repealing DACA," *Duke Journal of Constitutional Law & Public Policy Sidebar* 15 (2020): 99.

50 Fendrych, "DHS v Regents."

51 Department of Homeland Security, "Memorandum on Rescission of Deferred Action For Childhood Arrivals (DACA)," September 5, 2017, www.dhs.gov.

52 Wadhia, *Banned.*

53 Wadhia, *Banned.*

54 National Immigration Law Center, "Litigation Related to Deferred Action for Childhood Arrivals (DACA)," October 21, 2021, www.nilc.org.

55 Wadhia, *Banned.*

56 Wadhia, *Banned.*

57 Olivas, *Perchance to DREAM.*

58 Olivas, *Perchance to DREAM.*

59 Olivas, *Perchance to DREAM.*

60 Brian Wolfman, "The DACA Decision: Department of Homeland Security v. Regents of the University of California and Its Implications," *Georgetown Law Journal* 110, 135–142 (2021), http://dx.doi.org/10.2139/ssrn.3846903.

61 Olivas, *Perchance to DREAM.*

62 Olivas, *Perchance to DREAM.*

63 Olivas, *Perchance to DREAM*; Wadhia, *Banned.*

64 Wadhia, *Banned.*

65 Wadhia, *Banned*; Olivas, *Perchance to DREAM.*

66 Wadhia, *Banned*, 70.

67 Olivas, *Perchance to DREAM.*

68 Olivas, *Perchance to DREAM.*

69 Olivas, *Perchance to DREAM.*

70 Olivas, *Perchance to DREAM.*

71 Wolfman, "The DACA Decision"; Supreme Court of the United States, "Department of Homeland Security et al. v. Regents of the University of California et al.," June 18, 2020, www.supremecourt.gov.

72 Wolfman, "The DACA Decision."

73 Wolfman, "The DACA Decision," 5.

74 Wolfman, "The DACA Decision."

75 Wolfman, "The DACA Decision," 8.

76 Wolfman, "The DACA Decision."

77 Supreme Court of the United States, "Department of Homeland Security et al. v. Regents of the University of California et al.," 24.

78 Immigration Legal Resource Center, "Deferred Action for Childhood Arrivals: Practice Update," December 22, 2020, www.ilrc.org.

79 Immigration Legal Resource Center, "Deferred Action for Childhood Arrivals," 2.

80 Immigration Legal Resource Center, "Deferred Action for Childhood Arrivals," 2.

81 Department of Homeland Security, "Reconsideration of the June 15, 2012 Memorandums Entitled 'Exercising Prosecutorial Discretion with Respect to Individuals
Who Came to the United States as Children,'" July 28, 2020, www.dhs.gov.

82 Department of Homeland Security, "Reconsideration."

83 Department of Homeland Security, "Reconsideration."

84 National Immigration Law Center, "Litigation Related to Deferred Action."

85 National Immigration Law Center, "Litigation Related to Deferred Action."

86 Department of Homeland Security, "Deferred Action for Childhood Arrivals."

87 Immigration Legal Resource Center, "Deferred Action for Childhood Arrivals
(DACA) Final Rule Summary," September 12, 2022, www.ilrc.org; Immigrant
Legal Resource Center, "DACA."

88 Albarracín, *At the Core and in the Margins.*

89 Illinois Attorney General, "Law Enforcement and Immigration Law Enforcement
Guidance & Reporting on Compliance with the Illinois TRUST Act and VOICES
Act," 2023, https://illinoisattorneygeneral.gov.

90 Camilla Mroczkowski, "Illinois: A State-of-the-Art Model for State Immigration
Rulemaking," *DePaul Journal for Social Justice* 16 (2022): 1.

91 Heather Cherone, "What Does It Mean That Chicago Is a Sanctuary City? Here's
What to Know," October 20, 2023, https://news.wttw.com.

92 Zelideh Martinez Hoy and David H. K. Nguyen, "Higher Education Professionals
Navigating Anti-Immigration Policy for Undocumented Students." *Educational
Policy* 35, no. 7 (2021): 1163–1190, https://doi.org/10.1177/0895904819857823.

93 Leisy J. Abrego, "'I Can't Go to College Because I Don't Have Papers': Incorporation Patterns of Latino Undocumented Youth," *Latino Studies* 4 (2006): 212–31.

94 Higher Education Portal, "Tuition & Financial Aid Equity for Undocumented
Students," accessed December 5, 2023, www.higheredimmigrationportal.org.

95 Higher Education Portal, "Tuition & Financial Aid Equity for Undocumented
Students," accessed December 5, 2023, www.higheredimmigrationportal.org.

96 Higher Education Portal, "Tuition & Financial Aid Equity."

97 Higher Education Portal, "Tuition & Financial Aid Equity."

98 Higher Education Portal, "Tuition & Financial Aid Equity."

99 Higher Education Portal, "Tuition & Financial Aid Equity."

100 Illinois General Assembly, "Public Act 093–0007," accessed March 29, 2021, www
.ilga.gov.

101 Illinois General Assembly, "Full Text of HB2185," accessed March 29, 2021, www
.ilga.gov.

102 Illinois General Assembly, "Full Text of HB2691," accessed March 29, 2021, www
.ilga.gov.

103 Joseph M. Cervantes, Laura P. Minero, and Elivet Brito, "Tales of Survival 101
for Undocumented Latina/o Immigrant University Students: Commentary and
Recommendations from Qualitative Interviews," *Journal of Latina/o Psychology*,
June 8, 2015, https://psycnet.apa.org.

104 Cervantes et al., "Tales of Survival 101."

105 Basia D. Ellis, "The Psychology of Migrant 'Illegality': A General Theory," *Law & Social Inquiry* 46, no. 4 (2021): 1236–71.
106 Ko and Pereira, "'It Turned My World Upside Down.'"
107 Department of Homeland Security, "Deferred Action for Childhood Arrivals"; Nation World News Desk, "Biden Wants to Strengthen Protection for DACA Recipients."

CHAPTER 1. THE CROSSING

1 Illinois General Assembly, "Full Text of HB2691."
2 Krista M. Perreira and Lisa Spees, "Foiled Aspirations: The Influence of Unauthorized Status on the Educational Expectations of Latino Immigrant Youth," *Population Research and Policy Review* 34, no. 5 (2015): 641–64.
3 Perreira and Spees, "Foiled Aspirations."
4 Perreira and Spees, "Foiled Aspirations."
5 Perreira and Spees, "Foiled Aspirations."
6 Krista M. Perreira and India Ornelas, "Painful Passages: Traumatic Experiences and Post-Traumatic Stress among US Immigrant Latino Adolescents and Their Primary Caregivers," *International Migration Review* 47, no. 4 (2013): 976–1005.
7 Melanie M. Reyes, "Migration and Filipino Children Left Behind: A Literature Review," *Development (DFID)*, 2007.
8 Population Division United Nations Department of Economic and Social Affairs, "International Migration 2020 Highlights," 2020, www.un.org.
9 Jeanne Batalova, Mary Hanna, and Christopher Levesque, "Frequently Requested Statistics on Immigrants and Immigration in the United States," Spotlight, February 11, 2019, www.migrationpolicy.org.
10 Batalova et al., "Frequently Requested Statistics."
11 Stephen Castles, "Why Migration Policies Fail," *Ethnic and Racial Studies* 27, no. 2 (2004): 205–27.
12 Stephen Castles, Hein de Haas, and Mark Miller, *The Age of Migration: International Population Movements in the Modern World*, 5th ed. (New York: The Guilford Press, 2014).
13 Ran Abramitzky and Leah Boustan, "Immigration in American Economic History," *Journal of Economic Literature* 55, no. 4 (2017): 1311–45.
14 Abramitzky and Boustan, "Immigration in American Economic History"; J. William Ambrosini and Giovanni Peri, "The Determinants and the Selection of Mexico–US Migrants," *World Economy* 35, no. 2 (2012): 111–51.
15 Pia M. Orrenius and Madeline Zavodny, "Self-Selection among Undocumented Immigrants from Mexico," *Journal of Development Economics* 78, no. 1 (2005): 215–40.
16 Robert Kaestner and Ofer Malamud, "Self-Selection and International Migration: New Evidence from Mexico," *Review of Economics and Statistics* 96, no. 1 (2014): 78–91.
17 Raúl Delgado Wise and Humberto Márquez Covarrubias, "Capitalist Restructuring, Development and Labour Migration: The Mexico–US Case," *Third World Quarterly* 29, no. 7 (2008): 1359–74.

18 Wise and Covarrubias, "Capitalist Restructuring."

19 Philip Martin, "Mexico-US Migration, NAFTA and CAFTA, and US Immigration Policy," in *Migration, Nation States, and International Cooperation*, ed. Randall Hansen, Jobst Joehler, and Jeannette Money, vol. 23 (New York: Routledge, 2011), 75–86.

20 Duygu E. Şimşek, "Bidirectional Causal Relationship between Foreign Trade and Immigration: Evidence from NAFTA," in *Second InTraders International Conference on International Trade: Conference Book*, ed. Kürşat Çrapaz and Mustafa Yılmaz (Istanbul: Hiperlink, 2018).

21 Julia Albarracín, *At the Core and in the Margins: Incorporation of Mexican Immigrants in Two Rural Midwestern Communities* (East Lansing: Michigan State University Press, 2016); Douglas S. Massey, Karen A. Pren, and Jorge Durand, "Why Border Enforcement Backfired," *American Journal of Sociology* 121, no. 5 (2016): 1557–1600.

22 Douglas S. Massey and Karen A. Pren, "Unintended Consequences of US Immigration Policy: Explaining the Post-1965 Surge from Latin America," *Population and Development Review* 38, no. 1 (2012): 1–29.

23 Massey and Pren, "Unintended Consequences."

24 Castles et al., *The Age of Migration*.

25 Castles, "Why Migration Policies Fail."

26 Albarracín, *At the Core and in the Margins*.

27 Albarracín, *At the Core and in the Margins*; Castles, "Why Migration Policies Fail."

28 Ivan Light, Perminder Bhachu, and Stavros Karageorgis, "Migration Networks and Immigrant Entrepreneurship," in *Immigration and Entrepreneurship*, ed. Ivan Light and Parminder Bhachu (London: Taylor & Francis, 1989).

29 Saskia Sassen, "America's Immigration 'Problem,'" *World Policy Journal* 6, no. 4 (1989): 811–32.

30 Sassen, "America's Immigration 'Problem.'"

31 Sassen, "America's Immigration 'Problem,'" 818.

32 Michael B. Katz, Mark J. Stern, and Jamie J. Fader, "The Mexican Immigration Debate: The View from History," *Social Science History* 31, no. 2 (2007): 157–89.

33 Mae M. Ngai, *Impossible Subjects: Illegal Aliens and the Making of Modern America* (Princeton, NJ: Princeton University Press, 2004).

34 Kitty Calavita, *Inside the State: The Bracero Program, Immigration, and the INS* (Quid Pro Books, 2010).

35 Calavita, *Inside the State*, 3.

36 Abramitzky and Boustan, "Immigration in American Economic History."

37 Victor Leão Borges de Almeida, Carlos Esquivel, Juan Pablo Nicolini, and Timothy Kehoe, "Did the 1980s in Latin America Need to Be a Lost Decade?" 2018 Meeting Papers for the Society of Economic Dynamics, 2019.

38 Almeida et al., "Did the 1980s in Latin America Need to Be a Lost Decade?"

39 Asa Cristina Laurell, "Three Decades of Neoliberalism in Mexico: The Destruction of Society," *International Journal of Health Services* 45, no. 2 (2015): 246–64.

40 Laurell, "Three Decades of Neoliberalism in Mexico."

41 Laurell, "Three Decades of Neoliberalism in Mexico."

42 Ronelle Burger et al., "The Emergent Middle Class in Contemporary South Africa: Examining and Comparing Rival Approaches," *Development Southern Africa* 32, no. 1 (2015): 25–40.

43 Erik Olin Wright, "Class and Occupation," *Theory and Society* 9, no. 1 (1980): 177–214.

44 Castles, "Why Migration Policies Fail"; Castles et al., *The Age of Migration*.

45 Wanda A. Velez, "South America Immigration: Argentina," *Volume I: The Autobiographical Mode in Latin America Literature* (New Haven, CT: *Yale New Haven Teachers Institute*, 1990), 1.

46 John Bryant and Paul Merwood, "Reasons for Migrating and Settlement Outcomes: Evidence from the Longitudinal Immigration Survey New Zealand," *Labour, Employment and Work in New Zealand*, 2008. https://doi.org/10.26686/lew.v0i0.1628

47 Bryant and Merwood, "Reasons for Migrating and Settlement Outcomes."

48 Bryant and Merwood, "Reasons for Migrating and Settlement Outcomes."

49 Alberto Palloni, Douglas S. Massey, Miguel Ceballos, Kristin Espinosa, and Michael Spittel, "Social Capital and International Migration: A Test Using Information on Family Networks," *American Journal of Sociology* 106, no. 5 (2001): 1262–98.

50 Karen Musalo, "El Salvador: Root Causes and Just Asylum Policy Responses," *Hastings Race and Poverty Law Journal* 18, no. 2 (2021): 178.

51 Sebastián Calderón Bentin, "The Politics of Illusion: The Collapse of the Fujimori Regime in Peru," *Theatre Survey* 59, no. 1 (2018): 84–107.

52 Aristide R. Zolberg, *A Nation by Design: Immigration Policy in the Fashioning of America* (Cambridge, MA: Harvard University Press, 2009).

53 Elizabeth Petras, "The Role of National Boundaries in a Cross-national Labour Market," *International Journal of Urban and Regional Research* 4, no. 2 (1980): 157–95.

54 Nicholas De Genova, Sandro Mezzadra, and John Pickles, "New Keywords: Migration and Borders," *Cultural Studies* 29, no. 1 (2015): 55–87; Julia Albarracín, *Making Immigrants in Modern Argentina* (Notre Dame, IN: University of Notre Dame Pess, 2020).

55 Nicholas de Genova, "Spectacles of Migrant 'Illegality': The Scene of Exclusion, the Obscene of Inclusion," *Ethnic and Racial Studies* 36, no. 7 (2013): 1180–98.

56 De Genova, "Spectacles of Migrant 'Illegality'," 1182.

57 Peter Andreas, *Border Games* (Ithaca, NY: Cornell University Press, 2011); Albarracín, *Making Immigrants in Modern Argentina*.

58 De Genova, "Spectacles of Migrant 'Illegality.'"

59 Jeremy Slack, Daniel E. Martínez, Alison Elizabeth Lee, and Scott Whiteford, "The Geography of Border Militarization: Violence, Death and Health in Mexico and the United States," *Journal of Latin American Geography* 15, no. 1 (2016):

7–32; Perreira and Ornelas, "Painful Passages"; Michael A. de Arellano, Arthur R. Andrews, Kathy Reid-Quiñones, Desi Vasquez, Lauren Silcott Doherty, Carla K. Danielson, and Alyssa Rheingold, "Immigration Trauma among Hispanic Youth: Missed by Trauma Assessments and Predictive of Depression and PTSD Symptoms," *Journal of Latina/o Psychology* 6, no. 3 (2018): 159.

60 Slack et al., "The Geography of Border Militarization."

61 Pedro Paulo Orraca Romano and Francisco de Jesús Corona Villavicencio, "Risk of Death and Aggressions Encountered While Illegally Crossing the US-Mexico Border," *Migraciones Internacionales* 7, no. 3 (2014): 9–41.

62 Massey et al., "Why Border Enforcement Backfired."

63 Albarracín, *Making Immigrants in Modern Argentina*; de Genova et al., "New Keywords."

64 Romano and Villavicencio, "Risk of Death and Aggressions"; Massey et al., "Why Border Enforcement Backfired."

65 Massey et al., "Why Border Enforcement Backfired," 4.

66 Bradford S. Jones, Jeffrey W. Sherman, Natalie E. Rojas, Adrienne Hosek, David L. Vannette, Rene R. Rocha, Omar García-Ponce, Maria Pantoja, and Jesus Manuel García-Amador, "Trump-Induced Anxiety among Latina/os," *Group Processes & Intergroup Relations* 24, no. 1 (2021): 68–87.

67 Julie Hirschfeld Davis and Michael D. Shear, *Border Wars: Inside Trump's Assault on Immigration* (New York: Simon & Schuster, 2020).

68 Massey et al., "Why Border Enforcement Backfired."

69 Massey et al., "Why Border Enforcement Backfired," 1557–1600.

70 Romano and Villavicencio, "Risk of Death and Aggressions."

71 Romano and Villavicencio, "Risk of Death and Aggressions."

72 Amelia Cheatham, Claire Felter, and Zachary Laub, "How the U.S. Patrols Its Borders," April 12, 2021, Council on Foreign Relations, www.cfr.org.

73 US General Services Administration, "Land Ports of Entry, 2018," www.gsa.gov.

74 Cheatham et al., "How the U.S. Patrols Its Borders."

75 Howard Markel and Alexandra Minna Stern, "Which Face? Whose Nation? Immigration, Public Health, and the Construction of Disease at America's Ports and Borders, 1891–1928," *American Behavioral Scientist* 42, no. 9 (1999): 1314–31.

76 Bureau of Transportation Statistics, "2018 Traffic Data for U.S Airlines and Foreign Airlines U.S. Flights," April 30, 2020, www.bts.dot.gov.

77 Emily M. Cohodes, Sahana Kribakaran, Paola Odriozola, Sarah Bakirci, Sarah McCauley, H. R. Hodges, Lucinda M. Sisk, Sadie J. Zacharek, and Dylan G. Gee, "Migration-related Trauma and Mental Health among Migrant Children Emigrating from Mexico and Central America to the United States: Effects on Developmental Neurobiology and Implications for Policy," *Developmental Psychobiology* 63, no. 6 (2021): e22158.

78 Romano and Villavicencio, "Risk of Death and Aggressions."

79 Cohodes et al., "Migration-related Trauma and Mental Health."

80 Romano and Villavicencio, "Risk of Death and Aggressions."

81 Perreira and Ornelas, "Painful Passages."

82 Rose Cuison Villazor, "The Undocumented Closet," *North Carolina Law Review* 92 (2013): 1.

83 Sarah Dolfin and Garance Genicot, "What Do Networks Do? The Role of Networks on Migration and 'Coyote' Use," *Review of Development Economics* 14, no. 2 (2010): 343–59.

84 Dolfin and Genicot, "What Do Networks Do?"

85 Ko and Pereira, "'It Turned My World Upside Down.'"

86 Julia Albarracín, Guadalupe Cabedo-Timmons, and Gloria Delany-Barmann, "Factors Shaping Second Language Acquisition among Adult Mexican Immigrants in Rural Immigrant Destinations," *Hispanic Journal of Behavioral Sciences* 41, no. 1 (2019): 85–102.

87 Albarracín, *At the Core and in the Margins.*

88 Sean McMinn and Renee Klahr, "Where Does Illegal Immigration Mostly Occur? Here Is What the Data Tell Us," January 10, 2019, https://www.npr.org.

89 McMinn and Klahr. "Where Does Illegal Immigration Mostly Occur?"

90 Josiah McC Heyman, "Constructing a Virtual Wall: Race and Citizenship in US–Mexico Border Policing," *Journal of the Southwest* 50, no. 3 (2008): 305–33.

91 McC Heyman, "Constructing a Virtual Wall."

92 McC Heyman, "Constructing a Virtual Wall."

93 Rey Koslowski, *The Evolution of Border Controls as a Mechanism to Prevent Illegal Immigration* (Washington, DC: Migration Policy Institute, 2011). www.migrationpolicy.org.

94 Curt Pendergast, "Fraudulent ID Busts Downs at Border Ports of Entry," *Tucson. Com*, March 3, 2017, https://tucson.com.

95 Koslowski, *The Evolution of Border Controls.*

96 Koslowski, *The Evolution of Border Controls.*

97 US Department of State, "Visitor Visa," accessed September 16, 2021, https://travel.state.gov.

98 US Department of State, "Visitor Visa."

99 Reyes, "Migration and Filipino Children Left Behind," 1.

100 Maurizio Ambrosini, "Parenting from a Distance and Processes of Family Reunification: A Research on the Italian Case," *Ethnicities* 15, no. 3 (2015): 440–59.

101 Richard Mines and Douglas S. Massey, "Patterns of Migration to the United States from Two Mexican Communities," *Latin American Research Review* 20, no. 2 (1985): 104–23.

102 Ambrosini, "Parenting from a Distance and Processes of Family Reunification."

103 Reyes, "Migration and Filipino Children Left Behind."

104 Reyes, "Migration and Filipino Children Left Behind."

105 Castles et al., *The Age of Migration.*

106 Bryant and Merwood, "Reasons for Migrating and Settlement Outcomes."

107 Stephen Castles, Hein de Haas, and Mark Miller, "Theories of Migration," in *The Age of Migration: International Population Movements in the Modern World,* 5th

edition, ed. Stephen Castles, Hein de Hass, and Mark Miller (New York: The Guilford Press, 2014).

108 Albarracín, *At the Core and in the Margins*.

109 Castles, "Why Migration Policies Fail."

110 Albarracín, *Making Immigrants in Modern Argentina*.

111 Slack et al., "The Geography of Border Militarization."

112 Massey et al., "Why Border Enforcement Backfired."

113 Lenore Terr, "What Happens to Early Memories of Trauma? A Study of Twenty Children under Age Five at the Time of Documented Traumatic Events," *Journal of the American Academy of Child & Adolescent Psychiatry* 27, no. 1 (1988): 96–104.

114 Ambrosini, "Parenting from a Distance and Processes of Family Reunification."

CHAPTER 2. FINDING ONE'S PLACE

1 Gary Gerstle, "Historical and Contemporary Perspectives on Immigrant Political Incorporation: The American Experience," *International Labor and Working-Class History* 78, no. 1 (2010): 110–17.

2 Julia Albarracín, *At the Core and in the Margins: Incorporation of Mexican Immigrants in Two Rural Midwestern Communities* (East Lansing: Michigan State University Press, 2016).

3 Joseph M. Cervantes, Laura P. Minero, and Elivet Brito, "Tales of Survival 101 for Undocumented Latina/o Immigrant University Students: Commentary and Recommendations from Qualitative Interviews," *Journal of Latina/o Psychology*, June 8, 2015, https://psycnet.apa.org.

4 Albarracín, *At the Core and in the Margins*.

5 Cervantes et al., "Tales of Survival 101."

6 Albarracín, *At the Core and in the Margins*.

7 Albarracín, *At the Core and in the Margins*.

8 Roberto G. Gonzales, "Learning to Be Illegal: Undocumented Youth and Shifting Legal Contexts in the Transition to Adulthood," *American Sociological Review* 76, no. 4 (August 2011): 602–19, https://doi.org/10.1177/0003122411411901.

9 Albarracín, *At the Core and in the Margins*.

10 John W. Berry, "Immigration, Acculturation, and Adaptation," *Applied Psychology* 46, no. 1 (1997): 5–34.

11 Berry, "Immigration, Acculturation, and Adaptation."

12 Erwin Dimitri Selimos and Yvette Daniel, "The Role of Schools in Shaping the Settlement Experiences of Newcomer Immigrant and Refugee Youth," *International Journal of Child, Youth and Family Studies* 8, no. 2 (2017): 90–109; Arnold Van Gennep, *The Rites of Passage* (London: Routledge, 2013).

13 Van Gennep, *The Rites of Passage*.

14 Roberto G. Gonzales, Luisa L. Heredia, and Genevieve Negrón-Gonzales, "Untangling Plyler's Legacy: Undocumented Students, Schools, and Citizenship," *Harvard Educational Review* 85, no. 3 (2015): 318–41.

15 Linda K. Ko and Krista M. Pereira, "'It Turned My World Upside Down': Latino Youths' Perspectives on Immigration," *Journal of Adolescent Research* 25, no. 3 (2010): 465–93.
16 Selimos and Daniel, "The Role of Schools in Shaping the Settlement Experiences."
17 Selimos and Daniel, "The Role of Schools in Shaping the Settlement Experiences."
18 Erin Michaels, "Beyond Academic Achievement Outcomes: The Impact of School on the Immigrant Political Incorporation of Undocumented Latinx Youth," *Youth & Society* 52, no. 7 (2020): 1285–1311; Carola Suárez-Orozco, Frosso Motti-Stefanidi, Amy Marks, and Dalal Katsiaficas, "An Integrative Risk and Resilience Model for Understanding the Adaptation of Immigrant-Origin Children and Youth," *American Psychologist* 73, no. 6 (2018): 781.
19 Carola Suárez-Orozco, Hirokazu Yoshikawa, and Vivian Tseng, *Intersecting Inequalities: Research to Reduce Inequality for Immigrant-Origin Children and Youth* (New York: *William T. Grant Foundation*, 2015).
20 Suárez-Orozco et al., "Intersecting Inequalities."
21 Mambo Tabu Masinda, Marianne Jacquet, and Danièle Moore, "An Integrated Framework for Immigrant Children and Youth's School Integration: A Focus on African Francophone Students in British Columbia, Canada," *International Journal of Education* 6, no. 1 (2014): 90–107.
22 Roslyn Arlin Mickelson, "School Integration and K-12 Educational Outcomes: A Quick Synthesis of Social Science Evidence," *Research Brief. The National Coalition on School Diversity* 5 (2015), https://files.eric.ed.gov.
23 Suárez-Orozco et al., "An Integrative Risk and Resilience Model."
24 Suárez-Orozco et al., "An Integrative Risk and Resilience Model."
25 Albarracín, *At the Core and in the Margins*; Julia Albarracín, Guadalupe Cabedo-Timmons, and Gloria Delany-Barmann, "Factors Shaping Second Language Acquisition among Adult Mexican Immigrants in Rural Immigrant Destinations," *Hispanic Journal of Behavioral Sciences* 41, no. 1 (2019): 85–102.
26 Michael Evans and Yongcan Liu, "The Unfamiliar and the Indeterminate: Language, Identity and Social Integration in the School Experience of Newly-Arrived Migrant Children in England," *Journal of Language, Identity & Education* 17, no. 3 (2018): 152–67.
27 Shana Sanam Khan, "A Narrative Literature Review of the Identity Negotiation of Bilingual Students Who Are Labelled ESL," *Interchange* 51, no. 4 (2020): 361–83.
28 Khan, "A Narrative Literature Review of the Identity Negotiation of Bilingual Students."
29 Jean S. Phinney, "Ethnic Identity in Adolescents and Adults: Review of Research," *Psychological Bulletin* 108, no. 3 (1990): 499.
30 Bongki Woo, Wen Fan, Thanh V. Tran, and David T. Takeuchi, "The Role of Racial/Ethnic Identity in the Association between Racial Discrimination and Psychiatric Disorders: A Buffer or Exacerbator?" *SSM-Population Health* 7 (2019), DOI: 10.1016/j.ssmph.2019.100378.

31 Leisy J. Abrego, "Legal Consciousness of Undocumented Latinos: Fear and Stigma as Barriers to Claims-making for First-and 1.5-generation Immigrants," *Law & Society Review* 45, no. 2 (2011): 337–70; Roberto G. Gonzales and Leo R. Chavez, "'Awakening to a Nightmare': Abjectivity and Illegality in the Lives of Undocumented 1.5-Generation Latino Immigrants in the United States," *Current Anthropology* 53, no. 3 (June 2012): 255–81.

32 Gonzales, "Learning to Be Illegal"; Carlos E. Sluzki, "Migration and Family Conflict," *Family Process* 18, no. 4 (1979): 379–90.

33 Albarracín, *At the Core and in the Margins.*

34 Masinda et al., "An Integrated Framework for Immigrant Children and Youth's School Integration."

35 Ko and Pereira, "'It Turned My World Upside Down.'"

36 Carola Suárez-Orozco, Jean Rhodes, and Michael Milburn, "Unraveling the Immigrant Paradox: Academic Engagement and Disengagement among Recently Arrived Immigrant Youth," *Youth & Society* 41, no. 2 (2009): 151–85.

37 Suárez-Orozco et al., "Unraveling the Immigrant Paradox"; Suárez-Orozco et al., "An Integrative Risk and Resilience Model."

38 Selimos and Daniel, "The Role of Schools in Shaping the Settlement Experiences."

39 Stephanie Plenty and Jan O. Jonsson, "Social Exclusion among Peers: The Role of Immigrant Status and Classroom Immigrant Density," *Journal of Youth and Adolescence* 46, no. 6 (2017): 1275–88.

40 Philipp Jugert and Allard R. Feddes, "Children's and Adolescents' Cross-Ethnic Friendships," in *The Wiley Handbook of Group Processes in Children and Adolescents*, ed. Adam Rutland, Drew Nesdale, and Christia Spears Brown (New York: John Wiley and Sons, 2017), 373–92.

41 Walter G. Stephan and David Rosenfield, "Effects of Desegregation on Racial Attitudes," *Journal of Personality and Social Psychology* 36, no. 8 (1978): 795.

42 Jugert and Feddes, "Children's and Adolescents' Cross-Ethnic Friendships."

43 Lars Leszczensky, Philipp Jugert, and Sebastian Pink, "The Interplay of Group Identifications and Friendships: Evidence from Longitudinal Social Network Studies," *Journal of Social Issues* 75, no. 2 (2019): 460–85.

44 Leszczensky et al., "The Interplay of Group Identifications and Friendships"; Paul F. Lazarsfeld and Robert K. Merton, "Friendship as a Social Process: A Substantive and Methodological Analysis," *Freedom and Control in Modern Society* 18, no. 1 (1954): 18–66.

45 Berry, "Immigration, Acculturation, and Adaptation."

46 Melissa Michelson, "All Roads Lead to Rust: How Acculturation Erodes Latino Immigrant Trust in Government," *Aztlán: A Journal of Chicano Studies* 32, no. 2 (2007): 21–46; Suárez-Orozco et al., "An Integrative Risk and Resilience Model."

47 Suárez-Orozco et al., "An Integrative Risk and Resilience Model."

48 Suárez-Orozco et al., "An Integrative Risk and Resilience Model."

49 Woo et al., "The Role of Racial/Ethnic Identity."

50 Suárez-Orozco et al., "An Integrative Risk and Resilience Model."

51 Colorín Colorado, "Program Models for Teaching English Language Learners," 1993, www.colorincolorado.org.

52 Colorín Colorado, "Program Models for Teaching English Language Learners."

53 Colorín Colorado, "Program Models for Teaching English Language Learners."

54 Colorín Colorado, "Program Models for Teaching English Language Learners."

55 Albarracín, *At the Core and in the Margins*.

56 Laura Baecher, Tim Farnsworth, and Anne Ediger, "The Challenges of Planning Language Objectives in Content-Based ESL Instruction," *Language Teaching Research* 18, no. 1 (2014): 118–36.

57 Baecher et al., "The Challenges of Planning Language Objectives in Content-Based ESL Instruction."

58 Sarah Gallo, Holly Link, Elaine Allard, Stanton Wortham, and Katherine Mortimer, "Conflicting Ideologies of Mexican Immigrant English across Levels of Schooling," *International Multilingual Research Journal* 8, no. 2 (2014): 124–40.

59 Efren Velazquez and Melissa Avila, "Ethnic Labels, Pride, and Challenges: A Qualitative Study of Latinx Youth Living in a New Latinx Destination Community," *Journal of Ethnic and Cultural Studies* 4, no. 1 (2017): 1.

60 Velazquez and Avila, "Ethnic Labels, Pride, and Challenges."

61 Lucy Karanja, "ESL Learning Experiences of Immigrant Students in High Schools in a Small City," *TESL Canada Journal* 24, no. 2 (2007): 23–41.

62 Anna Trebits, Martin J. Koch, Katharina Ponto, Ann-Christin Bruhn, Marie Adler, and Kristin Kersten, "Cognitive Gains and Socioeconomic Status in Early Second Language Acquisition in Immersion and EFL Learning Settings," *International Journal of Bilingual Education and Bilingualism* 25, no. 7 (2021): 1–14.

63 Albarracín, *At the Core and in the Margins*; Albarracín et al., "Factors Shaping Second Language Acquisition among Adult Mexican Immigrants."

64 Tony Cline, Sarah Crafter, and Evangelina Prokopiou, *Child Language Brokering in School: Final Research Report* (London: Nuffield Foundation, 2014), 4, https://pure.northampton.ac.uk.

65 Rebecca Lowenhaupt, "Immigrant Acculturation in Suburban Schools Serving the New Latino Diaspora," *Peabody Journal of Education* 91, no. 3 (2016): 348–65.

66 Steven Talmy, "The Cultural Productions of the ESL Student at Tradewinds High: Contingency, Multidirectionality, and Identity in L2 Socialization," *Applied Linguistics* 29, no. 4 (2008): 619–44.

67 Albarracín, *At the Core and in the Margins*.

68 Berry, "Immigration, Acculturation, and Adaptation."

69 Berry, "Immigration, Acculturation, and Adaptation," 10.

70 Berry, "Immigration, Acculturation, and Adaptation," 10.

71 Berry, "Immigration, Acculturation, and Adaptation," 10.

72 Jacqueline Oxman-Martinez, Anneke J. Rummens, Jacques Moreau, Ye Ri Choi, Morton Beiser, Linda Ogilvie, and Robert Armstrong, "Perceived Ethnic Discrimination and Social Exclusion: Newcomer Immigrant Children in Canada," *American Journal of Orthopsychiatry* 82, no. 3 (2012): 376.

73 Alejandro Portes and József Böröcz, "Contemporary Immigration: Theoretical Perspectives on Its Determinants and Modes of Incorporation," *International Migration Review* 23, no. 3 (September 1989): 606–30, https://doi.org/10.1177/019791838902300311.

74 Berry, "Immigration, Acculturation, and Adaptation."

75 Berry, "Immigration, Acculturation, and Adaptation."

76 Berry, "Immigration, Acculturation, and Adaptation."

77 Christine Brigid Malsbary, "'It's Not Just Learning English, It's Learning Other Cultures': Belonging, Power, and Possibility in an Immigrant Contact Zone," *International Journal of Qualitative Studies in Education* 27, no. 10 (2014): 1312–36.

78 Sanne Smith, Frank Van Tubergen, Ineke Maas, and Daniel A. McFarland, "Ethnic Composition and Friendship Segregation: Differential Effects for Adolescent Natives and Immigrants," *American Journal of Sociology* 121, no. 4 (2016): 1223–72.

79 Malsbary, "'It's Not Just Learning English, It's Learning Other Cultures'"; Carola Suárez-Orozco, Marcelo M. Suárez-Orozco, and Irina Todorova, *Learning a New Land* (Cambridge, MA: Harvard University Press, 2008).

80 Sabahat C. Bagci, Adam Rutland, Madoka Kumashiro, Peter K. Smith, and Herbert Blumberg, "Are Minority Status Children's Cross-ethnic Friendships Beneficial in a Multiethnic Context?," *British Journal of Developmental Psychology* 32, no. 1 (2014): 107–15.

81 Bagci et al., "Are Minority Status Children's Cross-ethnic Friendships Beneficial in a Multiethnic Context?"

82 Berry, "Immigration, Acculturation, and Adaptation."

83 Berry, "Immigration, Acculturation, and Adaptation."

84 Leszczensky et al., "The Interplay of Group Identifications and Friendships"; Lazarsfeld and Merton, "Friendship as a Social Process."

85 Berry, "Immigration, Acculturation, and Adaptation."

86 Antonis Hatzigeorgiadis, Eleftheria Morela, Anne-Marie Elbe, Olga Kouli, and Xavier Sanchez, "The Integrative Role of Sport in Multicultural Societies," *European Psychologist* 18, no. 3 (2013): 191–202.

87 Hatzigeorgiadis et al., "The Integrative Role of Sport in Multicultural Societies."

88 Elisa Cavicchiolo, Sara Manganelli, Dora Bianchi, Valeria Biasi, Fabio Lucidi, Laura Girelli, Mauro Cozzolino, and Fabio Alivernini, "Social Inclusion of Immigrant Children at School: The Impact of Group, Family and Individual Characteristics, and the Role of Proficiency in the National Language," *International Journal of Inclusive Education* 27, no. 2 (2020): 146–66.

89 Bagci et al., "Are Minority Status Children's Cross-ethnic Friendships Beneficial in a Multiethnic Context?"

90 Bagci et al., "Are Minority Status Children's Cross-ethnic Friendships Beneficial in a Multiethnic Context?"

91 Berry, "Immigration, Acculturation, and Adaptation."

92 Andrea J. Romero, Henry Gonzalez, and Bryan A. Smith, "Qualitative Exploration of Adolescent Discrimination: Experiences and Responses of Mexican-
American Parents and Teens," *Journal of Child and Family Studies* 24, no. 6
(2015): 1531–43.

93 Jennifer Keys Adair, *The Impact of Discrimination on the Early Schooling Experiences of Children from Immigrant Families* (Washington, DC: Migration Policy
Institute, 2015).

94 American Immigration Council, "Immigrants in Florida," August 6, 2020, www
.americanimmigrationcouncil.org.

95 American Immigration Council, "Immigrants in Florida."

96 Alan A. Aja, *Miami's Forgotten Cubans: Race, Racialization, and the Miami Afro-
Cuban Experience* (New York: Springer, 2016).

97 Vilma Ortiz and Edward Telles, "Racial Identity and Racial Treatment of Mexican
Americans," *Race and Social Problems* 4, no. 1 (2012): 41–56.

98 Ortiz and Telles, Racial Identity and Racial Treatment of Mexican Americans," 2.

99 Lizette Ojeda, Rachel L. Navarro, Rocío Rosales Meza, and Consuelo Arbona,
"Too Latino and Not Latino Enough: The Role of Ethnicity-Related Stressors on
Latino College Students' Life Satisfaction," *Journal of Hispanic Higher Education*
11, no. 1 (2012): 14–28.

100 Edward D. Vargas, Nadia C. Winston, John A. Garcia, and Gabriel R. Sanchez,
"Latina/o or Mexicana/o? The Relationship between Socially Assigned Race and
Experiences with Discrimination," *Sociology of Race and Ethnicity* 2, no. 4 (2016):
498–515.

101 Heather Sandstrom and Sandra Huerta, "The Negative Effects of Instability on
Child Development: A Research Synthesis," Low-Income Working Families
(Urban Institute Washington, DC, 2013), www.urban.org.

102 Sandstrom and Huerta, "The Negative Effects of Instability on Child
Development."

103 Gonzales, *Lives in Limbo*; Heide Castañeda, *Borders of Belonging: Struggle and
Solidarity in Mixed-Status Immigrant Families* (Stanford, CA: Stanford University
Press, 2019).

104 Castañeda, *Borders of Belonging*.

105 Castañeda, *Borders of Belonging*, 72.

106 Selimos and Daniel, "The Role of Schools in Shaping the Settlement Experiences."

107 Suárez-Orozco et al., *Learning a New Land*.

108 Cline, Crafter, and Prokopiou, *Child Language Brokering in School*.

109 Karanja, "ESL Learning Experiences of Immigrant Students in High Schools in a
Small City."

110 Albarracín, *At the Core and in the Margins*.

111 James Cohen, "Imaginary Community of the Mainstream Classroom: Adolescent
Immigrants' Perspectives," *The Urban Review* 44, no. 2 (2012): 265–80.

112 Cohen, "Imaginary Community of the Mainstream Classroom."

113 Plenty and Jonsson, "Social Exclusion among Peers."

114 Berry, "Immigration, Acculturation, and Adaptation."

CHAPTER 3. SEARCHING FOR SUPPORT

1 Erwin Dimitri Selimos and Yvette Daniel, "The Role of Schools in Shaping the Settlement Experiences of Newcomer Immigrant and Refugee Youth," *International Journal of Child, Youth and Family Studies* 8, no. 2 (2017): 90–109; Carola Suárez-Orozco, Jean Rhodes, and Michael Milburn, "Unraveling the Immigrant Paradox: Academic Engagement and Disengagement among Recently Arrived Immigrant Youth," *Youth & Society* 41, no. 2 (2009): 151–85.

2 American School Counselor Association, "School Counselors Roles & Ratios," 2021, www.schoolcounselor.org.

3 Illinois General Assembly, "Public Act 093–0007," 2003, www.ilga.gov.

4 Selimos and Daniel, "The Role of Schools in Shaping the Settlement Experiences of Newcomer Immigrant and Refugee Youth"; Suárez-Orozco et al., "Unraveling the Immigrant Paradox."

5 Floralba Arbelo Marrero, "Barriers to School Success for Latino Students," *Journal of Education and Learning* 5, no. 2 (2016): 180–86.

6 Marrero, "Barriers to School Success for Latino Students," 180.

7 Maja K. Schachner, Linda Juang, Ursula Moffitt, and Fons J. R. van de Vijver, "Schools as Acculturative and Developmental Contexts for Youth of Immigrant and Refugee Background," *European Psychologist* 23, no. 1 (2018): 44–56; Nigar G. Khawaja, Emily Allan, and Robert D. Schweitzer, "The Role of School Connectedness and Social Support in the Acculturation in Culturally and Linguistically Diverse Youth in Australia," *Australian Psychologist* 53, no. 4 (2018): 355–64; Jason G. Irizarry and John Raible, "Beginning with El Barrio: Learning from Exemplary Teachers of Latino Students," *Journal of Latinos and Education* 10, no. 3 (2011): 186–203.

8 Linda K. Ko and Krista M. Pereira, "'It Turned My World Upside Down': Latino Youths' Perspectives on Immigration," *Journal of Adolescent Research* 25, no. 3 (2010): 465–93.

9 Schachner et al., "Schools as Acculturative and Developmental Contexts."

10 Schachner et al., "Schools as Acculturative and Developmental Contexts."

11 Ming Ming Chiu, Suet-ling Pong, Izumi Mori, and Bonnie Wing-Yin Chow, "Immigrant Students' Emotional and Cognitive Engagement at School: A Multilevel Analysis of Students in 41 Countries," *Journal of Youth and Adolescence* 41, no. 11 (2012): 1409–25.

12 Chiu et al., "Immigrant Students' Emotional and Cognitive Engagement at School."

13 Chiu et al., "Immigrant Students' Emotional and Cognitive Engagement at School."

14 Rebecca Lowenhaupt, "Immigrant Acculturation in Suburban Schools Serving the New Latino Diaspora," *Peabody Journal of Education* 91, no. 3 (2016): 348–65.

15 American School Counselor Association, "School Counselors Roles & Ratios."

16 Katherine E. Bernal-Arevalo, "Achieving the Dream: The High School Counselor Role in Supporting the Transition of Undocumented College-Bound Latino/a Students" (Master's thesis, California State, Fresno, 2019).

17 Aliza J. Gilbert, "Dreamers and the College Dream: A Case Study Analysis Examining the Influences of High Schools and High School Agents" (PhD dissertation, Loyola University, Chicago, August 2016).

18 Carolina Valdivia and Marisol Clark-Ibáñez, "'It Is Hard Right Now': High School Educators Working with Undocumented Students," *Latino Public Policy* 10 (July 31, 2018), https://scholar.smu.edu.

19 Valdivia and Clark-Ibáñez, "'It Is Hard Right Now.'"

20 Valdivia and Clark-Ibáñez, "'It Is Hard Right Now.'"

21 Marrero, "Barriers to School Success for Latino Students."

22 Linda Banks-Santilli, "First-Generation College Students and Their Pursuit of the American Dream," *Journal of Case Studies in Education* 5, 1-32 (2014).

23 Gilbert, "Dreamers and the College Dream."

24 Ariana Mangual Figueroa, "Speech or Silence: Undocumented Students' Decisions to Disclose or Disguise Their Citizenship Status in School," *American Educational Research Journal* 54, no. 3 (2017): 485–523.

25 H. Kenny Nienhusser, "Role of High Schools in Undocumented Students' College Choice," *Education Policy Analysis Archives* 21, no. 85 (2013): n85.

26 Nienhusser, "Role of High Schools in Undocumented Students' College Choice."

27 Lisa Barrow and Lisa Markman-Pithers, "Supporting Young English Learners in the United States," *The Future of Children* 26, no. 2 (2016): 159–83.

28 Ellen Bialystok, "Bilingual Education for Young Children: Review of the Effects and Consequences," *International Journal of Bilingual Education and Bilingualism* 21, no. 6 (2018): 666–79.

29 Suzanne García-Mateus and Deborah Palmer, "Translanguaging Pedagogies for Positive Identities in Two-Way Dual Language Bilingual Education," *Journal of Language, Identity & Education* 16, no. 4 (2017): 245–55.

30 Valerie A. Earnshaw et al., "Teacher Involvement as a Protective Factor from the Association between Race-Based Bullying and Smoking Initiation," *Social Psychology of Education* 17, no. 2 (2014): 197–209.

31 Karen Zeigler and Steven A. Camarota, "67.3 Million in the United States Spoke a Foreign Language at Home in 2018," *Center for Immigration Studies*, October 19, 2019, https://cis.org.

32 Irizarry and Raible, "Beginning with El Barrio."

33 Bialystok, "Bilingual Education for Young Children."

34 Irizarry and Raible, "Beginning with El Barrio."

35 Sabrina Zirkel, "Is There a Place for Me? Role Models and Academic Identity among White Students and Students of Color," *Teachers College Record* 104, no. 2 (2002): 357–76. Zirkel, "Is There a Place for Me?"

36 Irizarry and Raible, "Beginning with El Barrio."

37 Zirkel, "Is There a Place for Me?"; Christopher Redding, "A Teacher Like Me: A Review of the Effect of Student–Teacher Racial/Ethnic Matching on Teacher Perceptions of Students and Student Academic and Behavioral Outcomes," *Review of Educational Research* 89, no. 4 (2019): 499–535; Hua-Yu Sebastian Cherng and Peter F. Halpin, "The Importance of Minority Teachers: Student Perceptions of Minority versus White Teachers," *Educational Researcher* 45, no. 7 (2016): 407–20.

38 Jason T. Downer et al., "Teacher-Child Racial/Ethnic Match within Pre-Kindergarten Classrooms and Children's Early School Adjustment," *Early Childhood Research Quarterly* 37 (2016): 26–38; Redding, "A Teacher Like Me."

39 Lindsay Pérez Huber, "Discourses of Racist Nativism in California Public Education: English Dominance as Racist Nativist Microaggressions," *Educational Studies* 47, no. 4 (2011): 379–401; Anne Steketee, Monnica T. Williams, Beatriz T. Valencia, Destiny Printz, and Lisa M. Hooper, "Racial and Language Microaggressions in the School Ecology," *Perspectives on Psychological Science* 16, no. 5 (2021): 1075–98.

40 Steketee et al., "Racial and Language Microaggressions in the School Ecology."

41 Giselle Martinez Negrete, "'You Don't Speak Spanish in the Cafeteria': An Intersectional Analysis of Language and Social Constructions in a Kindergarten Dual Language Immersion Class," *International Journal of Bilingual Education and Bilingualism* 25, no. 5 (2020): 1–17.

42 Carola Suárez-Orozco, Frosso Motti-Stefanidi, Amy Marks, and Dalal Katsiaficas, "An Integrative Risk and Resilience Model for Understanding the Adaptation of Immigrant-Origin Children and Youth," *American Psychologist* 73, no. 6 (2018): 781.

43 Asghar Afshari, Zia Tajeddin, and Gholam-Reza Abbasian, "Sources of Demotivation among English Language Learners: Novice and Experienced Teachers' Beliefs," *Journal of Modern Research in English Language Studies* 6, no. 4 (2019): 59–81.

44 Irizarry and Raible, "Beginning with El Barrio."

45 Irizarry and Raible, "Beginning with El Barrio."

46 American School Counselor Association, "School Counselors Roles & Ratios."

47 Christine Mulhern, "Beyond Teachers: Estimating Individual Guidance Counselors' Effects on Educational Attainment," Institute of Education Sciences, Harvard University, 2020.

48 Clara Peña, Lisa Jones, Amy Orange, Felix Simieou, and Judith Márquez, "Academic Success and Resiliency Factors: A Case Study of Unaccompanied Immigrant Children," *American Journal of Qualitative Research* 2, no. 1 (2018): 162–81.

49 Bernal-Arevalo, "Achieving the Dream."

50 Cynthia T. Walley and Jasmine L. Knight, "The Road Less Traveled: School Counselors' Role in Helping Undocumented Students Move beyond College Enrollment," *Journal of School Counseling* 16, no. 26 (2018): n26.

51 Illinois Student Assistance Commission, "Golden Apple Scholarships of Illinois," 2021, www.isac.org.

52 Katherine E. Bernal-Arevalo, Sergio Pereyra, Dominiqua M. Griffin, and Gitima Sharma, "'They're in the Shadows': School Counselors Share the Lived Experiences of Latino/a Undocumented Students," *Journal of College Access* 6, no. 2 (2021): 8.

53 Regine M. Talleyrand and Jennifer Thanh-Giang Vojtech, "Potential Stressors of Undocumented Latinx Youth: Implications and Recommendations for School Counselors," *Professional School Counseling* 22, no. 1 (2019): 2156759X19847168.
54 Bernal-Arevalo et al., "'They're in the Shadows.'"
55 Illinois General Assembly, "Public Act 093–0007."
56 Illinois General Assembly, "Full Text of HB2185."
57 Illinois General Assembly. "Full Text of HB2691."
58 Illinois General Assembly, "Public Act 093–0007."
59 Valdivia and Clark-Ibáñez, "'It Is Hard Right Now.'"
60 Albarracín, *At the Core and in the Margins.*
61 Michael J. Trivette and David J. English, "Finding Freedom: Facilitating Postsecondary Pathways for Undocumented Students," *Educational Policy* 31, no. 6 (2017): 858–94.
62 American School Counselor Association, "School Counselors Roles & Ratios."
63 Sheila Cook and Iva Gaylord, "Navigating Graduate School: Resource Guide for Undocumented Students," *Santa Clara University Law School Digital Commons,* 2018, https://digitalcommons.law.scu.edu.
64 Gilbert, "Dreamers and the College Dream."
65 Illinois General Assembly, "Public Act 093–0007."
66 Bernal-Arevalo, "Achieving the Dream."
67 Ko and Pereira, "'It Turned My World Upside Down.'"
68 Marrero, "Barriers to School Success for Latino Students."
69 García-Mateus and Palmer, "Translanguaging Pedagogies for Positive Identities."
70 Earnshaw et al., "Teacher Involvement as a Protective Factor."
71 Cherng and Halpin, "The Importance of Minority Teachers"; Redding, "A Teacher like Me"; Zirkel, "Is There a Place for Me?"
72 Zirkel, "Is There a Place for Me?"
73 Irizarry and Raible, "Beginning with El Barrio."
74 Steketee et al., "Racial and Language Microaggressions in the School Ecology."
75 Rogelio Sáenz and Karen Manges Douglas, "A Call for the Racialization of Immigration Studies: On the Transition of Ethnic Immigrants to Racialized Immigrants," *Sociology of Race and Ethnicity* 1, no. 1 (2015): 166–80.
76 Illinois General Assembly, "Public Act 093–0007"; Illinois General Assembly, "Full Text of HB2691."
77 Bernal-Arevalo, "Achieving the Dream."
78 Valdivia and Clark-Ibáñez, "'It Is Hard Right Now.'"
79 Suárez-Orozco et al., "An Integrative Risk and Resilience Model."

CHAPTER 4. NO FUTURE IN SIGHT

1 Alejandro Portes and József Böröcz, "Contemporary Immigration: Theoretical Perspectives on Its Determinants and Modes of Incorporation," *International Migration Review* 23, no. 3 (1989): 606–30.
2 Portes and Böröcz, "Contemporary Immigration."

3 Rubén G. Rumbaut and Golnaz Komaie, "Immigration and Adult Transitions," *The Future of Children* 20, no. 1 (2010): 43–66.

4 Kara Cebulko, "Documented, Undocumented, and Liminally Legal: Legal Status during the Transition to Adulthood for 1.5-Generation Brazilian Immigrants," *Sociological Quarterly* 55, no. 1 (2014): 143–67; Cecilia Menjívar, "Liminal Legality: Salvadoran and Guatemalan Immigrants' Lives in the United States," *American Journal of Sociology* 111, no. 4 (2006): 999–1037; Loan Thi Dao, "Out and Asian: How Undocu/DACAmented Asian Americans and Pacific Islander Youth Navigate Dual Liminality in the Immigrant Rights Movement," *Societies* 7, no. 3 (2017): 17; Rebecca Maria Torres and Melissa Wicks-Asbun, "Undocumented Students' Narratives of Liminal Citizenship: High Aspirations, Exclusion, and 'in-between' Identities," *Professional Geographer* 66, no. 2 (2014): 195–204; Edelina M. Burciaga and Aaron Malone, "Intensified Liminal Legality: The Impact of the DACA Rescission for Undocumented Young Adults in Colorado," *Law & Social Inquiry*, 2021, 1092–1114; Benjamin J. Roth, "The Double Bind of DACA: Exploring the Legal Violence of Liminal Status for Undocumented Youth," *Ethnic and Racial Studies* 42, no. 15 (2019): 2548–65.

5 Joseph M. Cervantes, Laura P. Minero, and Elivet Brito, "Tales of Survival 101 for Undocumented Latina/o Immigrant University Students: Commentary and Recommendations from Qualitative Interviews," *Journal of Latina/o Psychology*, June 8, 2015, https://psycnet.apa.org.

6 Julia Albarracín, *At the Core and in the Margins: Incorporation of Mexican Immigrants in Two Rural Midwestern Communities* (East Lansing: Michigan State University Press, 2016); Portes and Böröcz, "Contemporary Immigration"; Xavier de Souza Briggs, "Conclusion Rethinking Immigrant Political Incorporation," in *Outsiders No More?: Models of Immigrant Political Incorporation*, ed. Jennifer Hochschild, Jacqueline Chattopadhyay, Claudine Gay, and Michael Jones-Correa (New York: Oxford University Press, 2013), 321.

7 Lauren M. Ellis and Eric C. Chen, "Negotiating Identity Development Among Undocumented Immigrant College Students: A Grounded Theory Study," *Journal of Counseling Psychology* 60, no. 2 (2013): 251–64.

8 Patricia Ewick and Susan S. Silbey, *The Common Place of Law: Stories from Everyday Life* (Chicago: University of Chicago Press, 1998).

9 Maria E. Zuniga, "Latino Immigrants: Patterns of Survival," *Journal of Human Behavior in the Social Environment* 5, no. 3–4 (2002): 137–55.

10 Leisy J. Abrego, "Legal Consciousness of Undocumented Latinos: Fear and Stigma as Barriers to Claims-making for First-and 1.5-generation Immigrants," *Law & Society Review* 45, no. 2 (2011): 337–70

11 Efrain Talamantes, Yadira Bribiesca, Bryan Rangel-Alvarez, Omar Viramontes, Marcela Zhou, Hemal Kanzaria, Mark G. Kuczewski, and Gerardo Moreno, "The Termination of Deferred Action for Childhood Arrival (DACA) Protections and Medical Education in the US," *Journal of Immigrant and Minority Health* 22 (2019): 353–58.

12 Zuniga, "Latino Immigrants: Patterns of Survival."

13 Cebulko, "Documented, Undocumented, and Liminally Legal"; Torres and Wicks-Asbun, "Undocumented Students' Narratives of Liminal Citizenship"; Roth, "The Double Bind of DACA."

14 Roberto G. Gonzales and Leo R. Chavez, "'Awakening to a Nightmare': Abjectivity and Illegality in the Lives of Undocumented 1.5-Generation Latino Immigrants in the United States," *Current Anthropology* 53, no. 3 (June 2012): 255–81.

15 Zuniga, "Latino Immigrants: Patterns of Survival."

16 Nicholas De Genova, "The Legal Production of Mexican/Migrant 'Illegality,'" *Latino Studies* 2, no. 2 (July 2004): 160–85.

17 Mae M. Ngai, *Impossible Subjects: Illegal Aliens and the Making of Modern America* (Princeton, NJ: Princeton University Press, 2004).; Roberto G. Gonzales, "Learning to Be Illegal: Undocumented Youth and Shifting Legal Contexts in the Transition to Adulthood," *American Sociological Review* 76, no. 4 (August 2011): 602–19, https://doi.org/10.1177/0003122411411901; De Genova, "The Legal Production of Mexican/Migrant 'Illegality.'"

18 Linda K. Ko and Krista M. Pereira, "'It Turned My World Upside Down': Latino Youths' Perspectives on Immigration," *Journal of Adolescent Research* 25, no. 3 (2010): 465–93.

19 De Genova, "The Legal Production of Mexican/Migrant 'Illegality.'"

20 De Genova, "The Legal Production of Mexican/Migrant 'Illegality.'"

21 Nicholas P. De Genova, "Migrant 'Illegality' and Deportability in Everyday Life," *Annual Review of Anthropology* 31, no. 1 (2002): 419–47.

22 De Genova, "Migrant 'Illegality' and Deportability in Everyday Life."

23 De Genova, "Migrant 'Illegality' and Deportability in Everyday Life."

24 Albarracín, *At the Core and in the Margins.*

25 Albarracín, *At the Core and in the Margins.*

26 Albarracín, *At the Core and in the Margins.*

27 Albarracín, *At the Core and in the Margins.*

28 Mark Hugo Lopez, Jeffrey S. Passel, and D'Vera Cohn, "Key Facts about the Changing U.S. Unauthorized Immigrant Population," Pew Research Center, April 13, 2021, www.pewresearch.org.

29 Ngai, *Impossible Subjects.*

30 Gonzales, "Learning to Be Illegal."

31 Cebulko, "Documented, Undocumented, and Liminally Legal."

32 Lorraine T. Benuto, Jena B. Casas, Caroline Cummings, and Rory Newlands, "Undocumented, to DACAmented, to DACAlimited: Narratives of Latino Students with DACA Status," *Hispanic Journal of Behavioral Sciences* 40, no. 3 (August 1, 2018): 259–78, https://doi.org/10.1177/0739986318776941.

33 Genevieve Negrón-Gonzales, "Navigating 'Illegality': Undocumented Youth and Oppositional Consciousness," *Children and Youth Services Review* 35 no. 8 (August 2013): 1284–90.

34 Dao, "Out and Asian"; Menjívar, "Liminal Legality"; Cebulko, "Documented, Undocumented, and Liminally Legal"; Torres and Wicks-Asbun, "Undocumented Students' Narratives of Liminal Citizenship"; Roth, "The Double Bind of DACA"; Zuniga, "Latino Immigrants: Patterns of Survival"; De Genova, "The Legal Production of Mexican/Migrant 'Illegality.'"

35 Torres and Wicks-Asbun, "Undocumented Students' Narratives of Liminal Citizenship."

36 Cebulko, "Documented, Undocumented, and Liminally Legal"; Torres and Wicks-Asbun, "Undocumented Students' Narratives of Liminal Citizenship."

37 Zuniga, "Latino Immigrants: Patterns of Survival."

38 Cebulko, "Documented, Undocumented, and Liminally Legal."

39 Cebulko, "Documented, Undocumented, and Liminally Legal."

40 Cebulko, "Documented, Undocumented, and Liminally Legal."

41 Zuniga, "Latino Immigrants: Patterns of Survival."

42 Michael A. Olivas, *Perchance to DREAM: A Legal and Political History of the DREAM Act and DACA* (New York: New York University Press, 2020).

43 Leisy Abrego, "Legitimacy, Social Identity, and the Mobilization of Law: The Effects of Assembly Bill 540 on Undocumented Students in California," *Law & Social Inquiry* 33, no. 3 (2008): 709–34.

44 Gonzales, "Learning to Be Illegal."

45 Sophia Rodriguez, "'I Was Born at the Border, Like the 'Wrong' Side of It': Undocumented Latinx Youth Experiences of Racialization in the US South," *Anthropology & Education Quarterly* 51, no. 4 (2020): 496–526.

46 Gonzales, *Lives in Limbo*; Ko and Pereira, "'It Turned My World Upside Down.'"

47 Gonzales, *Lives in Limbo.*

48 Nicholas De Genova, Sandro Mezzadra, and John Pickles, "New Keywords: Migration and Borders," *Cultural Studies* 29, no. 1 (2015): 55–87; Julia Albarracín, *Making Immigrants in Modern Argentina* (Notre Dame, IN: University of Notre Dame Pess, 2020); Peter Andreas, *Border Games* (Ithaca, NY: Cornell University Press, 2011).

49 De Genova, "Spectacles of Migrant 'Illegality,'" 1182.

50 De Genova, "Spectacles of Migrant 'Illegality.'"

51 Monica Cornejo, Jennifer A. Kam, and Tamara D. Afifi, "Discovering One's Undocumented Immigration Status through Family Disclosures: The Perspectives of US College Students with Deferred Action for Childhood Arrivals (DACA)," *Journal of Applied Communication Research* 49, no. 3 (2021): 267–85.

52 Heide Castañeda, *Borders of Belonging: Struggle and Solidarity in Mixed-Status Immigrant Families* (Stanford, CA: Stanford University Press, 2019).

53 Castañeda, *Borders of Belonging.*

54 Negrón-Gonzales, "Navigating 'Illegality.'"

55 Ko and Pereira, "'It Turned My World Upside Down.'"

56 Torres and Wicks-Asbun, "Undocumented Students' Narratives of Liminal Citizenship"; Roth, "The Double Bind of DACA"; Cecilia Menjivar, Victor

Agadjanian, and Byeongdon Oh, "The Contradictions of Liminal Legality: Economic Attainment and Civic Engagement of Central American Immigrants on Temporary Protected Status," *Social Problems* 69, no. 3 (2020): 678–98.

57 Roberto G. Gonzales, *Lives in Limbo: Undocumented and Coming of Age in America* (Berkeley: University of California Press, 2015).

58 Gonzales, "Learning to Be Illegal."

59 Gonzales, *Lives in Limbo.*

60 Gonzales, *Lives in Limbo.*

61 Akiko Yasuike, "Stigma Management and Resistance among High-Achieving Undocumented Students," *Sociological Inquiry* 89, no. 2 (2019): 191–213.

62 De Genova, "Migrant 'Illegality' and Deportability in Everyday Life."

63 De Genova, "Migrant 'Illegality' and Deportability in Everyday Life."

64 Albarracín, *At the Core and in the Margins.*

65 Gonzales, "Learning to Be Illegal."

66 Leisy J. Abrego, "'I Can't Go to College Because I Don't Have Papers': Incorporation Patterns of Latino Undocumented Youth," *Latino Studies* 4 (2006): 212–31.

67 Gonzales, "Learning to Be Illegal."

68 Illinois General Assembly, "Public Act 093–0007," 2003, www.ilga.gov.

69 Meggan Lee Madden, Paige E. Butler, and Nickie Smith, "'A Dream to Go Abroad': Undocumented Student Participation in Education Abroad," *Journal of Student Affairs Research and Practice* 57, no. 4 (2020): 457–69.

70 Madden et al., "'A Dream to Go Abroad.'"

71 Gonzales, *Lives in Limbo*; Gonzales, "Learning to Be Illegal"; Gonzales and Chavez, "'Awakening to a Nightmare'"; Roberto G. Gonzales, Carola Suárez-Orozco, and Maria Cecilia Dedios-Sanguineti, "No Place to Belong: Contextualizing Concepts of Mental Health among Undocumented Immigrant Youth in the United States," *American Behavioral Scientist* 57, no. 8 (2013): 1174–99; Abrego, "'I Can't Go to College Because I Don't Have Papers'"; Abrego, "Legitimacy, Social Identity, and the Mobilization of Law"; Carola Suárez-Orozco, Marcelo M. Suárez-Orozco, and Irina Todorova, *Learning a New Land* (Cambridge, MA: Harvard University Press, 2008); Luis Cisneros, "Undocumented Students Pursuing Higher Education," *UC Merced Undergraduate Research Journal* 5, no. 1 (2013): 192–204; Sharon Velarde Pierce, Alein Y. Haro, Cecilia Ayón, and Laura E. Enriquez, "Evaluating the Effect of Legal Vulnerabilities and Social Support on the Mental Health of Undocumented College Students," *Journal of Latinos and Education* 20, no. 3 (2021): 246–59; Benuto et al., "Undocumented, to DACAmented, to DACAlimited."

72 Gonzales et al., "No Place to Belong."

73 Gonzales, *Lives in Limbo.*

74 Gonzales, *Lives in Limbo.*

75 Benuto et al., "Undocumented, to DACAmented, to DACAlimited."

76 Carola Suárez-Orozco, Hirozaku Yoshikawa, Robert T. Teranishi, and Marcelo M. Suárez-Orozco, "Growing Up in the Shadows: The Developmental Implications of Unauthorized Status," *Harvard Educational Review* 81, no. 3 (2011): 438–73.

77 Cisneros, "Undocumented Students Pursuing Higher Education."

78 Cecilia Menjívar and L. J. Abrego, "Legal Violence: Immigration Law and the Lives of Central American Immigrants," *American Journal of Sociology* 117, no. 5 (March 2012): 1380–1421, https://doi.org/10.1086/663575.

79 Roth, "The Double Bind of DACA."

80 Abrego, "'I Can't Go to College Because I Don't Have Papers'"; Roth, "The Double Bind of DACA"; Lauren M. Ellis and Eric C. Chen, "Negotiating Identity Development Among Undocumented Immigrant College Students: A Grounded Theory Study," *Journal of Counseling Psychology* 60, no. 2 (2013): 251–64, https://doi.org/10.1037/a0031350.

81 Menjívar and Abrego, "Legal Violence."

82 Zuniga, "Latino Immigrants: Patterns of Survival"; De Genova, "Migrant 'Illegality' and Deportability in Everyday Life."

83 Negrón-Gonzales, "Navigating 'Illegality.'"

84 Gonzales et al., "No Place to Belong"; Ko and Pereira, "'It Turned My World Upside Down.'"

85 Lindsay Perez Huber, Robin N. Johnson, and Rita Kohli, "Naming Racism: A Conceptual Look at Internalized Racism in US Schools," *Chicano-Latino Law Review* 26 (2006): 183; Lindsay Pérez Huber, "Discourses of Racist Nativism in California Public Education: English Dominance as Racist Nativist Microaggressions," *Educational Studies* 47, no. 4 (2011): 379–401.

86 Yasuike, "Stigma Management and Resistance among High-Achieving Undocumented Students."

87 Jo Boyden, Andrew Dawes, Paul Dornan, and Colin Tredoux, "Adolescence and Youth: A Time of Responsibility and Transformation," in *Tracing the Consequences of Child Poverty* (Bristol: Policy Press, 2019), 101–32.

88 Ko and Pereira, "'It Turned My World Upside Down'"; Gonzales, *Lives in Limbo*.

89 Gonzales, *Lives in Limbo*.

90 Ko and Pereira, "'It Turned My World Upside Down.'"

91 Gonzales, *Lives in Limbo*.

92 Negrón-Gonzales, "Navigating 'Illegality.'"

93 Dao, "Out and Asian"; Menjívar, "Liminal Legality"; Cebulko, "Documented, Undocumented, and Liminally Legal"; Torres and Wicks-Asbun, "Undocumented Students' Narratives of Liminal Citizenship"; Roth, "The Double Bind of DACA"; Zuniga, "Latino Immigrants: Patterns of Survival"; De Genova, "The Legal Production of Mexican/Migrant 'Illegality.'"

94 Negrón-Gonzales, "Navigating 'Illegality.'"

95 Gonzales, *Lives in Limbo*; Benuto et al., "Undocumented, to DACAmented, to DACAlimited"; Suárez-Orozco et al., "Growing Up in the Shadows."

CHAPTER 5. DEFERRED ACTION

1 Rubén G. Rumbaut and Golnaz Komaie, "Immigration and Adult Transitions," *The Future of Children* 20, no. 1 (2010): 43–66.

2 Genevieve Negrón-Gonzales, "Navigating 'Illegality': Undocumented Youth and Oppositional Consciousness," *Children and Youth Services Review* 35 no. 8 (August 2013): 1284–90; Roberto G. Gonzales, Veronica Terriquez, and Stephen P. Ruszczyk, "Becoming DACAmented: Assessing the Short-Term Benefits of Deferred Action for Childhood Arrivals (DACA)," *American Behavioral Scientist* 58, no. 14 (2014): 1852–72; Roberto G. Gonzales, *Lives in Limbo: Undocumented and Coming of Age in America* (Berkeley: University of California Press, 2015); Roberto G. Gonzales, Sayil Camacho, Kristina Brant, and Carlos Aguilar, "The Long-Term Impact of DACA: Forging Futures Despite DACA's Uncertainty," *Report for the Immigration Initiative at Harvard and National UnDACAmented Research Project (NURP)*, 2019; Roberto G. Gonzales, Carola Suárez-Orozco, and Maria Cecilia Dedios-Sanguineti, "No Place to Belong: Contextualizing Concepts of Mental Health among Undocumented Immigrant Youth in the United States," *American Behavioral Scientist* 57, no. 8 (2013): 1174–99; Leisy J. Abrego, "Legal Consciousness of Undocumented Latinos: Fear and Stigma as Barriers to Claims-making for First-and 1.5-generation Immigrants," *Law & Society Review* 45, no. 2 (2011): 337–70; Leisy J. Abrego, "'I Can't Go to College Because I Don't Have Papers': Incorporation Patterns of Latino Undocumented Youth," *Latino Studies* 4 (2006): 212–31.

3 Gonzales et al., "Becoming DACAmented"; Caitlin Patler and Jorge A. Cabrera, "From Undocumented to DACAmented: Impacts of the Deferred Action for Childhood Arrivals (DACA) Program," *UCLA: Institute for Research on Labor and Employment*, 2015; Benjamin J. Roth, "The Double Bind of DACA: Exploring the Legal Violence of Liminal Status for Undocumented Youth," *Ethnic and Racial Studies* 42, no. 15 (2019): 2548–65; Catalina Amuedo-Dorantes and Francisca Antman, "Can Authorization Reduce Poverty among Undocumented Immigrants? Evidence from the Deferred Action for Childhood Arrivals Program," *Economics Letters* 147 (2016): 1–4; Julio C. Ramos et al., "The Impact of Deferred Action for Childhood Arrivals (DACA) Medical Students—a Scarce Resource to US Health Care," *American Journal of Public Health* 109, no. 3 (2019): 429–31; Martha Morales Hernandez and Laura E. Enriquez, "Life after College: Liminal Legality and Political Threats as Barriers to Undocumented Students' Career Preparation Pursuits," *Journal of Latinos and Education* 20, no. 3 (2021): 318–31; Caitlin Patler and Whitney Laster Pirtle, "From Undocumented to Lawfully Present: Do Changes to Legal Status Impact Psychological Wellbeing among Latino Immigrant Young Adults?," *Social Science & Medicine* 199 (2018): 39–48; Gonzales et al., "The Long-Term Impact of DACA."

4 Gonzales et al., "The Long-Term Impact of DACA"; Gonzales et al., "Becoming DACAmented"; Amuedo-Dorantes and Antman, "Can Authorization Reduce Poverty among Undocumented Immigrants?"; Ramos et al., "The Impact of Deferred Action for Childhood Arrivals (DACA) Medical Students."

5 Patler and Pirtle, "From Undocumented to Lawfully Present"; Oswaldo Moreno, Lisa Fuentes, Isis Garcia-Rodriguez, Rosalie Corona, and Germàn A. Cadenas, "Psychological Impact, Strengths, and Handling the Uncertainty Among Latinx DACA Recipients," *The Counseling Psychologist* 49, no. 5 (2021): 728–53; Rachel

Siemons, Marissa Raymond-Flesch, Colette L. Auerswald, and Claire D. Brindis, "Coming of Age on the Margins: Mental Health and Wellbeing among Latino Immigrant Young Adults Eligible for Deferred Action for Childhood Arrivals (DACA)," *Journal of Immigrant and Minority Health* 19, no. 3 (2017): 543–51.

6 Roth, "The Double Bind of DACA"; Morales Hernandez and Enriquez, "Life after College."

7 Catalina Amuedo-Dorantes, Esther Arenas-Arroyo, and Almudena Sevilla, "Labor Market Impacts of States Issuing of Driver's Licenses to Undocumented Immigrants," *Labour Economics* 63 (2020): 101805; Gonzales et al., "The Long-Term Impact of DACA"; Gonzales et al., "Becoming DACAmented"; Ramos et al., "The Impact of Deferred Action for Childhood Arrivals (DACA) Medical Students."

8 Gonzales et al., "Becoming DACAmented"; Gonzales et al., "The Long-Term Impact of DACA."

9 Gonzales et al., "Becoming DACAmented."

10 Gonzales et al., "Becoming DACAmented."

11 Gonzales et al., "The Long-Term Impact of DACA."

12 Gonzales et al., "The Long-Term Impact of DACA."

13 Amuedo-Dorantes and Antman, "Can Authorization Reduce Poverty among Undocumented Immigrants?"

14 Patler and Cabrera, "From Undocumented to DACAmented."

15 Patler and Pirtle, "From Undocumented to Lawfully Present"; Moreno et al., "Psychological Impact, Strengths, and Handling the Uncertainty Among Latinx DACA Recipients"; Siemons et al., "Coming of Age on the Margins."

16 Siemons et al., "Coming of Age on the Margins."

17 Siemons et al., "Coming of Age on the Margins."

18 Siemons et al., "Coming of Age on the Margins."

19 Siemons et al., "Coming of Age on the Margins."

20 Patler and Pirtle, "From Undocumented to Lawfully Present."

21 Patler and Pirtle, "From Undocumented to Lawfully Present."

22 Roth, "The Double Bind of DACA"; Morales Hernandez and Enriquez, "Life after College."

23 Roth, "The Double Bind of DACA."

24 Roth, "The Double Bind of DACA."

25 Roth, "The Double Bind of DACA."

26 Roth, "The Double Bind of DACA."

27 Morales Hernandez and Enriquez, "Life after College."

28 Morales Hernandez and Enriquez, "Life after College."

29 Amuedo-Dorantes and Antman, "Can Authorization Reduce Poverty among Undocumented Immigrants?"; Gonzales et al., "The Long-Term Impact of DACA"; Gonzales et al., "Becoming DACAmented."

30 Patler and Cabrera, "From Undocumented to DACAmented"; Patler and Pirtle, "From Undocumented to Lawfully Present"; Moreno et al., "Psychological Impact, Strengths, and Handling the Uncertainty Among Latinx DACA Recipients."

31 Patler and Pirtle, "From Undocumented to Lawfully Present."

32 Siemons et al., "Coming of Age on the Margins."

33 Morales Hernandez and Enriquez, "Life after College"; Roth, "The Double Bind of DACA."

34 Gonzales et al., "Becoming DACAmented."

35 Roberto G. Gonzales, Basia Ellis, Sarah A. Rendón-García, and Kristina Brant, "(Un)Authorized Transitions: Illegality, DACA, and the Life Course," *Research in Human Development* 15, no. 3–4 (2018): 345–59.

36 Amuedo-Dorantes and Antman, "Can Authorization Reduce Poverty among Undocumented Immigrants?"; Gonzales et al., "The Long-Term Impact of DACA."

37 Amuedo-Dorantes and Antman, "Can Authorization Reduce Poverty among Undocumented Immigrants?"

38 Nolan G. Pope, "The Effects of DACAmentation: The Impact of Deferred Action for Childhood Arrivals on Unauthorized Immigrants," *Journal of Public Economics* 143 (2016): 98–114.

39 Patler and Cabrera, "From Undocumented to DACAmented."

40 Pope, "The Effects of DACAmentation."

41 Gonzales et al., "The Long-Term Impact of DACA."

42 Pope, "The Effects of DACAmentation."

43 Gonzales et al., "The Long-Term Impact of DACA."

44 Amuedo-Dorantes and Antman, "Can Authorization Reduce Poverty among Undocumented Immigrants?"

45 Gonzales et al., "The Long-Term Impact of DACA."

46 Gonzales et al., "The Long-Term Impact of DACA."

47 Dalia Sofer, "DACA Recipients Seeking RN Licensure: On a Road to Nowhere?" *AJN The American Journal of Nursing* 119, no. 10 (2019): 12.

48 Gonzales et al., "The Long-Term Impact of DACA."

49 Morales Hernandez and Enriquez, "Life after College."

50 Morales Hernandez and Enriquez, "Life after College."

51 Gonzales et al., "The Long-Term Impact of DACA."

52 Gonzales et al., "The Long-Term Impact of DACA."

53 Gonzales et al., "The Long-Term Impact of DACA."

54 Siemons et al., "Coming of Age on the Margins."

55 Siemons et al., "Coming of Age on the Margins."

56 Patler and Pirtle, "From Undocumented to Lawfully Present."

57 Patler and Pirtle, "From Undocumented to Lawfully Present."

58 Siemons et al., "Coming of Age on the Margins."

59 Lindsay Perez Huber, "Como Una Jaula de Oro (It's Like a Golden Cage): The Impact of DACA and the California Dream Act on Documented Chicanas/Latinas," *Chicana/o-Latina/o Law Review* 33 (2015): 91.

60 Jessica Rosenberg et al., "What Happens to a Dream Deferred? Identity Formation and DACA," *Hispanic Journal of Behavioral Sciences* 42, no. 3 (2020): 275–99.

61 Siemons et al., "Coming of Age on the Margins."

62 Siemons et al., "Coming of Age on the Margins."

63 Roth, "The Double Bind of DACA."

64 Elira Kuka, Na'ama Shenhav, and Kevin Shih, "Do Human Capital Decisions Respond to the Returns to Education? Evidence from DACA," *American Economic Journal: Economic Policy* 12, no. 1 (2020): 293–324.

65 Edward L. Deci, "Effects of Externally Mediated Rewards on Intrinsic Motivation," *Journal of Personality and Social Psychology* 18, no. 1 (1971): 105; Mark R. Lepper, David Greene, and Richard E. Nisbett, "Undermining Children's Intrinsic Interest with Extrinsic Reward: A Test of the 'Overjustification' Hypothesis," *Journal of Personality and Social Psychology* 28, no. 1 (1973): 129.

66 Toshihiko Hayamizu, "Between Intrinsic and Extrinsic Motivation: Examination of Reasons for Academic Study Based on the Theory of Internalization," *Japanese Psychological Research* 39, no. 2 (1997): 98–108.

67 Judith M. Harackiewicz, "The Effects of Reward Contingency and Performance Feedback on Intrinsic Motivation," *Journal of Personality and Social Psychology* 37, no. 8 (1979): 1352.

68 Hayamizu, "Between Intrinsic and Extrinsic Motivation."

69 José F. Domene, Krista D. Socholotiuk, and Lyndsay A. Woitowicz, "Academic Motivation in Post-Secondary Students: Effects of Career Outcome Expectations and Type of Aspiration," *Canadian Journal of Education/Revue Canadienne de l'Éducation* 34, no. 1 (2011): 99–127.

70 Roth, "The Double Bind of DACA."

71 Elizabeth Aranda and Elizabeth Vaquera, "Racism, the Immigration Enforcement Regime, and the Implications for Racial Inequality in the Lives of Undocumented Young Adults," *Sociology of Race and Ethnicity* 1, no. 1 (2015): 88–104.

72 Aranda and Vaquera, "Racism, the Immigration Enforcement Regime, and the Implications for Racial Inequality"; Gonzales et al., "The Long-Term Impact of DACA."

73 Julia Albarracín, *At the Core and in the Margins: Incorporation of Mexican Immigrants in Two Rural Midwestern Communities* (East Lansing: Michigan State University Press, 2016).

74 Aranda and Vaquera, "Racism, the Immigration Enforcement Regime, and the Implications for Racial Inequality"; Gonzales et al., "The Long-Term Impact of DACA."

75 Aranda and Vaquera, "Racism, the Immigration Enforcement Regime, and the Implications for Racial Inequality."

76 Gonzales et al., "The Long-Term Impact of DACA."

77 Edelina M. Burciaga and Aaron Malone, "Intensified Liminal Legality: The Impact of the DACA Rescission for Undocumented Young Adults in Colorado," *Law & Social Inquiry* (2021): 1–23.

78 Burciaga and Malone, "Intensified Liminal Legality."

79 Gonzales, *Lives in Limbo*.

80 Siemons et al., "Coming of Age on the Margins"; Gonzales et al., "(Un)Authorized Transitions."

81 Genevieve Negrón-Gonzales, "Navigating 'Illegality': Undocumented Youth and Oppositional Consciousness," *Children and Youth Services Review* 35. no. 8 (August 2013): 1284–90.

82 Genevieve Negrón-Gonzales, "Undocumented, Unafraid and Unapologetic: Re-Articulatory Practices and Migrant Youth 'Illegality,'" *Latino Studies* 12, no. 2 (2014): 259–78, https://doi.org/10.1057/lst.2014.20.

83 Patler and Cabrera, "From Undocumented to DACAmented."

84 Cebulko, "Documented, Undocumented, and Liminally Legal"; Patler and Pirtle, "From Undocumented to Lawfully Present."

85 Gonzales et al., "(Un)Authorized Transitions."

86 Adrienne Pon, "The Dreamer Divide: Aspiring for a More Inclusive Immigrants' Rights Movement," *Stanford Journal of Civil Rights and Civil Liberties* 14, Special Issue (2018): 33–44.

87 Pon, "The Dreamer Divide."

88 Pon, "The Dreamer Divide."

89 Roth, "The Double Bind of DACA"; Morales Hernandez and Enriquez, "Life after College."

90 Roth, "The Double Bind of DACA."

91 Morales Hernandez and Enriquez, "Life after College."

92 Roth, "The Double Bind of DACA"; Morales Hernandez and Enriquez, "Life after College."

93 Morales Hernandez and Enriquez, "Life after College."

94 Roth, "The Double Bind of DACA."

95 Burciaga and Malone, "Intensified Liminal Legality."

96 Roth, "The Double Bind of DACA."

97 Roberto G. Gonzales, Luisa L. Heredia, and Genevieve Negrón-Gonzales, "Untangling Plyler's Legacy: Undocumented Students, Schools, and Citizenship," *Harvard Educational Review* 85, no. 3 (2015): 318–41.

98 Illinois General Assembly, "Public Act 093–0007."

99 Illinois General Assembly, "Full Text of HB2691."

100 Michael A. Olivas, *Perchance to DREAM: A Legal and Political History of the DREAM Act and DACA* (New York: New York University Press, 2020).

101 Sofer, "DACA Recipients Seeking RN Licensure."

102 Emir Estrada and Alissa Ruth, "Experiential Dual Frame of Reference: Family Consequences after DACA Youth Travel to Mexico through Advanced Parole," *Qualitative Sociology* 44, no. 2 (2021): 231–51.

103 Estrada and Ruth, "Experiential Dual Frame of Reference."

104 Louis DeSipio and O. Rodolfo, *US Immigration in the Twenty-First Century: Making Americans, Remaking America* (New York: Routledge, 2015).

105 DeSipio and Rodolfo, *US Immigration in the Twenty-First Century.*

106 DeSipio and Rodolfo, *US Immigration in the Twenty-First Century.*

107 Gonzales et al., "The Long-Term Impact of DACA."

108 Morales Hernandez and Enriquez, "Life after College."

109 Burciaga and Malone, "Intensified Liminal Legality"; Siemons et al., "Coming of Age on the Margins."

110 Antonio Olivo and Ellen Hirst, "Young Immigrants Packed Navy Pier to Seek Protected Status," *Chicago Tribune*, August 16, 2012.

111 Moreno et al., "Psychological Impact, Strengths, and Handling the Uncertainty Among Latinx DACA Recipients"; Patler and Pirtle, "From Undocumented to Lawfully Present"; Siemons et al., "Coming of Age on the Margins."

112 Gonzales et al., "The Long-Term Impact of DACA"; Gonzales et al., "Becoming DACAmented."

113 Gonzales et al., "The Long-Term Impact of DACA."

114 Amuedo-Dorantes and Antman, "Can Authorization Reduce Poverty among Undocumented Immigrants?"

115 Amuedo-Dorantes and Antman, "Can Authorization Reduce Poverty among Undocumented Immigrants?"

116 Moreno et al., "Psychological Impact, Strengths, and Handling the Uncertainty Among Latinx DACA Recipients"; Patler and Pirtle, "From Undocumented to Lawfully Present"; Siemons et al., "Coming of Age on the Margins."

117 Kuka et al., "Do Human Capital Decisions Respond to the Returns to Education?"

118 Aranda and Vaquera, "Racism, the Immigration Enforcement Regime, and the Implications for Racial Inequality."

119 Siemons et al., "Coming of Age on the Margins"; Gonzales et al., "(Un)Authorized Transitions."

120 Roth, "The Double Bind of DACA"; Morales Hernandez and Enriquez, "Life after College."

121 Roth, "The Double Bind of DACA"; Morales Hernandez and Enriquez, "Life after College."

122 Morales Hernandez and Enriquez, "Life after College."

123 Burciaga and Malone, "Intensified Liminal Legality."

124 Roth, "The Double Bind of DACA."

CHAPTER 6. DEPORTABLE AGAIN

1 Cecilia Menjívar and L. J. Abrego, "Legal Violence: Immigration Law and the Lives of Central American Immigrants," *American Journal of Sociology* 117, no. 5 (March 2012): 1380–1421, https://doi.org/10.1086/663575; Genevieve Negrón-Gonzales, "Navigating 'Illegality': Undocumented Youth and Oppositional Consciousness," *Children and Youth Services Review* 35, no. 8 (August 2013): 1284–90; Lorraine T. Benuto, Jena B. Casas, Caroline Cummings, and Rory Newlands, "Undocumented, to DACAmented, to DACAlimited: Narratives of Latino Students with DACA Status," *Hispanic Journal of Behavioral Sciences* 40, no. 3 (August 1, 2018): 259–78, https://doi.org/10.1177/0739986318776941; Carola Suárez-Orozco, Hirokazu Yoshikawa, Robert T. Teranishi, and Marcelo M.

Suárez-Orozco, "Growing Up in the Shadows: The Developmental Implications of Unauthorized Status," *Harvard Educational Review* 81, no. 3 (2011): 438–73; Roberto G. Gonzales, *Lives in Limbo: Undocumented and Coming of Age in America* (Berkeley: University of California Press, 2015).

2 Roberto G. Gonzales, Sayil Camacho, Kristina Brant, and Carlos Aguilar, "The Long-Term Impact of DACA: Forging Futures Despite DACA's Uncertainty," *Report for the Immigration Initiative at Harvard and National UnDACAmented Research Project (NURP)*, 2019; Roberto G. Gonzales, Veronica Terriquez, and Stephen P. Ruszczyk, "Becoming DACAmented: Assessing the Short-Term Benefits of Deferred Action for Childhood Arrivals (DACA)," *American Behavioral Scientist* 58, no. 14 (2014): 1852–72.

3 Oswaldo Moreno, Lisa Fuentes, Isis Garcia-Rodriguez, Rosalie Corona, and Germàn A. Cadenas, "Psychological Impact, Strengths, and Handling the Uncertainty Among Latinx DACA Recipients," *The Counseling Psychologist* 49, no. 5 (2021): 728–53; Caitlin Patler and Whitney Laster Pirtle, "From Undocumented to Lawfully Present: Do Changes to Legal Status Impact Psychological Wellbeing among Latino Immigrant Young Adults?," *Social Science & Medicine* 199 (2018): 39–48; Rachel Siemons, Marissa Raymond-Flesch, Colette L. Auerswald, and Claire D. Brindis, "Coming of Age on the Margins: Mental Health and Wellbeing among Latino Immigrant Young Adults Eligible for Deferred Action for Childhood Arrivals (DACA)," *Journal of Immigrant and Minority Health* 19, no. 3 (2017): 543–51.

4 Siemons et al., "Coming of Age on the Margins"; Roberto G. Gonzales, Basia Ellis, Sarah A. Rendón-García, and Kristina Brant, "(Un)Authorized Transitions: Illegality, DACA, and the Life Course," *Research in Human Development* 15, nos. 3–4 (2018): 345–59.

5 Department of Homeland Security, "Deferred Action for Childhood Arrivals"; Nation World News Desk, "Biden Wants to Strengthen Protection for DACA Recipients."

6 Marie L. Mallet-García and Lisa García-Bedolla, "Immigration Policy and Belonging: Ramifications for DACA Recipients' Sense of Belonging," *American Behavioral Scientist* 65, no. 9 (2021): 1165–79.

7 Mallet-García and García-Bedolla, "Immigration Policy and Belonging."

8 Rachel C. Kingsley, "'Legality' on Hold: An Exploratory Study on DACAmented Students' Experiences of Uncertainty and Fear" (Master's thesis, Oregon State University, 2019), http://ir.library.oregonstate.edu.

9 Kingsley, "'Legality' on Hold."

10 Gonzales, *Lives in Limbo*.

11 Benuto et al., "Undocumented, to DACAmented, to DACAlimited."

12 Suárez-Orozco et al., "Growing Up in the Shadows."

13 Luis Cisneros, "Undocumented Students Pursuing Higher Education," *UC Merced Undergraduate Research Journal* 5, no. 1 (2013): 192–204.

14 Kingsley, "'Legality' on Hold"; Mallet-García and García-Bedolla, "Immigration Policy and Belonging"; H. Kenny Nienhusser and Toko Oshio, "Awakened Hatred

and Heightened Fears: 'The Trump Effect' on the Lives of Mixed-Status Families," *Cultural Studies↔Critical Methodologies* 19(3) (December 2018), https://doi.org/10 .1177/1532708618817872.

15 Mallet-García and García-Bedolla, "Immigration Policy and Belonging."

16 Kingsley, "'Legality' on Hold."

17 Nienhusser and Oshio, "Awakened Hatred and Heightened Fears."

18 Cecilia Menjívar, William Paul Simmons, Daniel Alvord, and Elizabeth Salerno Valdez, "Immigration Enforcement, the Racialization of Legal Status, and Perceptions of the Police: Latinos in Chicago, Los Angeles, Houston, and Phoenix in Comparative Perspective," *Du Bois Review: Social Science Research on Race* 15, no. 1 (2018): 107–28.

19 Menjívar et al., "Immigration Enforcement."

20 Nik Theodore and Robert Habans, "Policing Immigrant Communities: Latino Perceptions of Police Involvement in Immigration Enforcement," *Journal of Ethnic and Migration Studies* 42, no. 6 (2016): 970–88.

21 Tom K. Wong, S. Deborah Kang, Carolina Valdivia, Josefina Espino, Michelle Gonzalez, and Elia Peralta, "How Interior Immigration Enforcement Affects Trust in Law Enforcement," *Perspectives on Politics* 19, no. 2 (2021): 357–70.

22 Stephanie L. Canizales and Jody Agius Vallejo, "Latinos & Racism in the Trump Era," *Daedalus* 150, no. 2 (2021): 150–64.

23 Cisneros, "Undocumented Students Pursuing Higher Education"; Gonzales, *Lives in Limbo*; Benuto et al., "Undocumented, to DACAmented, to DACAlimited"; Suárez-Orozco et al., "Growing Up in the Shadows."

24 Mallet-García and García-Bedolla, "Immigration Policy and Belonging."

25 Shoba Sivaprasad Wadhia, *Beyond Deportation: The Role of Prosecutorial Discretion in Immigration Cases* (New York: New York University Press, 2015).

26 Suárez-Orozco et al., "Growing Up in the Shadows."

27 Dolores Albarracín, Julia Albarracín, Man-pui Sally Chan, and Kathleen Hall Jamieson, *Creating Conspiracy Beliefs: How Our Thoughts Are Shaped* (New York: Cambridge University Press, 2021).

28 Albarracín et al., *Creating Conspiracy Beliefs*.

29 Albarracín et al., *Creating Conspiracy Beliefs*.

30 Benjamin J. Roth, "The Double Bind of DACA: Exploring the Legal Violence of Liminal Status for Undocumented Youth," *Ethnic and Racial Studies* 42, no. 15 (2019): 2548–65.

31 Cisneros, "Undocumented Students Pursuing Higher Education."

32 Edelina M. Burciaga and Aaron Malone, "Intensified Liminal Legality: The Impact of the DACA Rescission for Undocumented Young Adults in Colorado," *Law & Social Inquiry* (2021): 1–23.

33 Burciaga and Malone, "Intensified Liminal Legality."

34 Burciaga and Malone, "Intensified Liminal Legality."

35 Yamiche Alcindor, "With Nielsen's Departure, Trump's Cabinet Becomes Even Less Diverse," PBS, April 8, 2019, www.pbs.org.

36 Alcindor, "With Nielsen's Departure."

37 Wadhia, *Beyond Deportation*; Olivas, *Perchance to DREAM.*

38 Abrego, "'I Can't Go to College Because I Don't Have Papers'"; Roth, "The Double Bind of DACA"; Lauren M. Ellis and Eric C. Chen, "Negotiating Identity Development Among Undocumented Immigrant College Students: A Grounded Theory Study," *Journal of Counseling Psychology* 60, no. 2 (2013): 251–64, https://doi.org/10.1037/a0031350.

39 Mallet-García and García-Bedolla, "Immigration Policy and Belonging."

40 Mallet-García and García-Bedolla, "Immigration Policy and Belonging."

41 Joanna Méndez-Pounds, Denise A. Nicholas, Natali Gonzalez, and Jason B. Whiting, "'I Am Just Like Everyone Else, Except for a Nine-Digit Number': A Thematic Analysis of the Experiences of DREAMers," *The Qualitative Report* 23, no. 2 (2018): 442–56.

42 Maria Chávez, Jessica L. Lavariega Monforti, and Melissa R. Michelson, *Living the Dream: New Immigration Policies and the Lives of Undocumented Latino Youth* (New York: Routledge, 2015).

43 Adrienne Pon, "The Dreamer Divide: Aspiring for a More Inclusive Immigrants' Rights Movement," *Stanford Journal of Civil Rights and Civil Liberties* 14, Special Issue (2018): 33–44.

44 Pon, "The Dreamer Divide," 39.

45 Nicole Prchal Svajlenka, "A Demographic Profile of DACA Recipients on the Frontlines of the Coronavirus Response," April 6, 2020, www.americanprogress.org.

46 Camilo Montoya-Galvez, "Senate Parliamentarian Rejects Democrats' Latest Immigration Plan in Spending Bill," December 16, 2021, www.cbsnews.com.

47 Burciaga and Malone, "Intensified Liminal Legality."

48 Julia Albarracín, *At the Core and in the Margins: Incorporation of Mexican Immigrants in Two Rural Midwestern Communities* (East Lansing: Michigan State University Press, 2016).

49 Albarracín, *At the Core and in the Margins.*

50 Linda K. Ko and Krista M. Pereira, "'It Turned My World Upside Down': Latino Youths' Perspectives on Immigration," *Journal of Adolescent Research* 25, no. 3 (2010): 465–93; Amanda Morales, Socorro Herrera, and Kevin Murry, "Navigating the Waves of Social and Political Capriciousness: Inspiring Perspectives from DREAM-Eligible Immigrant Students," *Journal of Hispanic Higher Education* 10, no. 3 (July 2009): 266–83, https://doi.org/10.1177/1538192708330232; Genevieve Negrón-Gonzales, "Undocumented, Unafraid and Unapologetic: Re-Articulatory Practices and Migrant Youth 'Illegality,'" *Latino Studies* 12, no. 2 (2014): 259–78, https://doi.org/10.1057/lst.2014.20.

51 Christina M. Getrich, "'People Show Up in Different Ways': DACA Recipients' Everyday Activism in a Time of Heightened Immigration-Related Insecurity," *Human Organization* 80, no. 1 (2021): 27–36.

52 Department of Homeland Security, "Deferred Action for Childhood Arrivals."

53 Daniel T. Lichter, Zhenchao Qian, and Dmitry Tumin, "Whom Do Immigrants Marry? Emerging Patterns of Intermarriage and Integration in the United States," *ANNALS of the American Academy of Political and Social Science* 662, no. 1 (2015): 57–78.

54 Lichter et al., "Whom Do Immigrants Marry?"

55 Lichter et al., "Whom Do Immigrants Marry?"

56 Kingsley, "'Legality' on Hold."

57 Mallet-García and García-Bedolla, "Immigration Policy and Belonging."

58 Pon, "The Dreamer Divide."

59 Lichter et al., "Whom Do Immigrants Marry?"

60 Carola Suárez-Orozco, Frosso Motti-Stefanidi, Amy Marks, and Dalal Katsiaficas, "An Integrative Risk and Resilience Model for Understanding the Adaptation of Immigrant-Origin Children and Youth," *American Psychologist* 73, no. 6 (2018): 781.

CHAPTER 7. THE FIGHT IS NOT OVER

1 Julia Albarracín, *At the Core and in the Margins: Incorporation of Mexican Immigrants in Two Rural Midwestern Communities* (East Lansing: Michigan State University Press, 2016).

2 Albarracín, *At the Core and in the Margins.*

3 Walter J. Nicholls and Tara Fiorito, "Dreamers Unbound: Immigrant Youth Mobilizing," *New Labor Forum* 24, no. 1 (2015): 86–92.

4 Fanny Lauby, "Leaving the 'Perfect DREAMer' Behind? Narratives and Mobilization in Immigration Reform," *Social Movement Studies* 15, no. 4 (2016): 374–87; Nicholls and Fiorito, "Dreamers Unbound"; Estefanía Cruz, "Young Immigrants' Association and the Future Latino Leadership in the US: Dreamers' Social Capital and Political Engagement," *Norteamérica* 11, no. 2 (2016): 165–91; Tara R. Fiorito, "Beyond the Dreamers: Collective Identity and Subjectivity in the Undocumented Youth Movement," *Mobilization: An International Quarterly* 24, no. 3 (2019): 345–63; Maria Chávez, Jessica L. Lavariega Monforti, and Melissa R. Michelson, *Living the Dream: New Immigration Policies and the Lives of Undocumented Latino Youth* (New York: Routledge, 2015); Tom K. Wong, Angela S. García, and Carolina Valdivia, "The Political Incorporation of Undocumented Youth," *Social Problems* 66, no. 3 (2019): 356–72; Christina M. Getrich, "'People Show Up in Different Ways': DACA Recipients' Everyday Activism in a Time of Heightened Immigration-Related Insecurity," *Human Organization* 80, no. 1 (2021): 27–36; Loan Thi Dao, "Out and Asian: How Undocu/DACAmented Asian Americans and Pacific Islander Youth Navigate Dual Liminality in the Immigrant Rights Movement," *Societies* 7, no. 3 (2017): 17; Luis Fernando Baron, "An Alternative Social Space for Socio-Political Political Participation: Facebook and Youth of Social Movements Organizations in the US," *GlobDev* 8 (2014); William Perez et al., "Civic Engagement Patterns of Undocumented Mexican Students," *Journal of Hispanic Higher Education* 9, no. 3 (2010): 245–65; Dirk Eisema, Tara Fiorito, and

Martha Montero-Sieburth, "Beating the Odds: The Undocumented Youth Movement of Latinos as a Vehicle for Upward Social Mobility," *New Diversities* 16, no. 1 (2014): 23–39; Jessica Lavariega L. Monforti and Melissa R. Michelson, "Firme: Persistent Activism of Millennial Latino Immigrants in the Trump Era," *Aztlan: A Journal of Chicano Studies* 46, no. 2 (2021): 83–112; William E. Rosales, Laura E. Enriquez, and Jennifer R. Nájera, "Politically Excluded, Undocu-Engaged: The Perceived Effect of Hostile Immigration Policies on Undocumented Student Political Engagement," *Journal of Latinos and Education* 20, no. 3 (2021): 260–75; Emma Herlinger, "American Dreams: DACA Dreamers, Trump as a Political and Social Event, and the Performative Practice of Storytelling in the Age of Secondary Orality" (Senior thesis, Scripps College, 2017).

5 Albarracín, *At the Core and in the Margins.*

6 Robert D. Putnam, Robert Leonardi, and Raffaella Y. Nanetti, *Making Democracy Work* (Princeton, NJ: Princeton University Press, 1994).

7 Jennifer Hoschchild and John Mollenkopf, "Modelling Immigrant Political Incorporation," in *Brining Outsiders In; Transatlnatic Perpectives on Immigrant Political Incorporation*, ed. Jennifer Hoschchild and John Mollenkopf (Ithaca, NY: Cornell University Press, 2009).

8 Hoschchild and Mollenkopf, "Modelling Immigrant Political Incorporation," 15.

9 Sidney Verba, Kay Lehman Schlozman, and Henry E. Brady, *Voice and Equality: Civic Voluntarism in American Politics* (Cambridge, MA: Harvard University Press, 1995).

10 Verba et al., *Voice and Equality.*

11 Albarracín, *At the Core and in the Margins*; Julia Albarracín and Anna Valeva, "Political Participation and Social Capital among Mexicans and Mexican Americans in Central Illinois," *Hispanic Journal of Behavioral Sciences* 33, no. 4 (2011): 507–23.

12 Roberto G. Gonzales, Luisa L. Heredia, and Genevieve Negrón-Gonzales, "Untangling Plyler's Legacy: Undocumented Students, Schools, and Citizenship," *Harvard Educational Review* 85, no. 3 (2015): 318–41.

13 Gonzales et al., "Untangling Plyler's Legacy."

14 Gonzales et al., "Untangling Plyler's Legacy."

15 Linda DeAngelo, Maximilian T. Schuster, and Michael J. Stebleton, "California DREAMers: Activism, Identity, and Empowerment among Undocumented College Students," *Journal of Diversity in Higher Education* 9, no. 3 (2016): 216.

16 Illinois General Assembly, "Public Act 093-0007."

17 University of Illinois at Urbana-Champaign's La Casa Cultural Latina, "Undocumented Friendly Resources/Scholarships," accessed April 17, 2022, https://oiir .illinois.edu.

18 University of Illinois at Chicago, "Student Resources: Undocumented Students," accessed April 18, 2022, https://dream.uic.edu.

19 Northern Illinois University, "Dream Action NIU," accessed April 18, 2022, www .niu.edu.

20 Dominican University 2022, "Resources for DACA and Undocumented Students," https://research.dom.edu/.

21 Albarracín, *At the Core and in the Margins*.

22 Genevieve Negrón-Gonzales, "Political Possibilities: Lessons from the Undocumented Youth Movement for Resistance to the Trump Administration," *Anthropology & Education Quarterly* 48, no. 4 (2017): 420–26; Megan E. Morrissey, "A DREAM Disrupted: Undocumented Migrant Youth Disidentifications with US Citizenship," *Journal of International and Intercultural Communication* 6, no. 2 (2013): 145–62.

23 Morrissey, "A DREAM Disrupted."

24 Albarracín, *At the Core and in the Margins*.

25 Randy Shaw, *Beyond the Fields: Cesar Chavez, the UFW, and the Struggle for Justice in the 21st Century* (Berkeley: University of California Press, 2010).

26 Albarracín, *At the Core and in the Margins*; Matt A. Barreto et al., "Mobilization, Participation, and Solidaridad: Latino Participation in the 2006 Immigration Protest Rallies," *Urban Affairs Review* 44, no. 5 (2009): 736–64; Jonathan Benjamin-Alvarado, Louis DeSipio, and Celeste Montoya, "Latino Mobilization in New Immigrant Destinations: The Anti–HR 4437 Protest in Nebraska's Cities," *Urban Affairs Review* 44, no. 5 (2009): 718–35.

27 Dirk Eisema, Tara Fiorito, and Martha Montero-Sieburth, "Beating the Odds: The Undocumented Youth Movement of Latinos as a Vehicle for Upward Social Mobility," *New Diversities* 16, no. 1 (2014): 23–39; Negrón-Gonzales, "Political Possibilities"; Helge Schwiertz, "Transformations of the Undocumented Youth Movement and Radical Egalitarian Citizenship," *Citizenship Studies* 20, no. 5 (2016): 610–28; Veronica Terriquez, Tizoc Brenes, and Abdiel Lopez, "Intersectionality as a Multipurpose Collective Action Frame: The Case of the Undocumented Youth Movement," *Ethnicities* 18, no. 2 (2018): 260–76; Fiorito, "Beyond the Dreamers"; Nicholls and Fiorito, "Dreamers Unbound."

28 Roberto Vélez-Vélez and Jacqueline Villarrubia-Mendoza, "Interpreting Mobilization Dynamics through Art: A Look at the DREAMers Movement," *Current Sociology* 67, no. 1 (2019): 100–121.

29 Vélez-Vélez and Villarrubia-Mendoza, "Interpreting Mobilization Dynamics through Art."

30 Terriquez et al., "Intersectionality as a Multipurpose Collective Action Frame"; Negrón-Gonzales, "Undocumented, Unafraid and Unapologetic"; Morrissey, "A DREAM Disrupted."

31 René Galindo, "Undocumented & Unafraid: The DREAM Act 5 and the Public Disclosure of Undocumented Status as a Political Act," *Urban Review* 44, no. 5 (2012): 589–611.

32 Negrón-Gonzales, "Political Possibilities."

33 Negrón-Gonzales, "Political Possibilities"; Galindo, "Undocumented & Unafraid."

34 Christie Smith, "May Day Rallies Held in the Bay Area," NBC Bay Area, May 1, 2022, www.nbcbayarea.com; *The Wisconsin Examiner*, "May Day 2022: Wisconsin

Activists Continue Fighting for Immigrant Rights," *Milwaukee Independent*, May 3, 2022, www.milwaukeeindependent.com.

35 Jorge Mena Robles and Ruth Gomberg-Muñoz, "Activism After DACA: Lessons from Chicago's Immigrant Youth Justice League," *North American Dialogue* 19, no. 1 (2016): 46–54; Cruz, "Young Immigrants' Association and the Future Latino Leadership in the US."

36 Albarracín, *At the Core and in the Margins*.

37 Verba et al., *Voice and Equality*.

38 Cruz, "Young Immigrants' Association and the Future Latino Leadership in the US."

39 Nienhusser and Oshio, "Awakened Hatred and Heightened Fears."

40 Nienhusser and Oshio, "Awakened Hatred and Heightened Fears."

41 James C. Scott, *Domination and the Arts of Resistance* (New Haven, CT: Yale University Press, 2008).

42 James C. Scott, "Weapons of the Weak: Everyday Forms of Peasant Resistance," in *Weapons of the Weak* (New Haven, CT: Yale University Press, 1985).

43 Office of the Illinois Secretary of State, "Temporary Visitor Driver's License (TVDL) For Undocumented (Non-Visa Status) Individuals," accessed April 21, 2022, www.ilsos.gov.

44 Nienhusser and Oshio, "Awakened Hatred and Heightened Fears."

45 Akiko Yasuike, "Stigma Management and Resistance among High-Achieving Undocumented Students," *Sociological Inquiry* 89, no. 2 (2019): 191–213.

46 Dalal Katsiaficas et al., "The Role of Campus Support, Undocumented Identity, and Deferred Action for Childhood Arrivals on Civic Engagement for Latinx Undocumented Undergraduates," *Child Development* 90, no. 3 (2019): 790–807.

47 Carola Suárez-Orozco, María G Hernández, and Saskias Casanova, "'It's Sort of My Calling': The Civic Engagement and Social Responsibility of Latino Immigrant-Origin Young Adults," *Research in Human Development* 12, no. 1–2 (2015): 84–99.

48 DeAngelo et al., "California DREAMers."

49 Katsiaficas et al., "The Role of Campus Support, Undocumented Identity, and Deferred Action."

50 Clare Saunders et al., "Explaining Differential Protest Participation: Novices, Returners, Repeaters, and Stalwarts," *Mobilization: An International Quarterly* 17, no. 3 (2012): 263–80.

51 Lester W. Milbrath, "Predispositions toward Political Contention," *Western Political Quarterly* 13, no. 1 (1960): 5–18.

52 Antonio Olivo and Ellen Hirst, "Young Immigrants Packed Navy Pier to Seek Protected Status," *Chicago Tribune*, August 16, 2012.

53 Olivo and Hirst, "Young Immigrants Packed Navy Pier."

54 Jill Theresa Messing, David Becerra, Allison Ward-Lasher, and David K. Androff, "Latinas' Perceptions of Law Enforcement: Fear of Deportation, Crime Reporting,

and Trust in the System," *Affilia* 30, no. 3 (2015): 328–40; Amada Armenta and Rocío Rosales, "Beyond the Fear of Deportation: Understanding Unauthorized Immigrants' Ambivalence toward the Police," American Behavioral Scientist 63, no. 9 (2019): 1350–69; Consuelo Arbona, Norma Olvera, Nestor Rodriguez, Jacqueline Hagan, Adriana Linares, and Margit Wiesner, "Acculturative Stress among Documented and Undocumented Latino Immigrants in the United States," *Hispanic Journal of Behavioral Sciences* 32, no. 3 (2010): 362–84; Karen Hacker, Maria Anies, Barbara L. Folb, and Leah Zallman, "Barriers to Health Care for Undocumented Immigrants: A Literature Review," *Risk Management and Healthcare Policy* 8 (2015): 175.

55 Nienhusser and Oshio, "Awakened Hatred and Heightened Fears."

56 Julián Jefferies, "Fear of Deportation in High School: Implications for Breaking the Circle of Silence Surrounding Migration Status," *Journal of Latinos and Education* 13, no. 4 (2014): 278–95.

57 Nienhusser and Oshio, "Awakened Hatred and Heightened Fears."

58 Getrich, "'People Show Up in Different Ways.'"

59 Scott, "Weapons of the Weak."

60 Scott, "Weapons of the Weak."

61 Getrich, "'People Show Up in Different Ways.'"

62 Scott, "Weapons of the Weak," 33.

63 Scott, "Weapons of the Weak."

64 Office of the Illinois Secretary of State, "Temporary Visitor Driver's License (TVDL) For Undocumented (Non-Visa Status) Individuals."

65 Germán A. Cadenas, Jesús Cisneros, Nathan Todd, and Lisa Spanierman, "DREAMzone: Testing Two Vicarious Contact Interventions to Improve Attitudes toward Undocumented Immigrants," *Journal of Diversity in Higher Education* 11, no. 3 (2018): 295.

66 Cadenas et al., "DREAMzone."

67 Scott, *Domination and the Arts of Resistance.*

68 United We Dream, "Guiding Principles," accessed August 21, 2022, https://unitedwedream.org.

69 Scott, "Weapons of the Weak"; Scott, *Domination and the Arts of Resistance.*

70 Scott, *Domination and the Arts of Resistance.*

71 Scott, *Domination and the Arts of Resistance.*

72 Scott, "Weapons of the Weak."

73 Albarracín, *At the Core and in the Margins*; Office of the Illinois Secretary of State, "Temporary Visitor Driver's License (TVDL) For Undocumented (Non-Visa Status) Individuals."

74 Anne Nordberg, Marcus R. Crawford, Regina T. Praetorius, and Schnavia Smith Hatcher, "Exploring Minority Youths' Police Encounters: A Qualitative Interpretive Meta-Synthesis," *Child and Adolescent Social Work Journal* 33, no. 2 (2016): 137–49.

75 Nordberg et al., "Exploring Minority Youths' Police Encounters."

76 Tammy Rinehart Kochel, "Police Legitimacy and Resident Cooperation in Crime Hotspots: Effects of Victimisation Risk and Collective Efficacy," *Policing and Society* 28, no. 3 (2018): 251–70; Keisha April, Lindsey M. Cole, and Naomi E. S. Goldstein, "Let's 'Talk' about the Police: The Role of Race and Police Legitimacy Attitudes in the Legal Socialization of Youth," *Current Psychology* (2022): 1–16.

77 Armenta and Rosales, "Beyond the Fear of Deportation."

78 Cecilia Menjívar, William Paul Simmons, Daniel Alvord, and Elizabeth Salerno Valdez, "Immigration Enforcement, the Racialization of Legal Status, and Perceptions of the Police: Latinos in Chicago, Los Angeles, Houston, and Phoenix in Comparative Perspective," *Du Bois Review: Social Science Research on Race* 15, no. 1 (2018): 107–28.

79 Alejandro Portes and József Böröcz, "Contemporary Immigration: Theoretical Perspectives on Its Determinants and Modes of Incorporation," *International Migration Review* 23, no. 3 (1989): 606–30.

80 Menjívar et al., "Immigration Enforcement, the Racialization of Legal Status, and Perceptions of the Police."

81 Albarracín, *At the Core and in the Margins.*

82 Carolina Valdivia, "Expanding Geographies of Deportability: How Immigration Enforcement at the Local Level Affects Undocumented and Mixed-Status Families," *Law & Policy* 41, no. 1 (2019): 103–19.

83 Kyle E. Walker and Helga Leitner, "The Variegated Landscape of Local Immigration Policies in the United States," *Urban Geography* 32, no. 2 (2011): 156–78.

84 Valdivia, "Expanding Geographies of Deportability."

85 Valdivia, "Expanding Geographies of Deportability."

86 Monica W. Varsanyi, Paul G. Lewis, Doris Provine, and Scott Decker, "A Multilayered Jurisdictional Patchwork: Immigration Federalism in the United States," *Law & Policy* 34, no. 2 (2012): 138–58.

87 Albarracín, *At the Core and in the Margins.*

88 Illinois General Assembly, "General Provisions: (5 ILCS 805/) Illinois TRUST Act," accessed September 19, 2022, www.ilga.gov.

89 Illinois General Assembly, "General Provisions: (5 ILCS 805/) Illinois TRUST Act."

90 Albarracín, *At the Core and in the Margins.*

91 Albarracín, *At the Core and in the Margins.*

92 Armenta and Rosales, "Beyond the Fear of Deportation."

93 Scott, "Weapons of the Weak"; Scott, *Domination and the Arts of Resistance.*

94 Leisy J. Abrego, "Legal Consciousness of Undocumented Latinos: Fear and Stigma as Barriers to Claims-making for First-and 1.5-generation Immigrants," *Law & Society Review* 45, no. 2 (2011): 337–70.

95 Scott, "Weapons of the Weak."

96 Julia Albarracín, *Making Immigrants in Modern Argentina* (Notre Dame, IN: University of Notre Dame Press, 2020).

97 Kitty Calavita, "Immigration, Law, and Marginalization in a Global Economy: Notes from Spain," *Law & Society Review* 32 (1998): 529.

98 Tracy Lachica Buenavista, "Model (Undocumented) Minorities and 'Illegal' Immigrants: Centering Asian Americans and US Carcerality in Undocumented Student Discourse," *Race Ethnicity and Education* 21, no. 1 (2018): 78–91.

99 Armenta and Rosales, "Beyond the Fear of Deportation."

100 Bonnie Moradi, "Discrimination, Objectification, and Dehumanization: Toward a Pantheoretical Framework," in *Objectification and (de) Humanization* (New York: Springer, 2013), 153–81.

101 Abrego, "Legal Consciousness of Undocumented Latinos"; Messing et al., "Latinas' Perceptions of Law Enforcement"; David Becerra, M. Alex Wagaman, David Androff, Jill Messing, and Jason Castillo, "Policing Immigrants: Fear of Deportations and Perceptions of Law Enforcement and Criminal Justice," *Journal of Social Work* 17, no. 6 (2017): 715–31.

102 Albarracín, *At the Core and in the Margins.*

103 Armenta and Rosales, "Beyond the Fear of Deportation."

104 Armenta and Rosales, "Beyond the Fear of Deportation."

105 Yasuike, "Stigma Management and Resistance."

106 Yasuike, "Stigma Management and Resistance."

107 Yasuike, "Stigma Management and Resistance."

108 Michal Nowosielski and Witold Nowak, "(In) Formal Social Participation of Immigrants—Are Migrants from Poland Socially Active?" *CMR Spotlight* 1, no. 21 (2020): 2–6.

109 Armenta and Rosales, "Beyond the Fear of Deportation."

110 Putnam et al., *Making Democracy Work.*

111 Eisema et al., "Beating the Odds"; Negrón-Gonzales, "Political Possibilities"; Schwiertz, "Transformations of the Undocumented Youth Movement and Radical Egalitarian Citizenship"; Terriquez et al., "Intersectionality as a Multipurpose Collective Action Frame"; Fiorito, "Beyond the Dreamers"; Nicholls and Fiorito, "Dreamers Unbound."

112 Nowosielski and Nowak, "(In) Formal Social Participation of Immigrants."

113 Yasuike, "Stigma Management and Resistance among High-Achieving Undocumented Students."

114 Beleza Chan, "Not Just a Latino Issue: Undocumented Students in Higher Education," *Journal of College Admission* 206 (2010): 29–31.

115 Chan, "Not Just a Latino Issue."

116 DeAngelo et al., "California DREAMers."

117 Scott, "Weapons of the Weak"; Scott, *Domination and the Arts of Resistance.*

118 Calavita, "Immigration, Law, and Marginalization in a Global Economy."

119 Scott, "Weapons of the Weak."

CONCLUSION

1 National Immigration Law Center, "Deferred Action for Childhood Arrivals (DACA) Final Rule Summary," September 2022, www.ilrc.org.

2 National Immigration Law Center, "Deferred Action for Childhood Arrivals (DACA) Final Rule Summary."

3 Nation World News Desk, "Biden Wants to Strengthen Protection for DACA Recipients."

4 National Immigration Law Center, "Deferred Action for Childhood Arrivals (DACA) Final Rule Summary"; Immigrant Legal Resource Center, "DACA."

5 Pooja Slahotra, "Gov. Greg Abbott's Migrant Busing Program Costs Texas $12 Million," *Texas Tribune*, August 31, 2022, www.texastribune.org.

6 Slahotra, "Gov. Greg Abbott's Migrant Busing Program."

7 Dave Manning, "The Texas Border: A Volatile Mix of Border Patrol, Armed Militia, Texas National Guard and Questionable Law Enforcement Ties and Tactics," *Reform Austin*, September 10, 2022, www.reformaustin.org.

8 Manning, "The Texas Border."

9 Manning, "The Texas Border."

10 Joel Rose, "A Majority of Americans See an 'Invasion' at the Southern Border," August 18, 2022, www.npr.org.

11 Rose, "A Majority of Americans."

12 Rose, "A Majority of Americans."

13 Charlie Savage, Maggie Haberman, and Jonathan Swan, "Sweeping Raids, Giant Camps and Mass Deportations: Inside Trump's 2025 Immigration Plans," *New Tork Times*, November 11, 2023.

14 Titanilla Kiss and Shaki Asgari, "A Case Study of Personal Experiences of Undocumented Eastern European Immigrants Living in the United States," *Journal of Identity and Migration Studies* 9, no. 2 (2015): 42.

15 John Bryant and Paul Merwood, "Reasons for Migrating and Settlement Outcomes: Evidence from the Longitudinal Immigration Survey New Zealand," *Labour, Employment and Work in New Zealand*, 2008, https://doi.org/10.26686/lew.v0i0.1628.

16 Stephen Castles, "Why Migration Policies Fail," *Ethnic and Racial Studies* 27, no. 2 (2004): 205–27.

17 Karen Musalo, "El Salvador: Root Causes and Just Asylum Policy Responses," *Hastings Race and Poverty Law Journal* 18, no. 2 (2021): 178.

18 Julia Albarracín, *Making Immigrants in Modern Argentina* (Notre Dame, IN: University of Notre Dame Press, 2020).

19 Jeremy Slack, Daniel E. Martínez, Alison Elizabeth Lee, and Scott Whiteford, "The Geography of Border Militarization: Violence, Death and Health in Mexico and the United States," *Journal of Latin American Geography* 15, no. 1 (2016): 7–32.

20 Maurizio Ambrosini, "Parenting from a Distance and Processes of Family Reunification: A Research on the Italian Case," *Ethnicities* 15, no. 3 (2015): 440–59.

21 Erwin Dimitri Selimos and Yvette Daniel, "The Role of Schools in Shaping the Settlement Experiences of Newcomer Immigrant and Refugee Youth," *International Journal of Child, Youth and Family Studies* 8, no. 2 (2017): 90–109.

22 Stephanie Plenty and Jan O. Jonsson, "Social Exclusion among Peers: The Role of Immigrant Status and Classroom Immigrant Density," *Journal of Youth and Adolescence* 46, no. 6 (2017): 1275–88.

23 John W. Berry, "Immigration, Acculturation, and Adaptation," *Applied Psychology* 46, no. 1 (1997): 5–34.

24 Berry, "Immigration, Acculturation, and Adaptation."

25 Roberto G. Gonzales, Luisa L. Heredia, and Genevieve Negrón-Gonzales, "Untangling Plyler's Legacy: Undocumented Students, Schools, and Citizenship," *Harvard Educational Review* 85, no. 3 (2015): 318–41; Selimos and Daniel, "The Role of Schools in Shaping the Settlement Experiences of Newcomer Immigrant and Refugee Youth."

26 Floralba Arbelo Marrero, "Barriers to School Success for Latino Students," *Journal of Education and Learning* 5, no. 2 (2016): 180–86.

27 Hua-Yu Sebastian Cherng and Peter F. Halpin, "The Importance of Minority Teachers: Student Perceptions of Minority versus White Teachers," *Educational Researcher* 45, no. 7 (2016): 407–20.

28 Sabrina Zirkel, "Is There a Place for Me? Role Models and Academic Identity among White Students and Students of Color," *Teachers College Record* 104, no. 2 (2002): 357–76.

29 Jason G. Irizarry and John Raible, "Beginning with El Barrio: Learning from Exemplary Teachers of Latino Students," *Journal of Latinos and Education* 10, no. 3 (2011): 186–203.

30 Anne Steketee, Monnica T. Williams, Beatriz T. Valencia, Destiny Printz, and Lisa M. Hooper, "Racial and Language Microaggressions in the School Ecology," *Perspectives on Psychological Science* 16, no. 5 (2021): 1075–98.

31 Rogelio Sáenz and Karen Manges Douglas, "A Call for the Racialization of Immigration Studies: On the Transition of Ethnic Immigrants to Racialized Immigrants," *Sociology of Race and Ethnicity* 1, no. 1 (2015): 166–80.

32 Illinois General Assembly, "Public Act 093–0007"; Illinois General Assembly, "Full Text of SB2185."

33 Katherine E. Bernal-Arevalo, "Achieving the Dream: The High School Counselor Role Is Supporting the Transition of Undocumented College-Bound Latino/a Students" (Master's thesis, California State, Fresno, 2019).

34 Roberto G. Gonzales, *Lives in Limbo: Undocumented and Coming of Age in America* (Berkeley: University of California Press, 2015).

35 Linda K. Ko and Krista M. Pereira, "'It Turned My World Upside Down': Latino Youths' Perspectives on Immigration," *Journal of Adolescent Research* 25, no. 3 (2010): 465–93.

36 Loan Thi Dao, "Out and Asian: How Undocu/DACAmented Asian Americans and Pacific Islander Youth Navigate Dual Liminality in the Immigrant Rights Movement," *Societies* 7, no. 3 (2017): 17; Cecilia Menjívar, "Liminal Legality: Salvadoran and Guatemalan Immigrants' Lives in the United States," *American Journal of Sociology* 111, no. 4 (2006): 999–1037; Kara Cebulko, "Documented,

Undocumented, and Liminally Legal: Legal Status during the Transition to Adulthood for 1.5-Generation Brazilian Immigrants," *Sociological Quarterly* 55, no. 1 (2014): 143–67; Rebecca Maria Torres and Melissa Wicks-Asbun, "Undocumented Students' Narratives of Liminal Citizenship: High Aspirations, Exclusion, and 'in-between' Identities," *Professional Geographer* 66, no. 2 (2014): 195–204; Benjamin J. Roth, "The Double Bind of DACA: Exploring the Legal Violence of Liminal Status for Undocumented Youth," *Ethnic and Racial Studies* 42, no. 15 (2019): 2548–65; Maria E. Zuniga, "Latino Immigrants: Patterns of Survival," *Journal of Human Behavior in the Social Environment* 5, no. 3–4 (2002): 137–55; Nicholas De Genova, "The Legal Production of Mexican/Migrant 'Illegality,'" *Latino Studies* 2, no. 2 (July 2004): 160–85, https://doi.org/10.1057/palgrave.1st.8600085.

37 Genevieve Negrón-Gonzales, "Navigating 'Illegality': Undocumented Youth and Oppositional Consciousness," *Children and Youth Services Review* 35, no. 8 (August 2013): 1284–90.

38 Gonzales, *Lives in Limbo*; Benuto et al., "Undocumented, to DACAmented, to DACAlimited"; Suárez-Orozco et al., "Growing Up in the Shadows."

39 Lisa M. Martinez, "Dreams Deferred: The Impact of Legal Reforms on Undocumented Latino Youth," *American Behavioral Scientist* 58, no. 14 (December 26, 2014): 1873–90, https://doi.org/10.1177/0002764214550289.

40 Gonzales et al., "The Long-Term Impact of DACA."

41 Catalina Amuedo-Dorantes and Francisca Antman, "Can Authorization Reduce Poverty among Undocumented Immigrants? Evidence from the Deferred Action for Childhood Arrivals Program," *Economics Letters* 147 (2016): 1–4.

42 Gonzales et al., "The Long-Term Impact of DACA."

43 Oswaldo Moreno, Lisa Fuentes, Isis Garcia-Rodriguez, Rosalie Corona, and Germàn A. Cadenas, "Psychological Impact, Strengths, and Handling the Uncertainty Among Latinx DACA Recipients," *The Counseling Psychologist* 49, no. 5 (2021): 728–53; Caitlin Patler and Whitney Laster Pirtle, "From Undocumented to Lawfully Present: Do Changes to Legal Status Impact Psychological Wellbeing among Latino Immigrant Young Adults?," *Social Science & Medicine* 199 (2018): 39–48; Rachel Siemons, Marissa Raymond-Flesch, Colette L. Auerswald, and Claire D. Brindis, "Coming of Age on the Margins: Mental Health and Wellbeing among Latino Immigrant Young Adults Eligible for Deferred Action for Childhood Arrivals (DACA)," *Journal of Immigrant and Minority Health* 19, no. 3 (2017): 543–51.

44 Elira Kuka, Na'ama Shenhav, and Kevin Shih, "Do Human Capital Decisions Respond to the Returns to Education? Evidence from DACA," *American Economic Journal: Economic Policy* 12, no. 1 (2020): 293–324.

45 Siemons et al., "Coming of Age on the Margins"; Roberto G. Gonzales, Basia Ellis, Sarah A. Rendón-García, and Kristina Brant, "(Un)Authorized Transitions: Illegality, DACA, and the Life Course," *Research in Human Development* 15, no. 3–4 (2018): 345–59.

46 Roth, "The Double Bind of DACA"; Martha Morales Hernandez and Laura E. Enriquez, "Life after College: Liminal Legality and Political Threats as Barriers

to Undocumented Students' Career Preparation Pursuits," *Journal of Latinos and Education* 20, no. 3 (2021): 318–31.

47 Morales Hernandez and Enriquez, "Life after College."

48 Roth, "The Double Bind of DACA"; Morales Hernandez and Enriquez, "Life after College."

49 Edelina M. Burciaga and Aaron Malone, "Intensified Liminal Legality: The Impact of the DACA Rescission for Undocumented Young Adults in Colorado," *Law & Social Inquiry* (2021): 1–23.

50 Roth, "The Double Bind of DACA."

51 Daniel T. Lichter, Zhenchao Qian, and Dmitry Tumin, "Whom Do Immigrants Marry? Emerging Patterns of Intermarriage and Integration in the United States," *ANNALS of the American Academy of Political and Social Science* 662, no. 1 (2015): 57–78.

52 Marie L. Mallet-García and Lisa García-Bedolla, "Immigration Policy and Belonging: Ramifications for DACA Recipients' Sense of Belonging," *American Behavioral Scientist* 65, no. 9 (2021): 1165–79.

53 Adrienne Pon, "The Dreamer Divide: Aspiring for a More Inclusive Immigrants' Rights Movement," *Stanford Journal of Civil Rights and Civil Liberties* 14, Special Issue (2018): 33–44.

54 Carola Suárez-Orozco, Frosso Motti-Stefanidi, Amy Marks, and Dalal Katsiaficas, "An Integrative Risk and Resilience Model for Understanding the Adaptation of Immigrant-Origin Children and Youth," *American Psychologist* 73, no. 6 (2018): 781.

55 Dirk Eisema, Tara Fiorito, and Martha Montero-Sieburth, "Beating the Odds: The Undocumented Youth Movement of Latinos as a Vehicle for Upward Social Mobility," *New Diversities* 16, no. 1 (2014): 23–39; Tara R. Fiorito, "Beyond the Dreamers: Collective Identity and Subjectivity in the Undocumented Youth Movement," *Mobilization: An International Quarterly* 24, no. 3 (2019): 345–63; Genevieve Negrón-Gonzales, "Political Possibilities: Lessons from the Undocumented Youth Movement for Resistance to the Trump Administration," *Anthropology & Education Quarterly* 48, no. 4 (2017): 420–26; Walter J. Nicholls and Tara Fiorito, "Dreamers Unbound: Immigrant Youth Mobilizing," *New Labor Forum* 24, no. 1 (2015): 86–92; Helge Schwiertz, "Transformations of the Undocumented Youth Movement and Radical Egalitarian Citizenship," *Citizenship Studies* 20, no. 5 (2016): 610–28; Veronica Terriquez, Tizoc Brenes, and Abdiel Lopez, "Intersectionality as a Multipurpose Collective Action Frame: The Case of the Undocumented Youth Movement," *Ethnicities* 18, no. 2 (2018): 260–76.

56 Michal Nowosielski and Witold Nowak, "(In) Formal Social Participation of Immigrants—Are Migrants from Poland Socially Active?," *CMR Spotlight* 1, no. 21 (2020): 2–6.

57 Beleza Chan, "Not Just a Latino Issue: Undocumented Students in Higher Education," *Journal of College Admission* 206 (2010): 29–31.

58 Kevin R. Johnson, "Driver's Licenses and Undocumented Immigrants: The Future of Civil Rights Law," *Nevada Law Journal* 5 (2004): 213.

59 National Conference of State Legislators, "States Offering Driver's Licenses to Immigrants," September 20, 2022, www.ncsl.org.

60 Johnson, "Driver's Licenses and Undocumented Immigrants."

61 Catalina Amuedo-Dorantes, Esther Arenas-Arroyo, and Almudena Sevilla, "Labor Market Impacts of States Issuing of Driver's Licenses to Undocumented Immigrants," *Labour Economics* 63 (2020): 101805; Johnson, "Driver's Licenses and Undocumented Immigrants"; Heepyung Cho, "Driver's License Reforms and Job Accessibility among Undocumented Immigrants," *Labour Economics* 76 (2022): 102174.

62 Christie Smith, "May Day Rallies Held in the Bay Area," NBC Bay Area, May 1, 2022, www.nbcbayarea.com.

63 Jorge Mena Robles and Ruth Gomberg-Muñoz, "Activism After DACA: Lessons from Chicago's Immigrant Youth Justice League," *North American Dialogue* 19, no. 1 (2016): 46–54; Estefanía Cruz, "Young Immigrants' Association and the Future Latino Leadership in the US: Dreamers' Social Capital and Political Engagement," *Norteamérica* 11, no. 2 (2016): 165–91.

INDEX

Page numbers in italics indicate figures and tables

ABOUT THE AUTHOR

JULIA ALBARRACÍN is Professor of Political Science at Western Illinois University and author of *At the Core and in the Margins: Incorporation of Mexican Immigrants in Two Rural Midwestern Communities* (2016), *Making Immigrants in Modern Argentina* (2020), and a coauthor of *Creating Conspiracy Beliefs: How Our Thoughts Are Shaped* (2021). She is a 2022 recipient of the Hispanic Pride (Orgullo Hispano) Award from the International Press, Radio and TV Association and is currently a consulting editor for the *Hispanic Journal of Behavioral Sciences*. She has received grant funding from the US Department of Education and has earned numerous honors while at WIU, including 2022 Distinguished Faculty Lecturer, the 2015–2018 Dan and Laura Webb Professor of Political Science, and the 2023 College of Arts and Science's Outstanding Faculty Award in Research.

www.ingramcontent.com/pod-product-compliance
Lightning Source LLC
Chambersburg PA
CBHW031554060326
40783CB00026B/4074